Frommer's®

great
escapes
from NYC
without
wheels

by Lisa Marie Rovito

WILEY
Wiley Publishing, Inc.

Published by:

WILEY PUBLISHING, INC.
111 River St.
Hoboken, NJ 07030-5774

ISBN-13: 978-0-7645-9829-6
ISBN-10: 0-7645-9829-5

Editor: Alexis Lipsitz Flippin & Alexia Meyers
Production Editor: Heather Wilcox
Cartographer: Roberta Stockwell
Photo Editor: Richard Fox
Production by Wiley Indianapolis Composition Services

For information on our other products and services or to obtain technical support, please contact our Customer Care Department within the U.S. at
800/762-2974, outside the U.S. at 317/572-3993 or fax 317/572-4002.

Wiley also publishes its books in a variety of electronic formats. Some content
that appears in print may not be available in electronic formats.

Manufactured in the United States of America

5   4   3   2

Contents

List of Maps

ABOUT THE AUTHOR

Lisa Marie Rovito grew up in small-town Ohio, graduated from Ohio University, and has spent the past 10 years in Brooklyn, NY. In that time, she has traveled extensively, and has hiked along portions of the Appalachian Trail in five states—all via mass transit. Her work has appeared in *New York* magazine, citysearch.com, *Readymade* magazine, *Positive Thinking* magazine, and *Bridal Guide* magazine, in addition to freelance work for Chronicle Books and several public relations clients. Lisa Marie enjoys life as a passenger and has never owned a car.

ACKNOWLEDGMENTS

I would need an entire chapter to thank all of the people who were essential in the research, writing, and editing of this book. But I only have a page . . .

Michael Spring at Frommer's who pulled my pitch from the slush pile and believed in my idea.

Alexis Lipsitz Flippin for her masterful editing, encouragement, and laid back style.

Patrick Riley for dragging me to a Media Bistro pitch slam and not letting me give up.

Spencer Foxworth for giving my proposal a darn good copy edit before it went out.

Amy Wong, Julie Mehta, Heather Mac Donald, Matthew Raphael, Annette Blum, Catherine Arne, Kate Mathis, and my other friends who enthusiastically joined me on weekend research trips and made sure I didn't miss any details.

My manager and friend at The Princeton Review, Rob Franek, who put up with me being too tired to think on most Monday mornings for eight straight months.

All of the people who wrote sidebars and entries in this book including Alex Altman, Julie Mehta, Amy Wong, Rebecca Ciletti, Suzanne Podhurst, Robert Franek, Jen Adams, and Sarah Baker.

The tourism, advertising, marketing, public relations, general managers, and promotions staff people for most every destination in this book. They know their stuff and were more than willing to share their knowledge, their time, and their expertise.

A special and grateful nod to Cathy Ellis in the Ulster County Tourism Office who, if I had a county that needed promoting, I would hire in a hot second. Maureen Brooks at Adirondack Trailways was also especially helpful.

All the people whose weddings, birthday parties, and special events I missed because I was out of town. And all the people whose kind e-mails I forgot to return because all I could think about was bus schedules and train stations.

My neighbors at 20 Grand Avenue in Brooklyn, especially Darrell and Sarah Whitelaw, who lovingly and selflessly cared for our pets on more weekends than I can count.

My family (Mimi, Steve, and Markkus) and Alex's family (Irene, Alan, and Sue) for their never-ending interest and support. Mimi even flew out to join me on my travels twice. (I think the chocolate-themed spa in Hershey was the clincher.)

My dog Lilly, and cats, Poe and Petra, who had no idea why their mom deserted them every single weekend but who always forgave me as soon as I came home.

And of course, to my soulmate, Alex Altman, who makes all dreams come true—this book included.

AN INVITATION TO THE READER

In researching this book, we discovered many wonderful places—hotels, restaurants, shops, and more. We're sure you'll find others. Please tell us about them, so we can share the information with your fellow travelers in upcoming editions. If you were disappointed with a recommendation, we'd love to know that, too. Please write to:

Great Escapes from New York City without Wheels, 1st Edition
Wiley Publishing, Inc. • 111 River St. • Hoboken, NJ 07030-5774

AN ADDITIONAL NOTE

Please be advised that travel information is subject to change at any time—and this is especially true of prices. We therefore suggest that you write or call ahead for confirmation when making your travel plans. The authors, editors, and publisher cannot be held responsible for the experiences of readers while traveling. Your safety is important to us, however, so we encourage you to stay alert and be aware of your surroundings. Keep a close eye on cameras, purses, and wallets, all favorite targets of thieves and pickpockets.

Other Great Guides for Your Trip:

Frommer's New York State

Frommer's New York City

Frommer's New York City Day by Day

Frommer's New York City with Kids

Frommer's Portable New York City

Frommer's Memorable Walks in New York

Pauline Frommer's New York City

FROMMERS.COM

Now that you have the guidebook to a great trip, visit our website at **www.frommers.com** for travel information on more than 3,000 destinations. With features updated regularly, we give you instant access to the most current trip-planning information available. At Frommers.com, you'll also find the best prices on airfares, accommodations, and car rentals—and you can even book travel online through our travel booking partners. At Frommers.com, you'll also find the following:

◆ Online updates to our most popular guidebooks
◆ Vacation sweepstakes and contest giveaways
◆ Newsletter highlighting the hottest travel trends
◆ Online travel message boards with featured travel discussions

Introduction

IT'S FITTING THAT A GOOD PORTION OF THIS BOOK WAS ACTUALLY written aboard buses and trains going in and out of New York City. The benefit of being able to sit back and relax (or work on a laptop) while someone else contends with traffic, tolls, and navigation is worth more to me than the price of a round-trip ticket.

Bus travel to and from the city has come a long way. Once known for its colorful characters (remember Ratso Rizzo?), screaming babies, pit stops for smokers, and crumbs on the seat, these days the bus lines going in and out of the city and up and down the East Coast debunk those outdated stereotypes. In weekend travels I've often experienced a bus-wide calm and quiet so satisfying it has actually lulled me to sleep. Clean floors, roomy overhead bins, and reclining seats are standard issue. Laying down the law upfront, drivers give strict warnings about turning down the cellphone ring volume and keeping conversations soft-spoken and short. Adirondack Trailways buses even have mesh bags on the seat in front of you to hold magazines and snacks. A Peter Pan bus coming back from the Berkshires had mini–tray tables with drink holders. Even the Academy buses to Atlantic City were full of low-key regulars content to tilt their seats back and save their energy for the slots (for which you're awarded a $10 coupon on arrival). While many bus lines have TV screens, I have yet to see a movie played—leaving each and every passenger pleasantly undistracted.

Train travel in and out of New York City has its own list of positives. Without the tangle of highway traffic to contend with, trains for the most part leave and arrive on time. Bathrooms are bigger, and modest ticket prices (at least on Metro North and the Long Island Rail Road) make for some truly affordable and genuinely effortless getaways. Yes, you may have to switch trains midjourney, so pay attention during the 15 minutes prior to your stop for announcements concerning transfers. I once fell asleep on my way to Greenport and awoke only when we arrived for the transfer in Ronkonkoma. Not having heard the conductor say the train to Greenport was on the very same track but in front of our train (instead of across the track, like the subways), I missed the train completely. Cab ride out to Greenport to meet up with my scheduled tour group: $90 with tip. Ouch.

Amtrak has struggled in recent years, and the service on some of its trains reflects that. On one route you'll find a clean car with open seats and outlets for your laptop or cellphone charger. On another, the train will be dark, dingy, overcrowded, and delayed and the club car out of snacks and closed for the day. (One smart innovation that does work: Amtrak's "Quiet Car"—where riders are asked to turn off cellphones and talk quietly.) In the case of all mass transit—as the airlines have conditioned us to accept—there are no guarantees.

Why not just rent a car to get where you're going? Sure, you can rent a car. There are plenty of rental places in the city and the boroughs. But an average of $65 per day may or may not be within your weekend-travel budget. And that doesn't include all the extras that get tacked on to a car-rental bill: insurance, gas, and tolls. It can add up fast, and soon the tally for your quick weekend getaway—leaving Saturday morning and coming back Sunday evening—is exceeding $200 or more *just for the car.*

Then there's the often thorny reality of weekend car travel to and from the city. No matter which exit you take, driving out of the city on a postwork Friday can be harrowing and time-consuming—and the same is true of reentry on a Sunday afternoon. My feeling is, why wrestle with bumper-to-bumper traffic when you can leave and reenter the city with relative ease through mass transit? Yes, I know trains can run late and buses have to fight traffic, too (although special bus lanes are there to help minimize that problem), but in general it's a smoother process—especially when you leave the hassle of driving to someone else.

And let's face it: Many of the getaways in this book are places where you'll want to stay put once you get there anyway. Why on earth should you pay a car-rental fee if the only times you plan to use a car are for the trips there and back?

One aspect of suburban life I found fascinating was how the act of actually walking to get from one place to another is truly an anathema to many people outside NYC. In the Big Apple, we walk a lot because, well, it's easy, it's cheap, it's often the best way to get somewhere, and it can be vastly entertaining. On a recent trip to a charming small town, for example, I booked my weekend accommodations to be close to the bus station and the part of town where most of the activities take place. I was surprised when the innkeeper e-mailed to ask if I'd like to have a cab meet me at the station. "Is the inn far from the station?" I wrote back. "Not far," she replied. "Seven short blocks—but too far to walk with luggage." Geez: I was only coming for 2 nights—how much luggage could I have? She also mentioned that the sidewalks were bumpy. Out of politeness, I let her book the cab. The ride (I timed it) was less than 2 minutes.

On the other hand, it's important to note that many of the inns, spas, hotels, and other destinations in this book will arrange to pick you up when you get to town if they *aren't* located a short walk from mass transit. It pays to ask when you make your reservation. Some charge a nominal fee for the service, but plenty offer it for free. If not, taxis are usually readily available once you arrive at the station (though you may need to call one if none are waiting) for every place in this book.

If you do decide to rent a car, however, you can often find lower prices at the airport rental centers using Hotwire.com. However you choose to get there, do get out of the city once in a while. There are few faster ways of altering your perspective and your place in the universe than a couple days outside the Apple. And if you think you can't afford it, just consider how much you spend during a normal weekend in New York City.

Mass-transit travel may not give you the freedom to explore every back road or nook and cranny of a place. You may not be able to just up and go whenever and wherever you want. But it does free you from having to sit behind the wheel and wrestle with traffic when you could instead be reading, chatting, or daydreaming away the miles.

Note: The complete contact information for all the bus and train lines found in each chapter is located in appendix A, "Resources," at the end of the book.

Best of *Great Escapes from New York City without Wheels*

Y OU CAN ESCAPE NEW YORK CITY'S URBAN JUNGLE ANY NUMBER OF entertaining and enlightening ways throughout the Northeast Region—and you won't need wheels to touch down at many of my favorites. Here is a sampling of some of the best places to get away from it all just an hour or two from the mean streets of the Big Apple.

BEST PLACES TO SEE STARS

- **Appalachian Trail:** After a hard day of hiking, spotting a shooting star makes it all worthwhile. See p. 22.
- **Hudson River Museum Planetarium** (Yonkers, NY): Starry shows are free on Friday evenings. Special shows are also tailored to younger kids. See p. 224.
- **Saugerties Lighthouse** (Saugerties, NY): A wide-open sky over the Hudson River at night yields scads of brilliant constellations. See p. 57.

BEST PLACES TO PLAY *FEAR FACTOR*

- **Skydive the Ranch** (Gardiner, NY): How does if feel to jump out of a plane at 13,000 feet? Find out here. See p. 33.
- **EMS Climbing School** (New Paltz, NY): Scale the Gunks with an expert guide and find out what it means to be a rock star. See p. 45.
- **Kingda Ka at Six Flags** (Jackson, NJ): The highest, fastest ride in the world is just a bus ride away. See p. 240.
- **Skip Barber Racing School** (Lakeville, CT): Hit the curves like a pro with courses that last from 3 hours to 3 days. See p. 43.

New York City & the Northeast Region

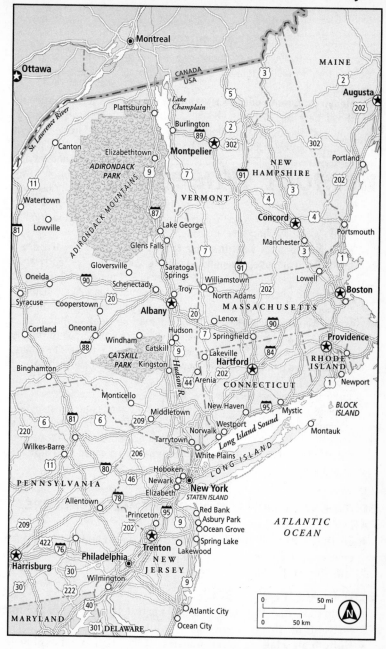

Montreal

Ottawa

MAINE

CANADA
USA

3

2

Augusta

202

Plattsburgh

Lake Champlain

5

Burlington

Canton

Elizabethtown

89

302

Montpelier

NEW
HAMPSHIRE

Portland

St. Lawrence River

ADIRONDACK
PARK

9

7

91

302

202

11

VERMONT

4

3

Watertown

87

Concord

4

Portsmouth

81

Lowville

Lake George

Manchester

3

1

Glens Falls

7

Gloversville

91

Williamstown

Lowell

Boston

Oneida

90

Saratoga
Springs

Lenox

North Adams

202

Syracuse

Schenectady

Troy

MASSACHUSETTS

Cooperstown

20

Albany

20

Cortland

Oneonta

Lenox

90

Windham

Hudson

7

Springfield

Providence

88

CATSKILL
PARK

Catskill

9

84

RHODE
ISLAND

Binghamton

Kingston

Lakeville

Hartford

Hudson R.

Arenia

202

1

Newport

Monticello

44

CONNECTICUT

BLOCK
ISLAND

81

6

209

Middletown

New Haven

95

Mystic

220

6

Westport

Montauk

Wilkes-Barre

Tarrytown

Norwalk

Long Island Sound

206

White Plains

LONG ISLAND

11

80

Hoboken

PENNSYLVANIA

46

Newark

New York

Allentown

78

Elizabeth

STATEN ISLAND

Princeton

95

Red Bank

*ATLANTIC
OCEAN*

209

202

9

Asbury Park
Ocean Grove

422

76

Trenton

Spring Lake

Harrisburg

30

Philadelphia

Lakewood

NEW
JERSEY

30

222

Wilmington

9

40

MARYLAND

Atlantic City

301 DELAWARE

Ocean City

0   50 mi

0   50 km

N

Top 5 Biggest Surprises about Regional Travel outside NYC

Even seasoned travelers may find some surprises in the regional landscape outside New York City. Here are a few of my own general finds and observations.

1. **Many restaurants outside NYC inflate their prices just as much as those here do.** Whether you're in a backyard garden restaurant in Lenox, Massachusetts, or dining along the pastoral Delaware River in Lambertville, New Jersey, don't be shocked to find that dinner is priced for upscale palates. This is especially true at popular weekend-escape spots that cater to tourists. If a bus or train makes a stop in town, chances are, so do weekending urbanites—and restaurants price their menus accordingly. Even restaurants sporting a casual look may charge double figures for a fettuccine dish and $26 or more for a steak.

2. **Most people don't walk in other towns.** Know that sidewalks are a quaint but dying phenomenon and not everyone out in the hinterlands can give you walking directions. They may in fact tell you that you need to call a cab when you are actually within comfortable walking distance of your destination. And they may stare at you like you're an alien if you're walking along the side of a road (alas, no sidewalks!) that sees relatively few pedestrians. But we New Yorkers walk in our town, and with or without a car at our disposal, we'll continue to walk in others. It's not just a point of pride, it's a perfectly practical means of getting around.

3. **Luxury condos are everywhere.** In the city, we see them all over the place. But I hadn't expected to find BUY NOW!" signs and construction equipment tearing up dirt lots in roughly 75% of the towns in this book. From Asbury Park, New Jersey, to Cooperstown, New York, and New Hope, Pennsylvania, condominiums are going up, up, up. For those

BEST DESTINATION FOR A SPA-THEMED BACHELORETTE PARTY

◆ **Gurney's Inn** (Montauk, NY): Pedicures with an ocean view, cottages on the beach, and a few bars along the main street in Montauk. See p. 132.

BEST PLACES FOR A BEER

◆ **Guinan's Irish Pub** (Garrison, NY): Just 10 steps from the train platform sits this riverside bar with lots of local color. See p. 118.

◆ **Bohemian Hall & Beer Garden** (Queens, NY): Possibly the largest bar in the city, this European-style beer garden has a seasonal garden for bratwurst and Czech beers. See p. 107.

in the market for a getaway condo, it's like Christmas in every town. Same for the eager real estate agents whose tourist-friendly offices sit right in the middle of the quaint downtown shops along Main Street, USA. For everyone else who lives there, the condo can single-handedly threaten to jack up the price of living, mar a view of the mountains, and swiftly redo a town's long-standing demographics. Or not. It remains to be seen what impact these luxury condos will have in the long run. My advice: Visit these spectacular towns before condo-ization goes too far.

4. **Nearly every town in this book has "resort maps" to help visitors get around.** They're free for the taking at local businesses, the visitor centers, and the chambers of commerce. These maps can be a real blessing when you're trying to get oriented in a jiffy. Many are large, kind of cartoonish hand-drawn maps with a border of ads around the outside. Every business that places an ad with the map company will have their business highlighted on the map. That's why only some, but not all, of a town's restaurants, inns, and landmark attractions are pointed out on the map. But the maps are an excellent resource regardless (www.resortmaps.com)—particularly for those on foot.

5. **Hitchhikers don't get rides.** Plus, it's illegal in many places, including, for instance, New Jersey. (Not that I've tried it . . . and definitely not in Jim Thorpe, Pennsylvania, when we were about to miss the last bus home for the night. No one picked us up, but we made the bus via a marathon run through town and a bus driver who was running behind schedule that night.) So plan your return home carefully—make sure you have the latest bus and train schedules on hand—and always carry the numbers of local cab companies with you in case you miss the last bus or train home. A 3-hour cab ride back to New York won't be cheap. But it *will* be a cab ride back to New York.

♦ **Harp & Hound** (Mystic, CT): A warm, atmospheric pub for a pint and an Irish session. See p. 166.

BEST PLACE TO DITCH YOUR DIET

♦ **Blue Hill at Stone Barns** (Pocantico Hills, NY): From the farm to your table, this amazing American fare prompts New Yorkers to reserve a table several months in advance. See p. 105.

BEST PLACES FOR A COZY WINTER WEEKEND

♦ **Troutbeck** (Amenia, NY): A country estate with logs on the fire, shelves of books for browsing, and a small bar for a cold evening's nightcap. See p. 85.

◆ **Inn at National Hall** (Westport, CT): Hole up in dramatic rooms with sitting areas and enormous bathtubs or head to the drawing room and watch the snow fall outside. See p. 70.

◆ **Lodge at Emerson Place** (Woodstock, NY): Ski the day at Belleayre, then come back to log-cabin charm with hotel amenities— and a room with a fireplace, plush robes, a sleeping loft, and a balcony overlooking the creek. See p. 30.

◆ **Silvermine Tavern** (Norwalk, CT): Live jazz and hearty New England fare warm up the tavern, where you can retire upstairs for a long winter's nap. See p. 109.

BEST PLACES TO STEP BACK IN TIME

◆ **Rye Playland** (Rye, NY): This seaside summer park hasn't changed much in 70 years, with its beach, a boardwalk, and old-fashioned rides. See p. 220.

◆ **Mystic Seaport** (Mystic, CT): Trace the origins of whaling and shipbuilding at this living re-creation of a 19th-century coastal community. See p. 166.

◆ **Williams Lake** (Rosendale, NY): Think there's no such thing as those *Dirty Dancing*–style lake resorts? Think again. Retro is the word at this family-friendly all-inclusive. See p. 226.

BEST PLACES TO GET IN THE CHRISTMAS SPIRIT

◆ **Festival of Light** (Hartford, CT): Starting Thanksgiving weekend, Hartford's Constitution Plaza twinkles with more than 250,000 little white lights. See p. 258.

◆ **Mystic Seaport** (Mystic, CT): It's Christmas 1876 during the lantern-light tours through this harbor-side museum set up like a colonial village. See p. 166.

BEST PLACES TO PROPOSE

◆ **Saugerties Lighthouse** (Saugerties, NY): Looking out over the Hudson River from the balcony of the light tower, you'll both be seeing stars. See p. 57.

◆ **Mohonk Mountain House** (New Paltz, NY): This old-fashioned resort is full of romantic nooks and crannies. See p. 88.

◆ **Castle on the Hudson** (Tarrytown, NY): The regal rooms here are worthy of an engagement *and* a honeymoon. See p. 54.

BEST GAY-FRIENDLY WEEKENDS

◆ **Lefèvre House** (New Paltz, NY): The beds wear Versace at this modern B&B, set in a town that proudly waves the rainbow flag. See p. 73.

Why I Love Adirondack Trailways

When you spend every weekend for 8 months on buses and trains, you become pretty sensitive to the details. Sometimes they're subtle—like the Adirondack Trailways buses that have net bags on the back of the seat in front of you so you can keep a magazine or bottle of water handy. At other times subtlety goes out the window, like when a driver for a competing bus company spent a good half-hour on the microphone explaining to our entire busload of Pennsylvania-bound travelers everything that's wrong with the company. New Yorkers are fortunate to have a bus line like Adirondack Trailways, a line that knows each experience you have on board will determine whether you ever buy another ticket. Trailways starts with a terrific website that lists all schedules and fares for their major destinations. Most destinations have a long list of arrivals and departures each day, and their fares are the same reasonable price no matter what day or time you ride. Their buses are clean, quiet, and on time. Their drivers are capable, safe, and willing to help. Not only that, but they travel to those Hudson Valley and Catskills towns with the best things to see and do. Trailways is the only bus line that consistently offers a trip so quiet and so pleasant that I've seen people fall asleep before the bus even pulls out of Port Authority. To plan your trip, go to www.trailwaysny.com.

♦ **Sky Lake Lodge Shambhala** (Rosendale, NY): Weekend workshops at this welcoming retreat incorporate yoga, meditation, and the tenets of Buddhism. See p. 146.

BEST PLACES FOR BIG SPENDERS

♦ **Skip Barber Racing School** (Lakeville, CT): The 3-day racing school puts you on track to your new favorite hobby. See p. 43.

♦ **Make Your Own Wine** (Elmsford, NY): Bottle a whole barrel of your own custom blend. See p. 112.

♦ **Long Island Wine Country's Wine Camp** (Southold, NY): Four days of living like you own a vineyard. See p. 121.

♦ **Inn at National Hall** (Westport, CT): A two-story suite with a winding staircase makes for a very nice break from your cramped city apartment. See p. 70.

♦ **Atlantic City, NJ:** Play the high-stakes tables, order two carts of room service, and reserve the couple's suite for treatments at the Borgata spa. See p. 60.

◆ **Castle on the Hudson** (Tarrytown, NY): Spacious rooms, multi-course dinners with fabulous wine, Bulgari bath products—but at a price tag fit for a king. See p. 54.

BEST PLACE TO TAKE A BATH (OR SWIM WHILE IT SNOWS)

◆ **The Porches Inn** (North Adams, MA): Claw-foot and whirlpool tubs sit deep and wide. Out back, next to the hot tub, the outdoor pool is kept warm enough for year-round swimming. See p. 208.

BEST PLACES FOR SHUTTERBUGS OR PAINTERS

◆ **Mohonk Mountain House** (New Paltz, NY): White cliffs, the Shawangunk Mountains, a half-mile-long lake—all beyond scenic and ready for your lens. See p. 88.

◆ **Stone Barns Center for Food & Agriculture** (Pocantico Hills, NY): Set up an easel and paint the rolling farms or old stone barns. See p. 103.

◆ **Sailing the *Cirrus*** (Kingston, NY): Sailing-and-painting excursions offer perspectives that harken back to the Hudson River School set. See p. 26.

BEST PLACES TO SWIM IN A LAKE

◆ **Interlaken Inn** (Lakeville, CT): No one can resist a jump in the lake so pretty they named the town for it. See p. 43.

◆ **Williams Lake** (Rosendale, NY): Kids love the cool lake here for swimming and canoeing; families find it an easy place to get together for family reunions. See p. 226.

◆ **Mohonk Mountain House** (New Paltz, NY): The lake here is abuzz with summer activity—swimming, boating, and fishing—in a dazzling mountain setting. See p. 88.

BEST GETAWAYS WITH YOUR DOG

◆ **Interlaken Inn** (Lakeville, CT): At the foothills of the Berkshires in the Litchfield Hills, dogs can run on the lawn, explore the woods, or swim in the lake at this inn with pet-friendly rooms. See p. 43.

◆ **Stone Barns Center for Food and Agriculture** (Pocantico Hills, NY): After roaming the fields and farms, walk the dog along the adjacent trails of Rockefeller State Park. See p. 103.

BEST TOWNS WITH A SEASONAL TROLLEY

◆ **Kingston, NY:** The three districts of the town include the harbor, museums, and historic stone houses—all along one route. See p. 28.

◆ **Beacon, NY:** The town trolley easily whisks you from the art at Dia: Beacon to the downtown restaurants, shops, and galleries. See p. 203.

Why I Love TripAdvisor.com

I don't remember how I finalized my hotel decisions before TripAdvisor.com. The website is filled with hotel reviews from regular, everyday people who have stayed the night and, afterward, wanted to—for better or worse—share their experiences with others. The website takes you behind the scenes and into the lobbies, restaurants, rooms, and service aspects of hotels around the globe. I learned that a hotel I was considering for the holidays in Jamaica has a seedy carryout store across the street that's a prime meeting place for local dealers. I read from many guests that an otherwise promising-looking hotel on the water in Upstate New York smells completely moldy, and that an innkeeper in Philadelphia has a long-standing reputation for rushing her guests through breakfast. Humph! On the flip side, I've read rave reviews of many hotels I have then booked and absolutely enjoyed. I don't want to imply that one bitter review of an otherwise shining property should be enough to turn you away. But I can say that I don't know of a better source for confirming that a hotel you've heard so many good things about is actually known for delivering on its promises. Here's to a good night's sleep wherever you go!

BEST BEACH ESCAPES
- ◆ **Block Island, RI:** Bike around the island, lie on the beach, check out the lighthouses, and go shopping in town. See p. 78.
- ◆ **Atlantic City, NJ:** Not just casinos anymore. The beach clubs are hopping 'til all hours of the morning. See p. 60.
- ◆ **Spring Lake, NJ:** This beach also features a lake, lovely Victorian B&Bs, and a good dose of peace and quiet. See p. 49.

BEST SPOOKY PLACE
- ◆ **New Hope, PA:** Brave souls can take a lantern-lit ghost tour and stay in a haunted hotel. See p. 190.

BEST GETAWAYS CLOSE TO THE CITY
- ◆ **Chinese Scholar's Garden** (Staten Island, NY): Built in China and transported here, this serene and uncrowded garden is just a quick bus ride from the Staten Island Ferry. See p. 128.
- ◆ **Noguchi Museum** (Long Island City, NY): An indoor-outdoor sculpture space with a spiritual ambience. See p. 214.
- ◆ **Kykuit** (Tarrytown, NY): This Rockefeller estate and its gardens, sculpture, and other artworks are the must-see gem of the Hudson. See p. 177.

Why I Love Metro North Railroad

Metro North trains go almost everywhere north of the city that you could want to go. You can choose to ride in seats facing backward or forward, the trains have decent bathrooms, and, if you can keep away from cellphone yappers, it's a quiet, scenic trip any season of the year (especially on the Hudson Line). You can even bring your bike if you get a $5 lifetime permit in advance.

But mainly I love Metro North because they don't mind toting along my dog, Lilly (as long as none of the nearby passengers mind her either). If you can get your dog to Grand Central, you can bring him or her on board a Metro North train inside a carrier or even on a secure and controlled leash. As long as you keep the leash short throughout the trip and your dog is not being a nuisance of noise, odor, or wild antics, you can ride up the Hudson to any number of patches of open land and let your furry friend run free.

Metro North does say that:

◆ Dogs cannot occupy a seat.

◆ Dogs are "subject to approval" by the conductor.

◆ Naturally, service animals are always welcome.

The trick, however, may be getting your dog to Grand Central in the first place—subways, buses, and the LIRR do *not* allow doggies unless they are safely tucked inside a kennel carrier. (Metro North seems to be the crunchy, animal-loving hippie of the MTA.) Living in Brooklyn, we have had good luck with several car services that are willing to pick us up and let our dog ride on our laps in the car, as long as we specify that we're bringing her when we call for a pickup. Cabs may or may not pick you up when you've got a leashed dog. As a last resort, you may end up having to get to the terminal on foot. But what dog doesn't mind an extra walk? For more information, go to www.mta.info and type "pets" in the Search text field.

◆ **Caramoor** (Katonah, NY): Treasures from around the world fill this elegant estate. Music events and afternoon teas complement the house tours. See p. 171.

BEST WAYS TO SEE IT ALL

◆ **Vintage Tours of Long Island Wine Country:** Tour, taste, and talk about wines when you spend a day in the heartland of some of the state's finest grapes. See p. 100.

◆ **Royal Rolling Chair Rides in Atlantic City, NJ:** Save your feet but see the boardwalk when you're pushed along the length of it swaddled in an old-fashioned wicker basket (www.rollingchairs.com). See p. 64.

BEST PLACES FOR A PICNIC

+ **West Mountain on the Appalachian Trail:** Spread out on the rocks with hawks above and a patchwork of farmland below. See p. 22.

+ **Olana** (Hudson, NY): Frederic Church shared the views from his hilltop estate with friends from across the world; now they are open to you, too. See p. 185.

BEST B&B BREAKFASTS

+ **Lefèvre House** (New Paltz, NY): Three decadent, chef-prepared courses in a metro-chic modern dining room. See p. 73.

+ **The Martin Coryell House** (Lambertville, NJ): Bountiful home-made breakfasts of stuffed French toast or blueberry waffles served on antique china. See p. 196.

BEST ART MUSEUM

+ **Williams College Museum of Art** and the **Clark Institute** (Williamstown, MA): Not far from the Porches Inn in North Adams, these are two of the most highly regarded art institutions in the country. See p. 212.

BEST ALTERNATIVE ART MUSEUMS

+ **Mass MoCA** (North Adams, MA): Postmodern art fills this former textile-printing plant across from the Porches Inn, where the workers used to live. See p. 208.

+ **Dia: Beacon** (Beacon, NY): Natural elements are a common medium in this quiet showplace for unconventional art. See p. 203.

The Nuts & Bolts of Mass Transit

THE MAJOR MASS TRANSIT PORTALS FOR NEW YORK CITY ARE **PORT Authority Bus Terminal** (buses), **Grand Central Terminal** (trains), and **Penn Station** (trains). Of course, if you've got the money (but still no car), there are any number of alternative ways to travel in and out of the city, including private jitneys and buses, limousines and town cars, fast-speed ferries, and (if money really *is* no object) helicopter and plane services. In this chapter, however, we concentrate on the Big Three mass transit options and provide insider tips on how to maneuver your way through some of the world's busiest transportation hubs. Complete contact information for bus and train lines can be found in the "Resources" appendix at the end of the book.

Port Authority Bus Terminal

The **Port Authority Bus Terminal** (625 Eighth Ave.; customer hot line ⊘ **800/221-9903**, automated bus information 212/564-8484; www.panynj.gov/CommutingTravel/bus/html/pa.html) is the world's busiest bus terminal. Its North Wing (42nd St. and Eighth Ave.) and South Wing (41st St. and Eighth Ave.) are connected on the second level and on the subway level through hallways, and on the street level by walking outside through a set of doors near the front of each building.

TIPS FOR USING PORT AUTHORITY BUS TERMINAL

- ◆ The ticket counters for NJ Transit, Academy, Martz, and Trans-Bridge bus lines are toward the back of the South Wing on the street level.
- ◆ The ticket counter for Short Line/Coach USA is on the second level of the North Wing.

- There are ticket counters for Trailways, Peter Pan/Bonanza, and Greyhound in both buildings. The ones on the street level of the South Wing tend to have shorter lines than those on the subway level of the North Wing.

- Most bus companies start boarding their buses 5 or 10 minutes early so they can leave right on time. Unlike the airlines, buses with late departures are very rare—so try not to cut it close and force yourself to make a run for it. Chances are you won't make it.

- Most buses have a restroom on board and do not make stops for food, smoking, or anything else.

- The bus rules are common-sense ones: no smoking, no radios without headphones, keep your conversations at a reasonable level. For many, this is naptime.

- Many buses also make an announcement about limiting the use of your cellphone. So don't plan to use your 3-hour ride to catch up with everyone listed in your phone.

- There are no guarantees, but most buses arrive at their destinations on time—barring traffic caused by an accident, for example, or a particularly heavy rush hour. Traffic can delay a trip, but oftentimes projected traffic delays have already been factored into the published arrival time.

- Buses like to travel full, so don't expect two seats to yourself. That said, you'll sometimes be able to score two seats for less popular destinations and travel times.

- In some cases, you can buy your ticket back to NYC on board the bus if the company does not have a station in town or if it is closed at the time of your departure. But if you're traveling round-trip, it's easier to buy the round-trip ticket upfront. Agents at the ticket counter may ask you what day and time you're coming back, but you're rarely locked into a specific trip and can use the ticket anytime.

- Best tip: If you know you can't get to the station until shortly before the bus departs, buy your ticket days in advance at the ticket counter or online. A half-hour before a bus leaves, the line is generally short. But by 15 to 20 minutes before departure, the line is often wrapping around itself and bumping into lines for other gates. If you're traveling with a friend, have one person go to the gate while the other buys tickets. If you get to the gate with only a few minutes to spare, you may not find two seats together.

- Best on-the-go food: Au Bon Pain on the street level of the South Wing. Beyond bagels and pastries, grab a wrap, salad, fresh-fruit cup, pack of carrot and celery sticks, soup, gourmet cheese, or an M&M cookie.

◆ Best place to pick up something you forgot: Duane Reade on the street level of the South Wing. The many Hudson News stands throughout the terminals also carry headache medicine, bags of trail mix, bottled water, and soft drinks.

◆ Best restrooms: On the second level of the North Wing. Not glitzy, but a step above those near the gates downstairs.

Grand Central Terminal

Grand Central Terminal (42nd St. and Park Ave.; events hot line ✆ **212/340-2210;** www.grandcentralterminal.com) is the hub for **Metro-North** commuter trains (✆ **212/532-4900;** www.mta.nyc.ny. us/mnr) that run from the city to points north in New York and Connecticut and back. Other than the subways 4, 5, 6, 7, and S (shuttle to Times Sq.), Metro-North is the only mode of transportation based in this station.

As most New Yorkers know, Grand Central is a destination in itself—even if you're not using the transportation system, it's a great place to meet for lunch or dinner or for a drink—even to pick up dinner (whether from the Dining Concourse in the station's lower level or from Grand Central Market on the main level). Believe it or not, this beautiful public space was on its way to suffering the fate of its sister terminal, the original Penn Station, a neoclassical masterwork that was demolished to make way for a more modern structure. But Grand Central was spared the wrecking ball through a landmarks preservation campaign led by such famous New Yorkers as Jacqueline Kennedy Onassis. A multimillion-dollar renovation completed in 1998 modernized the building and restored its show-stopping luster.

TIPS FOR USING GRAND CENTRAL

◆ There are three Metro-North lines. They are, from west to east: the Hudson line (it goes up the east bank of the Hudson River), the Harlem line (runs roughly parallel to the NY–CT border), and the New Haven line (travels along the CT coast, with several branch lines). The screens in the terminal that post departure times, as well as the paper maps and schedules, are coded by color: green, blue, and red, respectively. Tickets for all three lines are available from ticket machines or the ticket counters. (*Note:* Bike permits are available only at window no. 27.)

◆ Fares are divided into peak (rush hour) and off-peak (non–rush hour, weekends, and holidays). Traveling off-peak can save a few bucks each way, depending on the fare. Tickets purchased on board trains have an additional surcharge of $4.75 and $5.50 and credit cards are not accepted. (Avoid this if at all possible!) If you are returning to the city from a station where there are no ticket machines on the platform and the ticket office is closed, you will not be forced to pay the surcharge for an onboard purchase. Web tickets purchased in advance online offer a 5% savings over those purchased at the station.

◆ It makes sense to buy a round-trip ticket upfront. You won't be tied into coming back on a certain day or time. Know, however, that if you buy an off-peak ticket and use the ticket during peak times, you'll need to pay the difference.

◆ The clock-topped information kiosk in the center of the terminal is your one-stop shop for schedules, maps, and a real live person to answer your questions.

◆ Tracks 11 to 42 are on the main floor; tracks 101 to 117 are on the lower level (where the Food Court is located).

◆ Metro-North trains run a tight ship. They tend to leave on the dot and arrive right on time. Trains are generally quite full and at rush hours can be packed. Store larger bags overhead on luggage racks or under your seat.

◆ Some seats face forward and some backward. If you're easily affected by a landscape that moves backward, board early to grab a forward-facing seat.

◆ While some trains are quiet, there are plenty of cellphone yakkers who don't mind sharing their conversations with the whole train. You have been warned.

◆ Metro-North trains have restrooms, but they are sometimes few and far between along the train, or even locked during certain hours (post-cleaning, for security reasons, and so forth).

◆ If you have extra time, you'll have plenty of browsing options here, from the New York City Transit Museum store (great bags) and Papyrus paper to Our Name is Mud pottery and several boutiques with high-end accessories.

◆ Ever noticed the StoryCorps booth in the Biltmore Room on the main level next to tracks 41 and 42? Inside this soundproof box is a studio where you can record your story or the stories of your loved ones on CD. For more information, go to **www.storycorps.net**.

◆ **Free tours:** The Municipal Arts Society sponsors a free tour every Wednesday at 12:30pm. Meet the tour guide at the center information booth on the Main Concourse. For more information, call ✆ **212/935-3960.** The Grand Central Partnership sponsors a free 90-minute walking tour of Grand Central Terminal and the surrounding neighborhood on Friday at 12:30pm. The tour meets in the Sculpture Court of the Whitney Museum at Altria on East 42nd Street, across from Grand Central. For more information, call ✆ **212/883-2420** or visit www.grandcentralpartnership.org.

◆ **Best places to meet someone:** A conservative 95% of New Yorkers meet at the central information kiosk smack-dab in the middle of Grand Central—it's easy to find and centrally located. But if you don't know what the people you're meeting look like, you'll have a hard time finding them among the sea of other people waiting there. Across from the information center, along the wall, is an I LOVE NY TOURISM window. Brochures for Broadway shows and the like are laid out here. The window is usually devoid of people, making it an easy place to find someone you haven't already met. The currency-exchange window to its left is another good option.

◆ **Best place to nosh:** Just about anywhere! The Dining Concourse, which takes up the entire lower level of Grand Central, is a monster food court with serious food (from sushi to Creole to Indian to pizza) with places to sit, too. On the main level, Zaro's Bread Basket, Starbucks, and others offer takeout options. The classic Oyster Bar restaurant (on the lower level) cultivates fans with its 25 types of fish and up to 30 varieties of oysters. Cipriani Dolci, Charlie Palmer's Métrazur, and Michael Jordan's The Steak House N.Y.C. are the restaurants on the Balcony Level.

◆ **Best food for picnic fare:** The food hall called Grand Central Market, at the east end of the terminal. Here you can get gourmet prepared foods, cheeses, seafood, fruit, nuts—even fresh flowers.

◆ **Best place to pick up something you forgot:** Rite-Aid in the Shuttle Passage of the main level. The many Hudson News stands throughout the terminals also carry headache medicine, bags of trail mix, bottled water, and the like.

◆ **Best places for last-minute gifts:** Grande Harvest Wines, and Flowers on Lexington, both next to Grand Central Market, if you need a last-minute gift. Treats and kitchen gifts can be found in the market as well.

◆ **Best places for a drink:** The Saloon at the Oyster Bar or the Campbell Apartment cocktail lounge on the Balcony Level. The former is down-to-earth and richly atmospheric; the latter is sophisticated, old-world, and serves drinks the price of some train tickets. (It was the former office and salon of 1920s tycoon John W. Campbell.) During the evening rush hour, beer is actually sold at the entrance to some of the tracks.

♦ Best little-known facts: The Beaux Arts interior of Grand Central is truly striking. The floors are made of Tennessee marble, and the large, bare-bulb chandeliers are made of real gold. The ceiling of the main terminal is covered in an astronomical mural by French painter Paul Helleu. It depicts the Mediterranean sky—with an October–March zodiac and 2,500 stars. In one corner you can see a dark rectangle that is actually dirt! When the ceiling was cleaned as part of a major restoration in 1996, the patch of dirt was left to remind everyone why the ceiling would be kept clean from then on.

Penn Station

Of the three major mass transit terminals in NYC, **Penn Station** (Eighth Ave. between 31st and 33rd sts.; ✆ **212/630-6401**) is the gloomiest and least up-to-date space. It replaced the grand, much lamented McKim, Mead & White 1910 structure, which was demolished in 1964 to make way for the current building—now, in an ironic nod to the past, scheduled to be replaced in the near future by another historic McKim, Mead & White landmark, the 1914 post office, nearby. Until then, however, **Amtrak** (www.amtrak.com), **Long Island Rail Road** (**LIRR;** www.mta.nyc.ny.us/lirr), and **NJ Transit** (www.njtransit.com) trains all use separate areas of the current building. Each area has its own ticket counters.

TIPS FOR USING PENN STATION

♦ Amtrak, LIRR, and NJ Transit all offer quick-ticket kiosks that make purchasing tickets with a credit or debit card much faster than waiting in line for the ticket counters. Never wait in those lines (especially the LIRR ones on a summer weekend) unless you have some long-winded question. Bring a credit card and use the kiosks.

♦ Amtrak has a waiting area with seating, but you must show a ticket to enter.

♦ Amtrak track announcements are made about 10 minutes before departure, and are posted on the large board by the tracks. There's usually a mad rush downstairs to the tracks once the track number is posted. When the conductor takes your ticket, it must be signed in the upper-left corner, and he or she may also ask for photo ID. Most Amtrak trains offer tray-tables, power outlets, restrooms, and a cafe car with simple snacks and beverages. Some trains have separate cars for coach class and business class. Some even have "quiet cars" that ban cellphone use.

◆ LIRR and NJ Transit run fairly close to schedule. Amtrak makes an effort but suffers from periodic delays.

◆ For the LIRR, ticket prices vary by time of day (categorized as peak and off-peak fares). Avoid rush hours, which are more crowded and have peak fares, if possible. Tickets purchased on board trains cost $4.75 to $5.50 more than tickets bought before boarding at ticket machines or ticket windows and credit cards are not accepted. This higher onboard fare does not apply to customers boarding at stations without a ticket office/ticket machine. Web tickets can be purchased online in advance for a 5% savings.

◆ NJ Transit will also allow you to purchase tickets on board, which are subject to a surcharge unless the station has no agents or ticket machines.

◆ The LIRR offers service between NYC and Queens, Brooklyn, and 134 Long Island communities. Destinations include Belmont Park (horse racetrack), Shea Stadium (Mets baseball), the Hamptons, Montauk, Long Beach, Jones Beach, and Long Island wine country.

◆ The LIRR, Amtrak, and NJ Transit trains all have restrooms.

◆ Collapsible bicycles are permitted on NJ Transit trains at all times. Standard-frame bicycles may be carried on board during off-peak hours (weekdays 9:30am–4pm and 7pm–5am) and all day Saturday and Sunday.

◆ Best tip: Don't use the Taxi Dispatch line to wait for a cab. Few cabs travel down this side street and it's much faster to walk over to Eighth Avenue and hail one yourself.

◆ Other best tip: Arrive early enough to catch your train but not so early that you have too much time to hang out. The station is rather dismal in most parts, and because track numbers aren't announced more than 15 minutes in advance, there's no point in arriving 45 minutes early to secure a prime seat.

◆ Best non–fast food: After Krispy Kreme and Nathan's comes Tracks Raw Bar & Grill. Penn Station is all about fast food. Even eateries that aren't actually "fast food" have the look and feel of fast food. Tracks is the exception to this rule. It may shock you that Grand Central isn't the only terminal with an oyster bar, but this is 34th Street's answer to fresh shucked oysters and clams in a dozen varieties, served with a well-poured pint of Guinness. Sure, it's pricey: Burgers and sandwiches are $8.95, entrees are $14 to $20, but it's clean and you won't find anything better for blocks and blocks. The atmosphere could be improved, but the food is consistently tasty. Tracks is on the LIRR concourse off Seventh Avenue (✆ **212/244-6350;** www.tracksbargrill.com).

◆ Best history fact: The original station was a work of art when it opened in 1910, with 15-foot ceilings and a waiting room designed to resemble the Roman Baths of Caracalla and the Basilica of Constantine. Twenty-two stone eagles, each weighing a ton, crowned the building. Almost nothing remains of old Penn Station; look for the two original stone eagles outside the Seventh Avenue entrance. Another sits in the courtyard of a building down on Third Avenue near St. Mark's Place.

Outdoor Activities

I T'S HARD NOT TO GET JEALOUS TALKING TO FRIENDS WHO LIVE IN places with an abundance of outdoor adventures to be had out their front door. Talk of kayaking in Seattle, skiing in Colorado, golfing in Palm Springs, or hiking up in Maine sure can get under the skin.

It's not as if New York City has no outdoor recreation. You can paddle in a kayak on the Hudson River for free at Pier 26 or fly through the air at the riverfront trapeze school downtown. You can ice-skate in Rockefeller Center or freestyle roller-skate in Central Park. You can ride your bike, jog, or stroll in the city's many parks. The extreme sport of waiting in lines behind velvet ropes in the freezing cold to get into a nightclub? You can do that here as well.

Okay, maybe NYC doesn't offer the kind of just-out-your-front-door outdoor adventures you can get in, say, Portland, Oregon, or Boulder, Colorado. But serious nature-centric opportunities are just an hour or two away. For scenic peaks, we've got the Catskills, the Berkshires, and the Appalachian Trail. For watersports, there's the Atlantic Ocean, the Delaware Water Gap, and the Esopus Creek. Sky diving, race-car driving, sailing, tubing, and rafting are all a bus or train ride away. And for those of us who take their sports with less horsepower, the New York/Northeast Region offers plenty of great green fairways, gin-clear swimming holes, and gentle trails through glorious woodlands.

Appalachian Trail Day Hike

Pawling, NY 12564
☏ 201/512-9348 · www.nynjtc.org

Getting there: Metro-North Harlem line train from Grand Central to the Appalachian Trail stop.
Subways: 4, 5, 6, 7, S to Grand Central.
Approximate travel time: 1 hr., 55 min. each way.
Schedule: Trains leave Grand Central twice in the morning Sat-Sun and return from the Appalachian Trail 3 times in the afternoon.

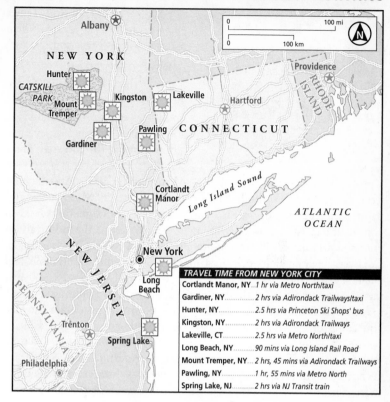

Albany

NEW YORK

Hunter

CATSKILL
PARK Mount
Tremper

Kingston   Lakeville   Hartford

Gardiner

Pawling   C O N N E C T I C U T

Providence

RHODE ISLAND

Cortlandt
Manor

Long Island Sound

ATLANTIC
OCEAN

New York

Long
Beach

NEW JERSEY

PENNSYLVANIA

Trenton

Spring Lake

Philadelphia

0   100 mi
0   100 km

TRAVEL TIME FROM NEW YORK CITY	
Cortlandt Manor, NY	1 hr via Metro North/taxi
Gardiner, NY	2 hrs via Adirondack Trailways/taxi
Hunter, NY	2.5 hrs via Princeton Ski Shops' bus
Kingston, NY	2 hrs via Adirondack Trailways
Lakeville, CT	2.5 hrs via Metro North/taxi
Long Beach, NY	90 mins via Long Island Rail Road
Mount Tremper, NY	2 hrs, 45 mins via Adirondack Trailways
Pawling, NY	1 hr, 55 mins via Metro North
Spring Lake, NJ	2 hrs via NJ Transit train

Season: Year-round, weekends only.
Cost: $23 round-trip off-peak; trail use is free.

This peak-driven day hike offers an ample trekking challenge for sea-soned and unseasoned hikers alike. A quick train ride from the city lets you off right *on* the Appalachian Trail—which just happens to stretch 2,160 miles from Georgia to Maine. This section of the AT is chock-full of uphill terrain, leisurely flatlands, cool woods, flowered fields, and, at the summit, a rewarding view of **West Mountain,** where you can stretch out on the rocks and feast on a picnic lunch.

TRANSIT FACTS

This is a weekend-only train stop, just before Pawling, New York. Trains leave Grand Central at two different times in the morning and make three return trips in the afternoon/early evening. The AT attracts a decent number of hikers in good weather, but, just to be safe, mention to the train conductor as you board that you're getting off at the Appalachian Trail stop. Times change, so check Metro-North for schedule information.

HIKING THE TRAIL

Exiting the train, head south, away from nearby Route 22. You'll trek through a marshy area and an open field before eventually beginning the forested, fairly steep, ¼-mile ascent up **West Mountain.** The Appalachian Trail is well marked, with white "blazes"—vertical white rectangles painted on trees, rocks, or other landmarks—in both directions to keep you on track. At the top, 3⅓ miles in, veer off onto the side trail on your right. Here, you'll get a mountaineer's view to go with your lunch. Look east over a patchwork of farmland and beautiful countryside, and get dizzy watching hawks as they circle above. Elevation: 1,100 feet (just 300 or so ft. shy of the top of the Empire State Building).

After lunch it's as easy as heading back down the mountain the way you came up. The round-trip trek is a moderate 6¼ miles and, of course, goes by faster on the return trip downhill. You'll want to time your hike to allow plenty of time to make the return train to New York. (Write that time on your arm if you have to—there are only three trains back each day!) Catch the train on the same platform on which you arrived.

Pace yourself, drink plenty of water, and stop as often as you need to. Because part of the hike is through open fields, the sun in the warmer months can really give you a beating. There are no food or restroom facilities on the trail, so plan accordingly. Pack out any trash. The average time for this round-trip hike is 7 hours—including 1 hour for lunch and several short breaks.

For an **alternate day hike,** get off at the Appalachian Trail stop but head north, crossing the highway, Route 22, that runs parallel to the train tracks. Follow the AT's white blazes, turning left onto paved Hurds Corner Road, then right to enter the woods and Pawling Nature Reserve. Keep a keen eye on the time and allow a solid window of time to be back for your return train.

For an **overnight hike,** catch the Saturday morning train and camp out 3 miles in at the Telephone Pioneers shelter (or, for speed demons, 10 miles in at the Morgan Stewart Memorial shelter). Head back the next day and hop the last train on Sunday evening. You'll be home in time to drop your bag and order a pizza. You've earned it.

Maps and detailed guidebooks are available from local Eastern Mountain Sports stores or the Appalachian Trail Conference (✆ **201/ 512-9348;** www.nynjtc.org).

If you like this hike, you can find other trails that are accessible without a car at **www.nynjtc.org/trails/no-car.html**.

New York Golf Shuttle

P.O. Box 40165, Glen Oaks, NY 11004
✆ **800/679-7011** • www.nygolfshuttle.com

Getting there: Shuttle will pick you up at an NYC location you arrange in advance.
Approximate travel time: Varies depending on the course you choose.
Schedule: Pickup and drop-off are built around your tee time.
Season: Call for tee times. Season runs Apr–Nov.
Cost: Varies by course and increases if you need rentals.

Why should suits get to have all the fun? The New York Golf Shuttle may have been concocted so those with expense accounts can impress their best clients, but it works just as well for the casual duffer or the weekend warrior. Whether it's a birthday on the links, a couple of couples going head to head, or a day of serious golf, if you have no personal means of transportation and you lack the time for mass transit, New York Golf Shuttle is there to fill in the gaps. If you've always wanted to test your mettle out on **Bethpage Black** (home of the 2002 and 2009 U.S. Open championships), you can do it in style, with round-trip limo transport from the city to your links of choice. They'll make the reservation, too—and not only tee times but caddies and rentals as well. Just give them the date and they'll take care of the rest. The all-inclusive packages include the greens fees, carts, and luxury transportation.

A DAY OF GOLF

New York Golf Shuttle provides reservation booking and transportation to municipal courses, semiprivate courses, and the Bethpage courses. Reservations can be made up to a year in advance, or as spontaneously as the day before, provided there's still availability. You don't have to worry about booking a tee time or figuring out mass-transit arrangements—they do it all for you.

Normally the shuttle picks up passengers from Manhattan hotels, but you can arrange to be met wherever in the city works best for you. **Be warned:** Some courses ask that you be there an hour in advance to claim your reservation. Use the time to grab a snack at the clubhouse or to work the kinks out on the range. You may or may not have the option to use a caddy depending on where you play, but in general, most area courses use golf carts. This is done primarily for speed of play.

Your limo will be waiting at the course for you so you can hop right back in as soon as you're done with your round . . . or your after-round drinks.

WHERE TO EAT

Isn't booking your tee time, getting you there, and renting your clubs enough? New York Golf Shuttle isn't going to pack a picnic for you. You'll have to eat the traditional way—with the rest of the duffers at the snack bars and halfway houses at the golf course.

> **Tip**
>
> Check out the links on the company's website for their other shuttles: NY Ski Shuttle and Casino Shuttle.
>
> –Alex Altman

WHERE TO SHOP

The pro shops at the courses can rent out clubs to you. But you never know what you'll get until you're out there. Some sets may be mismatched, beat up, or too old for your taste. You can rent premium clubs in advance through NY Golf Shuttle for $75 per set per day. You'll be paying a little extra, but that set of Callaways may be worth it.

Sail the *Cirrus*

Rondout Harbor, Kingston, NY 12402
☏ **845/687-2440** • www.hudsonsailing.com

Getting there: Adirondack Trailways from Port Authority to Kingston, then a cab to the harbor.
Subways: A, C, E to 42nd St./Port Authority or N, Q, R, S, W, 1, 2, 3, 7 to 42nd St./Times Sq.

Approximate travel time: 2-2½ hr.

Schedule: Buses leave Port Authority once or twice an hour and return from Kingston on a similar schedule.

Alternate transit: Should you decide to take an Amtrak train to Rhinecliff (on the other side of the Hudson) and spend the weekend in small-town Rhinebeck instead, the *Cirrus* can pick you up at the docks there for your sail. From Penn Station to Rhinecliff, the train fare is $60-$70 round-trip and takes about 1 hr., 40 min. For more information, go to www.rhinebeck chamber.com.

Season: Spring-fall, depending on the weather.

Cost: $43 round-trip; charter excursions start at $75 per person for half-day, $150 per person for full day; lessons start at $250 per person for half-day, $650 for 3 half-days.

One of the most unassuming boats among the string of vessels in Kingston's Rondout Harbor, the *Cirrus* is also one of the fastest—having logged speeds of up to 18 knots, maybe more. It's no yacht, to be sure. There's no polished wood deck or cigar-smoking guy behind the wheel in white pants and docksiders. This is a water-skimming, smooth-riding trimaran racer. And whether you choose to hang on for a few hours of tanning and sailing or learn the ropes as the Hudson goes by on either side, you're in for one fine ride.

SAILING THE *CIRRUS*

A trimaran is made of a main hull and two smaller outrigger hulls (amas), attached to the main hull with lateral struts. The entire boat sits low to the water, providing what feels like a dolphin's-eye perspective. (The first trimarans were actually built by the Polynesians almost 4,000 years ago.) In the case of the *Cirrus*, in back are a few fiberglass seats, the sides of the cabin have meshy, trampoline-type areas, and up front there's just enough room to catch some rays. The small cabin has a minikitchen and a tiny head (that's ship talk for restroom). Its taut white wings are two sails and a spinnaker. All this adds up to a streamlined vessel that's low and light and slices and glides its way up, down, and across the river.

Captain Dan takes charters of up to six people—which can get pretty cozy once you add him and his mate. But that's not a bad thing. Dan isn't the kind of person with whom you'd mind being stuck out at sea, anyway (and you're not going to get stuck). He's a U.S. Coast Guard–licensed captain who has been sailing and racing on all kinds of boats for most of his life. You might also like to know that Corsair trimarans are unsinkable due to the closed-cell foam sandwich construction of their hulls. But beyond sailing, Dan is also a former instructor with the National Outdoor Leadership School and has experience climbing, mountaineering, ski patrolling, and teaching Nordic skiing. The man has things to talk about. In a way, he's some kind of Renaissance man—guys like him, girls dig him, and he looks like he was just born to sit on the back of a boat smoking a cigarette and getting ready to take the next gust of wind by the horns.

From a morning sail to pushing off as dusk moves in, there isn't a bad time of day or evening to sail the *Cirrus*. Those who book a morning sail can wake up and have their breakfast out on the water. On a brilliant afternoon, Dan will find some safe water where you can jump in and cool off if you like. If you go in the evening, you don't have to mess with slathering on the sunscreen. Along the ride you'll see lighthouses, an island, and estates that look out onto the water. The trimaran is true sailing at its best—in which you're close to the water, catching even the lightest of breezes, and feeling the boat respond to your every command.

If you sign on for the three-lesson beginner's course, you'll go through all the basics: sailing theory, safety, rules, rigging, points of sail, upwind sailing, downwind sailing, mooring, docking, and single-handing. You'll spend half of each day on the water, with the other half left to explore Kingston, our state's first capital city.

Built in 1998, the 28-foot *Cirrus* is a former national champion. She's fast, safe, stable, and sails with minimum heel (tilt) due to the buoyancy of the amas (the outboard hulls). She makes an excellent boat on which to learn sailing foundation, improve your racing skills, or relax away a Hudson River day.

GETTING AROUND

The bus drops passengers off at 400 Washington Ave. From there, it's a short walk to the Holiday Inn (503 Washington Ave.). If you're staying down by the waterfront in the Rondout section, you can hop on the **seasonal trolley** (see below), grab the **Citibus** (which runs several routes throughout the city for $1 per ride), or catch a **cab** by calling **Kingston Kabs** (∅ 845/331-8294, -8200), **Royal Taxi** (∅ 845/338-9420), or **New Cabs** (∅ 845/336-2400).

The harbor sits at the foot of downtown Kingston—also called the Rondout. This is one of three main areas of town. The midtown section is the middle area that runs along Broadway and links downtown with uptown, the third area, which is also called the Historic Stockade District. The three areas are too spread out to walk between them, but a seasonal trolley, the **Kingston Trolley Bus,** runs from one end of town through to the other, hitting all the must-see stops in between.

Events: Painting Cruises

The *Cirrus* also offers full-day "painting cruises" for those who dream of following in the footsteps of the Hudson River School painters. The day combines sailing and painting with a barbecue on the beach. Painting excursions are $150 per person with a four-person minimum. Call ✆ **845/687-2440** or go to www.hudsonsailing.com for details.

Operating weekends May through October, it costs just $1 for the day, including the tour you'll get along the way. Hours are 10am to 6pm, with extended hours until 8pm on Friday and Saturday in the summer.

WHAT TO DO NEARBY

Kingston is full of galleries, shops, museums, restaurants, and enough stuff to fill up a weekend for any history buff. The **Trolley Museum and Maritime Museum** (89 E. Strand; ✆ 845/331-3399; www.tmny. org) is a quick walk from where the *Cirrus* docks, the *Rip Van Winkle* (Rondout Landing; ✆ **845/843-7472**; www.hudsonrivercruises.com) offers narrated sightseeing cruises and a Friday-night music cruise, and the Stockade District has street after street of old stone houses. Guided **Historic Walking Tours** of the Uptown Stockade and Rondout Waterfront districts are held May through October on the first Saturday (2pm) and the third Saturday (11am) of the month. The tours are free, but you'll need to make reservations in advance (✆ **845/339-0720**). If you can't make a tour, pick up a map at the downtown Rondout visitor center at 20 Broadway, just up the street from the harbor (✆ **845/331-7517**) and take a self-guided tour of your own.

WHERE TO STAY

In Kingston, **Miss Gussie Bug B&B** (37 Broadway; ✆ **914/334-9110**; www.missgussiebug.com) is right along the waterfront. **Rondout B&B** (88 W. Chestnut St.; ✆ **845/331-8144**) is within walking distance, and the revamped **Holiday Inn** (503 Washington Ave.; ✆ **845/338-0400**; www.hikingston.com) is uptown, within a quick ride on the trolley, Citibus, or in a cab.

WHERE TO EAT

Feel free to bring some snacks and beverages with you on your sail. Pack a picnic lunch, or order one from chef Graziano Tecchio of the **Downtown Cafe** in Kingston through the captain. After your sail you'll find plenty of good restaurants along the harbor from which to choose (with seating both on the water and across the street), as well as in the Stockade District. Ask Captain Dan for his recommendations.

The Lodge at Emerson Place & Belleayre Mountain

The Lodge: 5340 Rte. 28, Mount Tremper, NY 12457
⌀ **845/688-2451** · www.emersonplace.com
Belleayre Mountain: Highmount, NY 12441
⌀ **845/254-5600** · www.belleayre.com

Getting there: Adirondack Trailways to Mt. Pleasant, at the intersection of Mt. Pleasant Rd. and Rte. 28.

Subways: A, C, E to Port Authority or N, Q, R, S, W, 1, 2, 3, 7 to Times Sq./42nd St.

Approximate travel time: 2 hr., 45 min.

Schedule: Buses leave Port Authority about 6 times a day (7am–5pm) and return from Mt. Pleasant on a similar schedule.

Alternate Transit: If you prefer to take an Amtrak train to Rhinecliff, NY (on the other side of the Hudson River), a car service can be arranged for guests. This service must be reserved in advance and a fee is charged. Alternatively, you can take an Adirondack Trailways bus into Kingston, NY, and have the resort arrange for car service from there, again for a fee. Trailways runs this route more often than the Mt. Tremper route so flexibility in scheduling is the advantage.

Season: The Lodge is open year-round; ski season runs roughly Nov–Mar.

Transit cost: $56 round-trip.

Lodge/ski rates: Doubles $190–$400 per night; 1-day lift tickets $46 per person on a weekend or holiday ($80 for a 2-day ticket), $37 midweek, and $28–$36 for half-day (noon–4pm).

Anyone who loves the idea of a log cabin but hates the idea of roughing it will take a quick shine to the cozy comforts of this log-construction Catskills lodge at the edge of the Catskill Forest Preserve. Guests are greeted with a fire in the lobby and the key to an equally welcoming retreat of a room. Thick Woolrich blankets dress twig furniture beds, and subtle bear and moose motifs show up in the decor.

The property used to be an 1800s dairy barn. Now the grain silo is a giant kaleidoscope, a walking trail runs along the creek in back, and Manhattanites come here in droves for the weekend to ski, shop, eat, rest, and sit by the fireplace they wish they had at home.

Even the standard rooms are a treat at the Lodge at Emerson Place, where the menu of accommodations includes two room types, three types of suites, and Frette robes, layers of blankets, and European bathroom amenities. From there, add a king-size bed, whirlpool tub, sitting area, and/or vaulted ceiling for ambience. Special-occasion guests might want to consider a suite with a second-floor bedroom, minibar, whirlpool tub, and a balcony with mountain views. Luxury suites have a private porch overlooking the creek and a gas fireplace.

Spring, summer, and fall are beautiful here, but winter brings in some of the biggest crowds. Book as far in advance as possible at any time of year to make sure you get your desired room type.

GETTING AROUND

Let the bus driver know when you board that you are going to Emerson Place. As long as advance notice is given, he or she will make a special stop at the intersection of Mount Pleasant Road and Route 28. Be sure to inform the reservations department that you'll be arriving by bus so someone will be there to greet you at the bus stop near the entrance to Emerson Place.

Emerson Place can arrange to shuttle you up to the ski mountains of Belleayre. Everything else you need is right on the property—a restaurant, a spa, a coffee bar, shopping, a walk along the stream, and plenty of Catskill views.

WHAT TO DO

Belleayre Mountain   Just a few minutes west of the Lodge at Emerson Place is Belleayre Mountain. Unlike other ski resorts, where condos creep ever closer, this one's beauty is pristine and shall remain so by law—Belleayre's snowy peaks are part of the protected Catskill Forest Preserve. The resort itself is actually owned and operated by the State of New York's Department of Environmental Conservation, and the slopes sit on what has been forever deemed wild land.

Belleayre is one of the best places to learn to ski in the East. Each lift ticket comes with access to a teaching circle where instructors guide first-time skiers down a green hill. For all levels, a 1½-hour group skiing or snowboarding class starts at $21. Nearly 60% of Belleayre's 42 slopes and trails are for intermediate skiers, with the rest divided almost evenly among beginner and expert hills. It's a great place to learn, but it's also a great place to ski while a companion is along to learn. By the afternoon, you may be meeting in the middle on a blue-square hill. Ask the lodge about ski packages (and the "Ski Free on Weekdays" packages) when you call to make a reservation. What's also

---

Events: Bonfire Nights

Every Friday night the Lodge hosts a bonfire to get guests together and make merry along the stream. Bonfires on the River Walk warm you up from 8 to 11pm and include campfire music, storytelling, champagne, wine, brandy, and beer.

important to note is that Belleayre's amazingly peaceful setting has in recent years helped to turn it into a four-season resort. When the snow melts, Belleayre Beach at Pine Hill Lake offers boating, fishing, hiking, biking, a sky ride to the summit, and a summer concert series. Year-round Belleayre packs a full events schedule, too.

Note: If you're simply heading to Belleayre, the Adirondack Trailways Ski Bus leaves daily from Port Authority. Tickets are $62 round-trip and include your lift ticket. (Rental is extra.) Belleayre's Overnight Ski Bus packages are available for 1- or 2-night stays and include lodging, lift tickets, and shuttle service to and from Belleayre Mountain. Call ∅ **800/431-4555** or 800/942-6904 for more information.

Emerson Place Spa   The decor is Asian Zen, but the treatments include ayurvedic rituals, reiki, mud wraps, aromatherapy, prenatal massage, manicures/pedicures, Indian head massage, yoga classes, and private yoga training and cardio hikes. Much is done with warm infused oils and herbal concoctions. Treat yourself to one of three 110-minute packages ($149–$200). Spa guests are welcome to use the steam room, sauna, whirlpool, resistance pool, and exercise equipment in the small fitness center.

> **Tip**
>
> Throughout the year, Emerson Place can coordinate a private guide to take you into the great outdoors for fishing, hiking, boating, mountain biking, or whatever other activity these mountains inspire you to tackle. Ideally, you'll want to reserve this service when you make your reservation.

The kaleidoscope   Maybe it wasn't a goal in life to see the world's largest kaleidoscope. But now that it's right in front of your nose, you might find it worth a look. It's official: The Guinness Book of World Records has declared that this kaleidoscope, created inside a former farm silo, is the world's biggest. It can hold a dozen or more people inside at a time, who then lie on the floor and look up to watch a 10-minute Surround Sound show that reflects onto 1½ tons of mirrors. Admission is $7. Afterward, see spots (and stars and fractals) in the adjacent **Kaleidostore.**

WHERE TO EAT

At the Lodge at Emerson Place, **The Catamount** has a casual, ski-lodge feel. It serves hearty American fare and is decorated with vaulted, beamed ceilings and antler chandeliers. Prime seating is fireside in winter and on the patio overlooking the Esopus Creek in summer. Start with fried calamari or a jumbo-shrimp cocktail and move to a choice of chops, ribs, steaks, and seafood dishes. Weekend nights sometimes feature live bands. The restaurant serves breakfast, dinner, and Sunday brunch; entrees run from $12 to $28.

Belleayre Mountain has several lodges for eating, drinking, and warming up with a view of the slopes, including the **Sunset Lodge,** at its highest elevation of 3,325 feet.

WHERE TO SHOP

The Emporium at Emerson Place This indoor plaza of a few select shops has an open floor plan that lets one store blend into the next. The tie that binds them together is a focus on country elegance and luxury goods. After browsing antiques and home furnishings, clothing, spa and beauty products, glassware, pottery, and linens, stop by the general store and the coffee bar. Here you can pick up gourmet snacks for later or sit down with a cappuccino and leaf through a book from the regionally focused library. Many of the books by local authors, maps, cookbooks, art books, outdoor recreation books, and history books are Catskills-themed.

Skydive the Ranch

45 Sandhill Rd., Gardiner, NY 12525
✆ **845/255-4033** · www.skydivetheranch.com

Getting there: Adirondack Trailways bus from Port Authority to New Paltz, then a cab from station.

Subways: A, C, E to 42nd St./Port Authority or N, Q, R, S, W, 1, 2, 3, 7 to 42nd St./Times Sq.

Approximate travel time: 1 hr., 45 min., plus 15-min. cab ride.

Schedule: The Ranch is open daily 8am (9am on weekdays) until sunset spring-fall. 7 or so buses throughout the day leave NYC for New Paltz and return on a similar schedule.

Alternate transit: Metro-North Hudson Line train to Poughkeepsie, take a cab from the station. The train ride takes 1 hr. 50 min.; the fare is $26 round-trip off-peak.

Season: Spring-fall, depending on the weather.

Hours: On weekends, time slots are available 8am-4pm; weekdays are flexible. Reservations are highly recommended.

Cost: $38 round-trip, plus cab fare.

Skydive jump cost: $180 for your 1st tandem jump.

"The Ranch" looks like a circus that set up years ago and never left town. The instructors roll and pack their chutes under a big striped tent, and an old, wheel-less bus is forever grounded nearby. Bathrooms are inside a shed, as are jumpsuits, goggles, and other equipment. A trailer houses the pro shop, where you can purchase your souvenir T-shirt. Everyone's having a great time, but it's not because they're clowning around. The ringmaster running this operation is a man named Joe Richards, who co-owns the ranch and has himself jumped more than 4,000 times. His instructors have received extensive training, and safety is the top priority here.

Don't head up to Gardiner expecting to jump without making a reservation first. And once you do, you'll want to keep an eye on the weather. If it's not cooperating—as in, a major downpour—they'll be happy to move your reservation to another day. Someone from the outfit will call you a few days in advance to take your credit card information for a $40 deposit; you can call and cancel without a penalty if you chicken out. The only way you'll lose your deposit is if you don't show up and never called to cancel or to reschedule for a different day. If you can't tell if the weather is skydive-friendly or not, give them a call the morning of your jump, before you leave for the bus station.

So who can skydive? Just about anyone in good health who weighs less than 225 pounds. If you're worried about finding the guts to actually jump out the plane window when the moment comes, your tandem master takes care of that for you. On, "ready, set, go" he jumps forward and you're along for the ride, whether you've come to terms with the view at 13,000 feet or not. And honestly, that's a good thing. The plane might be circling until it runs out of fuel if your group has to wait for each person to wrestle with his or her own personal fear-of-heights demons.

GETTING AROUND

New Paltz has only one cab company: **New Paltz Taxi** (∅ **845/255-1550**). The good news is that their office is right at the bus station. The bad news is that they may only have three cars running per shift. When you finish your dive, call for a pickup—then chill out at the picnic tables while you wait.

THE SKYDIVE

From a group of picnic tables, you can watch the groups scheduled before yours as they slide into soft landings on the adjacent grassy tarmac. But that's only after you've piled into the old bus to fill out seven pages of I-will-not-sue-you-and-neither-will-my-heirs paperwork and to view a totally dated-looking video on safety and procedure. Once you're signed and all paid up (add an extra $90 if you want the 10-min. video of your jump), you'll get a brief practice session about what you do when you're up in the air. The truth is, you don't need to do much—which makes most people very happy. Here's what you learn in the practice session: After the jump from the plane, you put your arms out to the sides, do a feel for the rip cord, and then check your altimeter. At 6,000 feet you activate your chute. Don't worry: If in the event you forget to do so, your instructor *will* do it for you.

Before you go anywhere, though, you're suited up in an optional jumpsuit, plus cap, goggles, and altimeter. (*Note:* It's a good idea to go for the Snoopy/Red Baron jumpsuit. Not only does it keep your clothing free from grass stains upon landing, it also provides an extra layer for the freezing temps during the freefall. And hey, it looks official for the video and any pre- and post-jump photos as well!)

They run a tight ship here, and unless they're mobbed, you'll be up in a plane in no time. Each plane holds up to 22 people, so be prepped to get a little cozy with your instructor—not a bad thing, as all are great. Jonathan is a sweetheart, Sebastien loves to do spins and flips if you're up for it, and Zak is known for wearing a helmet covered in bright blue fun fur. The instructors will adjust your harness and cap and go over last-minute instructions on the ride up—and it only takes a few minutes to reach jump-appropriate altitude, hovering somewhere in the range of 13,000 feet. If you've opted for the video, your cameraperson will actually be jumping out with you and shooting every expression you make from jump to grass landing.

What can be said about the jump other than that you get a loud, cold, and adrenaline-pumping minute of free fall followed by a graceful featherlike float? It's different for everyone, of course, but it's something I'll never forget. One of the reasons they push for the video here (aside from the $90) is that many people say it's like a wedding day—it's such a whirlwind, you kind of blank on the details once it's over. So the video—done on DVD—is actually money well spent. Your cameraperson records you on the ground beforehand and in the plane, jumps with you to get your goofy, play-by-play facial expressions, then captures you on the ground once it's all over. It's put together in about 15 or 20 minutes after you land, edited with some zany music and the date added, and ready to take home for your many screenings to come. (If you can't wait, you can preview the masterful creation on a TV and DVD player on the porch off the editing room.) Before you leave, your

> **Tip**
>
> To speed up the time from arriving to jumping, you can print out and sign all of the paperwork online, as well as watch the safety video. Go to www.skydive theranch.com.

instructor will sign a certificate and issue you an official bumper sticker and coupon for $24 off your next jump.

WHERE TO STAY

See the **Lefèvre House** entry in chapter 4, "Romantic Weekends," if you want to stay overnight in the area and make a real trip of it.

WHERE TO EAT

If you've brought along a lunch (you can pick up subs at one of several places near the New Paltz bus station before you head for the Ranch), spread out at the picnic tables to relive the jump and plan your next visit. Or take a cab and eat at any of the pubs and restaurants along the main street back in town. For an added dimension to your day, make a detour to the **Mountain Brauhaus Restaurant** (at the intersection of Rte. 44/55 and Rte. 299; ∅ **845/255-9766;** www.mountainbrauhaus. com), about 10 minutes away in a cab. It serves massive portions of hearty German fare like schnitzels and wursts and big pints of German beer.

Surf 2 Live Lessons

830 E. Chester St., Long Beach, NY 11561
∅ **516/973-7873** · surf2live.com

Getting there: Long Island Rail Road to Long Beach, NY. At Penn Station, purchase the train-and-beach-pass combination ticket for $17.
Approximate travel time: 90 min.
Schedule: Surf 2 Live teaches daily July–Sept, by appointment.
Hours: On weekends, time slots are available from 10am on, depending on the waves. Evening classes 6:30–8pm Mon–Fri, 6–7:30pm weekends. Reservations are required.
Cost: $17 round-trip including beach pass; group lessons are $60, private lessons are $100.

You may not realize it, but the coast of Long Island has plenty of gnarly waves. The laid-back crew of Surf 2 Live makes Long Beach their playground. Don't look for a sign, there isn't any; rather, the group can be spotted by their red and yellow boards. Or by their fearless leader, Elliot Zuckerman, a friendly, bronzed charmer (especially with the ladies) who has been catching waves for more than 40 years.

If you've always wanted to learn to surf but never had the opportunity, the Surf 2 Live lessons are a good place to start. Most anyone can do it, but it helps to have catlike agility and good balance. If you're worried about safety, Elliot keeps a keen eye on the group to make sure no one goes too close to the nearby jetty. And even if your "ride" lasts but a few seconds, for many it's glorious just being out in the waves with the Long Island sun beaming overhead. And we all know that carrying a surfboard automatically makes you cool. You are brave and fearless in the eyes of the sun-worshippers watching from the safety of their towels. It's a sport for rebels and renegades—just like you, dude.

GETTING AROUND

Once you exit the station at Long Beach, cross Park Avenue and follow the crowds to the boardwalk, take a left (keeping the ocean on your right) and walk until you reach Monroe Boulevard. You'll see the colored boards in the "Surfing Only" area.

SURF'S UP

First of all, be sure to make a reservation; these are required with a 50% deposit (and cancellations must be made 24 hr. in advance for a full refund). The only time class is canceled is if there is severe weather or a high surf advisory. All equipment (wet suits and surfboards) is provided. Make sure to arrive at least 15 minutes before the class starts, if not sooner. If you get there late, the group might already be in the water.

At the beginning of the class, you'll fill out paperwork and don wet suits. You'll get on-land instruction first—the basics of how to pop up and where to position your feet—but like most sports, surfing is really more a learn-by-doing activity. The surfboards are lined in a row facing the soon-to-be-tackled surf. Each person lies belly-down on a surfboard. The boards are made of Styrofoam, so they're less likely to cause injury should you run into your classmates or get hit by waves. When Elliot yells "Up!" you spring from a push-up position to standing. It's one quick motion, the more solid, the better. No wobbling here.

After about 15 minutes of on-land practicing, it's time to rip. Using the Velcro cuff, you attach the leash to your ankle and head out with the board tucked under your arm or overhead. Elliot leads the way into the water along with a few helpful assistants. Paddling out can be a challenge if the waves are big, but don't even try until they dissipate; otherwise, you could be painfully clobbered, like being trapped in a giant washing machine.

When learning how to surf, "standing up" is everyone's goal. Depending on your level of athleticism and balance, you might get it on the first try. With a 3:1 ratio of instructors to students, you get ample opportunity. Elliot and his assistants watch for the waves, then push your board into the surf and at the appropriate time yell "Pop up!" From there, it's up to you to rise and ride.

For some it's easy; for others it can be challenging. But if you do manage to stand up and catch the wave, it's a pure thrill. You're stoked, and Elliot's crew happily cheers you on. You might even ride a wave almost all the way to the shore. Once you find you can stand, the challenge then becomes staying on the board instead of wiping out. And just when you think you're too waterlogged to continue, Elliot shouts "last wave" and there you are making one last go of it, shredding the whitecaps.

Onshore, wet suits are peeled off, the assistants run for food before their next lesson, and you're already dreaming of moving to San Diego. Chances are, you've worked up an appetite. Before boarding the train, head back to Long Beach's Park Avenue to **Gino's** pizzeria, an institution since 1962, for a slice (16 W. Park Ave.; ✆ **516/432-8193**).

—Rebecca Ciletti

Hunter Mountain Skiing & Snowboarding

P.O. Box 295, Hunter, NY 12442
✆ **800/HUNTER-MTN** • www.huntermtn.com

Getting there: Princeton Ski Shops' weekend bus.
Subways: N, R, 6 to 23rd St.
Schedule: Buses leave from Princeton Ski Shops at 21 E. 22nd St. (btwn Park Ave. S. and Broadway) at 6am Sat–Sun and arrive back in the city at 8:30pm.
Approximate travel time: 2½ hr. each way.
Season: Winter weekends only.
Cost: $60 per person for 1-day trip includes transportation, lift ticket, and light breakfast (lessons and equipment rental are extra).

Billed as "The Snowmaking Capital of the World," Hunter Mountain has been a favorite powder mound with ski-bound New Yorkers since 1960. Its easy accessibility—it's the closest big mountain to the city—and impressive summits (the vertical drop here is 1,600 ft.) combine to make it a great day trip from early November through March. In addition to 53 **skiing and snowboarding trails**—and a crew to groom them 'round the clock in high season—snowboarders can bump and jump in **Terrain Park,** complete with a half-pipe, double-rail slide, tabletop, and Funbox. Beginners can purchase a 1½-hour "Guaranteed to Learn to Ski or Snowboard" group lesson ($20) to get started.

Or sit back and let gravity do the work: Rent a **snow tube** ($20 per day on weekends) and cruise down Hunter's 12 chiseled snow chutes.

If you're a novice seeking the thrill of the hill, this definitely beats the bunny slopes. Three rope tows hoist you back to the top.

If you're planning to visit Hunter just for the day, here's a **suggested equipment list:** ski jacket, snow pants, hat, gloves, scarf, sunscreen, lip balm, plus ski or snowboard equipment if you've got it. And snacks or breakfast for the bus.

TRANSIT FACTS

Princeton Ski Shops (✆ **212/228-4400;** www.princetonski.com) is one of the only outfitters in the city that offers trips to Hunter Mountain, but being somewhat lesser-known, it tends to attract a smaller, older crowd of serious skiers. (Think a less spring break–ish bus ride.) Bus-and-lift-ticket packages include a simple breakfast you can bring on the bus. You'll need to reserve—and pay for—your trip in advance. Total ski time: about 8 to 9 hours.

WHERE TO STAY

The Hunter Mountain website provides details on and links to area hotels, motels, and B&Bs, or you can call their **reservation hot line** at ✆ **800/775-4641** for lodging options. *Note:* For overnight trips, consider catching Adirondack Trailways to Hunter, New York ($59 per person round-trip). It may take a bit longer—up to 3½ hours each way—but the bus drops you off across the street from the resort, where you can purchase your lift tickets. Adirondack offers three buses coming and going each day.

WHERE TO EAT

Hunter Mountain's 11 slope-side eateries range from typical (soups, sandwiches, burgers, and pizzas) to the next big thing. Andre's **Slope-side Barbeque** grills burgers, dogs, and chicken, while the **Summit Lounge** is open from noon to 5pm for sushi and cocktails.

WHERE TO SHOP

Hunter has one shop for skiing and one for snowboarding. Both carry big names in gear, clothing, and accessories in case you forgot something that you can't live without.

Atlantic Kayak Tours

Annsville Creek Paddlesport Center, Cortlandt Manor, NY 10566
Office: ✆ **845/246-2187;** paddle-sport center: ✆ **914/739-2588**
www.atlantickayaktours.com

Getting there: For tours departing from the paddle-sport center, take a Metro-North Hudson line train from Grand Central to Peekskill, then a cab to the center. Other tours typically involve a trip on a Metro-North or Amtrak train, followed by a short walk or cab ride to the put-in point.
Subways: 4, 5, 6, 7, S to Grand Central Terminal.
Approximate travel time: 1 hr. to Peekskill, plus a short cab ride.
Schedule: Most tours meet Sat-Sun at 9:30am and finish between 3:30 and 4:30pm. The weeknight Sunset Paddle begins promptly at 5:30pm.
Season: Late Apr through early Nov.
Cost: $18 round-trip off-peak
Kayak tours: Most tours are $50, plus $45 for equipment rental.

Never tried kayaking and want to get your feet wet? Taking one of the guided beginner tours offered by Atlantic Kayak Tours is a great way to do it. Atlantic operates the only kayak center on the lower Hudson River, and the company's 100-boat rental fleet and 7-month schedule of tours provide plenty of options for just the right fit. The guides are friendly, patient, and knowledgeable. Their goal is to make sure you stay safe and have fun. If you capsize, they'll have you back in your boat in minutes. If you take to kayaking and want to learn a few tricks, they'll be happy to teach you.

Anyone who's in good health and knows how to swim can kayak. (They won't let you out on the water without a life jacket, but better safe than sorry.) If you're looking for a serious full-body work-out—arms, legs, glutes, core—kayaking will get you there. Note to first-timers: You're gonna be sore . . . but in a good way!

> **Tip**
>
> When choosing a **mass-transit-friendly tour,** just look for the trips that have a train or taxi icon on Atlantic's website or brochure. These tours have a meeting point that is within walking distance or a short cab ride from the train station. Several depart from the paddle-sport center. Others have put-in points that are readily accessible via Metro-North or Amtrak.

GETTING AROUND

Taxis are usually waiting at the Peekskill station to meet the trains; the ride costs between $5 and $10. Get the taxi driver's or company's phone number so you can call for a pickup from the paddle-sport center. For the return trip to the train station, try **Hudson River Taxi** (⊘ 914/788-6477) or **Bynum Taxi** (⊘ 914/737-3753). For tours leaving from the paddle-sport center, your best weekend train bet is the 7:51am out of Grand Central, which gets you into Peekskill at 8:55am.

Note: If your trip leaves from somewhere other than the Annsville Creek Paddlesport Center in Peekskill, be sure to get mass-transit instructions and a taxi number if necessary from the center when you make your reservation. They get a lot of paddlers up from the city and are happy to help.

A KAYAKING TOUR

Atlantic offers eight beginner tours that are mass-transit-friendly. The 3-hour **Annsville Easy Tour** is a fine introduction to kayaking—long enough to whet your appetite for more, short enough not to exhaust you during your first time out on the water, and a good value at $65 including equipment rental. For this tour, guides fit each person into a boat (they'll have you try out a few until you find one that's comfortable) and give the group a brief paddle lesson at the Annsville Creek Paddlesport Center. Then you're off, heading up the Hudson toward the Bear Mountain Bridge or exploring the creek. (Or both if time and conditions allow.) The guides move among the group, giving pointers as needed. This tour finishes around 1:30pm, and you're free to paddle on your own all afternoon. Other beginner tours are longer and put in at Cold Spring, New York; Rhinecliff, New York; Hudson, New York; and other points along the Hudson. On these trips you'll kayak all morning, break for lunch, then paddle back in the afternoon. The Constitution Island trip should be interesting for history buffs: Once you land on the island, you'll get a tour of Revolutionary War sites that are usually off-limits to the public. There's also a trip on the Saugatuck River in Connecticut.

> **Tip**
>
> If you want to rent a kayak or canoe and hit the water on your own from June through September, the paddle-sport center is open from 10am to 6pm on weekends; 11am to 7pm Monday, Wednesday, and Friday; and noon to 8pm on Thursday. The center operates on a more limited schedule in spring and after Labor Day. Kayak and canoe rentals range from $35 to $50 for a half-day, $45 to $60 for a full day.
>
> —Amy Wong

For more seasoned kayakers, Atlantic Kayak offers six intermediate tours and three advanced tours that have put-in points near train stations. For superstrong paddlers, there's even a sea-kayak version of the Circle Line cruise—a 10-hour, 30-mile trip circumnavigating Manhattan. Rental equipment is limited on these trips, so call or e-mail ahead to make sure you'll have the equipment you need. And expect rough water, especially with the advanced tours—a good reason not to lie about your level of experience.

Here's a **suggested equipment list** for your kayaking tour: Wear clothes made out of synthetic materials (they dry faster), and aqua socks, sport sandals, or old sneakers. A hat and sunglasses help cut the glare off the water. Slather on the sunscreen, too. Bring lunch (the delis near the train station may not be open when you arrive) and plenty of drinking water, along with a change of clothes just in case you fall in.

The paddle-sport center is well stocked with equipment, gear, maps, and a refrigerated case full of bottled water and sports drinks. The facilities are minimal, however: a shed with one of those eco-conscious no-flush toilets, no sinks or showers, two changing rooms, and a wall of open cubbies to stash your stuff. You can leave keys, cellphones, and other valuables in a drawer behind the counter.

Skip Barber Racing School & the Interlaken Inn

Inn: 74 Interlaken Rd., Lakeville, CT 06039
✆ **800/222-2909** · www.interlakeninn.com
Racing School: ✆ **800/221-1131** · www.skipbarber.com

Getting there: Metro-North Harlem line train from Grand Central to Wassaic, NY, then a cab to the inn.
Subways: 4, 5, 6, 7, S to Grand Central.
Approximate travel time: 2 hr., 15 min. on the train, plus a 15-min. cab ride.
Schedule: Trains leave Grand Central every couple hours and return from Wassaic on a similar schedule.
Season: Interlaken is open year-round; Skip Barber holds classes at Lime Rock Apr–Nov.
Cost: Train fare is $27 round-trip off-peak, plus $15 each way for the cab to the inn.
Inn rates: Doubles start at $139 per night.
Racing school costs: Racing school starts at $595 a class.

This is one trip that doesn't make you decide between a romantic weekend getaway in the gorgeous countryside and the high-speed adventure of a lifetime. How often does *that* happen? Up in northwest Connecticut's Litchfield Hills, the Interlaken Inn offers a swimming lake, shady porches, and romance packages a mere 3 miles down the road from the Skip Barber Racing School—where hundreds of current racers got their start.

Fido Is More than Welcome

If you've got a pup, bring him along, too (although, not to the racetrack, of course). Interlaken not only allows pets, it embraces them, with pet-walking trails, off-leash play areas, and wholehearted permission to swim in the lake. There's a $10 fee for the privilege of your pooch's company, but he'll be welcome almost everywhere on the property (aside from the restaurant). If he's been on his best behavior lately, treat him to the hotel's **PUPS Amenity Package** ($30), complete with bowl, spring water, treats, imitation bone, and a "we're glad you're here" toy.

Headquartered at Lime Rock Park, Skip Barber's school welcomes anyone with a driver's license to come out for an action-packed day behind the wheel. Skip Barber is a notable racing figure who went on to open the first-of-its-kind racing school, one that is headquartered right here in hilly Lakeville, Connecticut (several other schools have since opened in other parts of the country). Expect to have a lot of fun, but this is serious business: According to the website, "Not only have Skip Barber–trained drivers won every major U.S. road-racing championship but, on average, a third of the drivers in the Indy 500 and any Nextel Cup race are Skip Barber graduates." Whether you take a racing class or a defensive-driving class, you'll learn and practice the same techniques the school taught to Jeff Gordon, Michael Andretti, and hundreds of other famous drivers. Plus, because of the small class sizes and the high ratio of instructors to students, you'll be lavished with personal attention.

TRANSIT FACTS

A few trains run express, but for most trains to Wassaic, you'll need to transfer at the Southeast station for another train that goes on up to the end of the line. (The transfer adds only a few minutes to the trip.)

GETTING AROUND

From the Wassaic station, you'll need to take a cab (across state lines, no less) to the inn. Interlaken recommends calling ahead to be sure a taxi is waiting at the station. Try **DeLango Taxi** (✆ 845/877-9000) or **Lakeville Taxi** (✆ 860/435-9999). The cost is about $15 one-way.

The Interlaken Inn is just a 4-minute drive down the road from Lime Rock Park where all of the racing events and the racing schools are held. Interlaken Inn happily transports their speed-demon guests to and from the park.

A DAY OF DRIVING AT SKIP BARBER

The **Intro to Racing class** includes an hour of lap time and a crash course in accelerating, braking, cornering, and downshifting in a sleek and mighty Formula Dodge. In the **One-Day Driving School,** you'll learn the finest defensive-driving techniques, car-control skills, and tips that could save your life—working your way up to a 500-horse-power Viper sports car. You'll learn how to make an emergency lane change to avoid a deer or oncoming car, how to come out of and recover from a skid, how to drive under all sorts of conditions, and generally how to handle the sticky situations that every driver eventually faces. The school also offers a **racing-driving combo class** and classes that span the course of several days.

Which should you go for, the racing or driving classes? The Skip Barber Racing School requires knowledge of stick-shift driving for the racing program. For the driving program, they highly recommend it but will teach it to you if necessary. (You can learn to drive stick in the 1-day New Driver program.) If you want some crazy fun, the racing school is the best. But if you want fun and some skills you can actually take with you on the road, the driving program is worth its weight in gold.

Rates start at $595 for a 3-hour Introduction to Racing course and go up from there. The One-Day Driving School is $795; a One-Day Driving-Racing Combo Class is $995; and, if you just won Mega Millions, reserve your spot in the Three-Day Racing Class for $3,695, for which the Skip Barber school gained its initial notoriety. There you'll confront an intense series of slalom, braking, and downshifting exercises, some high-speed lapping sessions where you'll use your new-found knowledge of racing theory and advanced braking techniques, and get drilled on passing and racing in the rain, double-file race starts, and single-file restarts. All without owning a car.

WHERE TO STAY

When your class is over for the day, head to your room at the **Inter-laken Inn.** Summer is the biggest season at the inn, when people come

---

Events: Lime Rock Park

Lime Rock Park isn't used for Skip Barber students alone, of course. The Ferrari/Maserati Racing Days, Rolex-sponsored Vintage Festival, American Le Mans Series, Busch-North Series NASCAR events, and other notable events take to the park and attract loyal spectators. Go to **www.limerock. com** for schedule information.

Events: Theme Weekends at Interlaken

Canoeing, tennis, hiking, fly-fishing, gardening, painting, and the liberal arts are some of the learn-and-stay weekend packages offered that take advantage of the inn's fabulous natural setting,

---

to enjoy a plunge in the lake or a paddle out to the middle in a canoe. The inn also has a swimming pool and tennis courts in excellent condition for a morning match. Winter is nice as well, with ski resorts and sleigh rides at the woodsy 21-acre Loon Meadow Farm, both a short cab ride away.

Interlaken's varied rooms are divided among the main building and four separate outbuildings, all with a style of their own. Some rooms go for Victorian inn appeal—notably, Sunnyside, part of the original inn back in the late 1800s. Each of the 12 rooms has a sunny bed-and-breakfast charm—with wicker and floral prints—and some have direct access out their doors to the wraparound porch. Rooms in the main building have a clean-lined, modern look, while the ground-floor Woodside rooms have vaulted ceilings, dark woods, and French doors opening onto the bath. (Check out the website for photos and detailed descriptions of the buildings and their rooms.) Be sure to notice the artwork and sculpture throughout the public areas of the property: The inn has a partnership with a local artists' guild to display the artworks on loan.

Many of the Skip Barber race-car instructors, drivers, and their entourage stay at the Interlaken, so it's no surprise that they now offer spa services. A staff of massage therapists is available any day of the week for a massage, facial, manicure, or pedicure. End your day with a walk down to the lake, dinner up the road in Millerton, and a cocktail back at the inn's bar, where live jazz plays on weekends. Isn't driving a race car romantic?

WHERE TO EAT
Morgan's, the sunny dining room at the Interlaken Inn, serves one fine organic, grass-fed burger. The restaurant offers seasonally inspired entrees as well, along with a tapas-style menu of sharable small plates. Friday and Saturday nights, jazz music sets the atmosphere for dinner or a glass of red at the bar. Service here is subtle and superb. On Sunday morning, wake to the brunch buffet. Entrees run from $13 to $26.

Rock Climbing in the Gunks with the Eastern Mountain Sports School

3124 Routes 44/55, Gardiner, NY 12525
☎ **800/310-4504** · www.emsclimb.com

Getting there: Adirondack Trailways bus line from Port Authority to New Paltz, NY, then a cab from the station to the school.
Subways: A, C, E to 42nd St./Port Authority or N, Q, R, S, W, 1, 2, 3, 7 to 42nd St./Times Sq.
Approximate travel time: 1 hr., 55 min., plus 10- to 15-min. cab ride.
Schedule: Buses leave Port Authority more than a dozen times daily between 7am and 11:30pm and return from New Paltz on a similar schedule.
Season: Rock-climbing season runs from early Apr through early Nov.
Hours: Class meets at the EMS school at 8:30am and ends anytime between 3:30 and 5pm.
Cost: $38 round-trip; cab fare is less than $15.
Climbing school cost: A 1-day intro class is $195, with slight discounts given for parties of 2 or 3.

While the Shawangunk Mountains of upstate New York offer miles of pristine rock face and attract able-bodied climbers from across the globe, they are also one heck of a place to get started in the sport. Considered to be some of the finest climbing on the East Coast, "the Gunks" (as fans know them) stand tall in the scenic Mohonk Preserve with plenty of height, a variety of rock surfaces, and motivatingly beautiful views from the top.

True, the area becomes a crunch-ified nirvana for local climbers on weekends, when its cliquey subculture of gear-laden devotees can look mighty intimidating to those who can't tell a caribiner from a crash pad. But heading out to the climbs with a seasoned EMS (Eastern Mountain Sports) instructor gives you instant trail cred. Absorb their wise words and you will be relaxed, rehearsed, and ready to ascend on your first climb long before lunch break.

> **Tip**
>
> From January through the end of March, the EMS school offers a rock alternative: **ice climbing.** The New Paltz school location remains the meeting point, but classes then head an hour north into the Catskills for instruction.

The New Paltz location is one of EMS's four East Coast climbing schools, the first of which opened back in 1968. It's worth noting that the school is accredited by, and all guides are certified by, the American

Mountain Guides Association. EMS is the largest school in the region and employs up to 12 guides in the summer, leading trips every day of the week. Each guide trains continuously (even after certification) in the areas of technical skill, teaching, and first aid. And it shows. Safety is the top priority, but passion for the sport is a close second. The majority of guides have been teaching for more than 5 years and climbing for more than double that. Even while classes begin daily at 8:30am, some guides have been known to head out to the rock before class to squeeze in a few quiet hours of climbing at sunrise.

GETTING AROUND

The New Paltz bus station doubles as headquarters for the only taxi service in town: **New Paltz Taxi** (✆ **845/255-1550**). Arrange as soon as you arrive for a taxi to your accommodations or the school. While you wait, you can grab an ice cream, snack, or beverage from the station cafe.

You'll need to take a cab from the bus station to the school (about 10–15 min. away), but instructors are often kind enough to give you a lift back to the bus station or to your overnight accommodations after class if they're heading in that direction.

CLIMBING THE GUNKS

With a maximum of three students per class, you'll swiftly cover the basics of knots and commands and get on to the fun parts of belaying, movement, and climbing technique. Throughout the day, on climbs (specific routes up the rock face where it is safe to set up your equipment) with names like "Betty," "Funny Face," and "Beginner's Delight," you'll work your way up varied terrain that may include face, slab, crack, and chimney features. Multi-pitch climbs—that require several different ropes to be set one after the other in order to reach the top—can easily take

> **Tip**
> Don't forget to tip your guide; 15% to 20% is customary.

you up 250 feet or more, even if it's your first time out. The best part is that because your teacher will be customizing the class to your skill level and personal interests, you can learn the ropes at your own pace and comfort. And if that comfort happens to be a 5.9 climb with an overhang the size of a small car, your EMS guide is happy to oblige.

EMS offers 1- to 4-day basic classes. For the more advanced, it has intermediate classes and specialized courses in learning to lead, self-rescue efforts, setting up a top-rope pitch, and adventure racing. All classes are offered 7 days a week. Cancellations due to rain are at your own discretion—if you still want to climb, they still want to teach—except in cases of severe weather. For weekend climbing, reservations should be made by phone or online 1 to 2 weeks in advance to ensure availability.

Here's a **suggested equipment list** for your climb: At least 1 liter of water (more when it's hot outside), lunch and snacks, sunscreen, trail shoes or sneakers, an extra layer in case of temperature change, and a backpack for transporting all this plus your equipment to the trail. Antibacterial hand gel isn't a bad idea either, unless you like eating lunch with hands that are black from sliding them along the ropes as you rappel. If you don't have your own equipment, EMS will let you borrow shoes, a harness, a helmet, and chalk, all of which are included in the price of your class.

WHERE TO STAY

Several **free camping areas** in the area are popular with climbers. Facilities are limited to an outhouse and a patch of land, but you can't beat the price. EMS staff can point you in the right direction in terms of getting there. One camping area is within walking distance of the Near Trapps climbing area.

Lefèvre House If your climbing class factors into a romantic weekend away, head back to New Paltz for at least 1 night at this highly modern and comfortably plush B&B. A good soak in the hot tub on their landscaped stone terrace is a well-earned reward for those multi-pitch endeavors. (See details on the Lefèvre House in chapter 4.)

Minnewaska Lodge Just 400 yards away from Eastern Mountain Sports, this modern mountain lodge of a hotel means you can walk to the EMS center the morning of your class. Some rooms have balconies with view of the cliffs or the woods; a state park adjoins the grounds. Rates start at $125 for midweek November through April (including a continental breakfast) and $199 on weekends May through October. Rte. 44/55, Gardiner. ⌀ **845/255-1110.** www.minnewaskalodge.com.

New Paltz Hostel Right next door to the bus station is this cheery white house with shared and private rooms, starting at a mere $25 a night. Provided are linens, a fully equipped kitchen, Internet access, board games, a garden, and a friendly staff who can make good recommendations about what to do, see, and eat around town. Drugs, alcohol and smoking are against house rules. Interaction with other guests is center to the experience; you won't find a TV on the premises. 145 Main St. ⌀ **845/255-6676.** www.newpaltzhostel.com. $25 per night per person shared room; private rooms available.

WHERE TO EAT

You'll need to pack your lunch and bring it along with you. The **Bistro Mountain Store** right next to the school is a modest carryout that opens early and stocks food to fuel the climbing set—power bars, energy drinks, dried fruit, nuts, pretzels, and jerky. They will also make you a hot bacon, egg, and cheese sandwich at breakfast or your choice of deli sandwiches to go. There's an ATM, too.

After class, head back to town for your pick of restaurants along Main Street. Or head across the highway from the school to **Mountain Brauhaus Restaurant** for stick-to-your-ribs German fare and over-sized steins of beer (✆ **845/255-9766**).

WHERE TO SHOP

The EMS Climbing School has a small, climber-staffed tech shop on-site filled with climbing gear and accessories. At lesson's close, you will also receive a coupon for 15% off shoes, a helmet, or a climbing rope that you can use back at one of the two EMS stores in the city.

Spring Lake, New Jersey

Spring Lake, NJ 07762
✆ **732/449-0577** · www.springlake.org

Getting there: NJ Transit Long Branch train from New York Penn Station to Spring Lake, NJ.
Subways: 1, 2, 3 to 34th St./Penn Station or A, C, E to 34th St./Eighth Ave.
Approximate travel time: 2 hr.
Schedule: Trains leave Penn Station about once an hour and return from Spring Lake on a similar schedule.
Cost: $20 round-trip off-peak.

Spend some time in Spring Lake and you'll probably start wondering if you've stumbled onto a movie set. Sprawling Victorian mansions with wraparound porches. Impeccably manicured lawns. Swans swimming serenely across a pond. Rest assured, though, this idyllic town on the Jersey Shore is the real thing. With 2 miles of the most uncluttered and uncrowded beach you'll find anywhere near New York City, this spot is a haven for families seeking good, clean beach fun and couples and singles in need of a quiet getaway.

Spring Lake began as a summer resort in the late 1800s when some of the houses shown in the Philadelphia Centennial Exposition were transported to the area. Soon Victorian houses of a similar style were springing up all over the community. Today, these spectacular homes—with countless windows, gables, and turrets—front the sandy beach. While many are summer residences, Spring Lake now has about 3,500 permanent residents as well.

Still, it's the honking of geese, not cars, that wakes you in the morning. Or perhaps it's the friendly chugging of a train passing through town. One of the best things about this small town is that even on a short walk, you're bound to come across a body of water. Spring Lake is bordered by Lake Como to the north, Wreck Pond to the south, and the Atlantic Ocean to the east. And then, right smack dab in the middle of it all, there's another lake—the town's namesake—fed by bubbling underground springs.

Everywhere you look nature is preening—from fuchsia and indigo hydrangeas to sprouting clusters of mushrooms to wild bunnies scurrying amid the underbrush. Baby ducks swim in slow procession behind their mother. Owls call from the shadows of lush trees. All around the lake you'll discover nooks and crannies ideal for hiding out with a book or a journal—and lo and behold, a bench is right there, awaiting your arrival.

Two wooden footbridges lead over the lake into the sleepy downtown area with its high-end clothing and furniture shops. There are no traffic lights or parking meters. A baby blue water tower is the tallest thing around.

So what about the beach, you ask? In a word, it's lovely. And along the beach runs the longest noncommercial boardwalk in New Jersey—made of recycled grocery bags and sawdust (but very solid). No dogs or food is allowed on the beach (there's a reason it's so clean!), but you can buy snacks and eat at the tables in one of the two pavilions near either end of the beach. The pavilions also have large green saltwater pools, kiddie pools, lockers, and bathrooms. Head up to the balcony and plant yourself in one of the wicker rocking chairs for a seagull's-eye view of this practically perfect piece of shore.

TRANSIT FACTS

Most trains run on the North Jersey Coast Line (Long Branch–NJCLL). About 90 minutes into your trip, you'll need to get off at Long Branch and walk across the track to get on a local train that will depart about 5 minutes later. You'll pass one quaint oceanside town after another, each prettier than the next, until you reach Spring Lake about 15 minutes later. Occasionally, trains have an hour-long layover in Long Branch. Check the schedule for connection times before starting out.

Additional trains to Spring Lake run several times a day on the Northeast Corridor Line. If you're on one of these trains, you'll instead need to transfer at Newark Penn Station (about 45 min. into your trip).

GETTING AROUND

Once you arrive in Spring Lake, you can either walk to your hotel or B&B or call **Coast City Taxi** (∅ 732/449-1414) for a ride. Spring Lake is extremely walkable. Swans way outnumber cars, and the biggest thing you have to watch out for is the geese droppings on the sidewalks near the pond. Street names are printed on low, rather inconspicuous white posts. Take along a map when you explore.

Biking is also a great way to see the town. Most B&Bs have bikes available for free or a small fee. Just keep in mind that they're only allowed on the boardwalk before 9am.

WHAT TO DO

Well, you've got the beach and ocean, of course, and great biking (see "Getting Around," above). At the corner of Third and Madison avenues is the ivy-covered brick building that houses the **Spring Lake Theatre Company** (∅ 732/449-4530; www.springlaketheatre.com), a widely respected community theater group that stages lavish productions of Broadway favorites like *South Pacific*, *Into the Woods*, and *Scrooge*.

WHERE TO STAY

Chateau Inn & Suites All rooms have marble bathrooms, refrigerators, two telephones with personal voice mail, and in-room safes. Some suites have Jacuzzi tubs and fireplaces. The hotel offers complimentary tennis passes to nearby Divine Park courts. 500 Warren Ave. ∅ **732/974-2000.** Doubles $99–$219.

Normandy Inn A half-block from the ocean, this beauty is on the National Register of Historic Places. Rooms feature period antiques, fireplaces, or Jacuzzis. In addition to breakfast, the inn serves up treats for afternoon tea and cordials in the evening. 21 Tuttle Ave. ∅ **732/449-7172.** Doubles $115–$305.

Events: Cookies & Candlelight Christmas Inn Tour

Spring Lake's beautiful B&Bs get decked in holiday lights and other festive dress at Christmastime. During this annual event to kick off the holiday season, visitors are invited to step inside participating inns, sample holiday cookies, and collect the recipes used to bake them. Tickets are $30, $25 if purchased before Labor Day, and free if you're staying at one of the inns on the tour (∅ **732/449-6685**).

White Lilac Inn   This pretty little inn is just steps away from Wreck Pond and an easy walk to downtown. Owner Mari Kennelly decorated the 10-room B&B herself with carousel horses, collectible dolls, tea sets, crystal decanters, and plenty of books. Each room has a theme (Mary's favorite has a fishing motif) and a stuffed teddy bear on the bed waiting to welcome guests. Jacuzzis and fireplaces are available in many rooms. Beach badges, bike rentals, beach chairs, and towels are all complimentary. 414 Central Ave. ⌀ **732/449-0211.** www.whitelilacinn.com. Doubles $139–$259.

> **Tip**
>
> If you don't have the funds to spring for an overnight stay, try a day trip. An adult beach pass for the day costs $7. Children under 11 are free.
>
> –Julie Mehta

WHERE TO EAT

Cucina Café   Check out this cute, casual downtown cafe with freshly baked cookies, sandwiches, quiches, and delectable desserts. Prices are low, so buy some extra treats to take with you. 219B Morris Ave. ⌀ **732/974-3433.** Entrees under $10.

Island Palm Grill   This is the poshest restaurant downtown and serves pricey Latin-influenced meat and seafood dishes. Close to Spring Lake Theatre Company, it's a convenient choice for a preshow meal. 1321 Third Ave. ⌀ **732/449-1909.** www.islandpalmgrill.com. Entrees $21–$27.

The Breakers   With a view of the ocean, live piano music, and rich decor, this hotel restaurant offers elegant yet affordable meals. The cuisine is Italian, with many choices for vegetarians. 1507 Ocean Ave. ⌀ **732/449-7700.** www.breakershotel.com. Entrees $8.95–$37.

WHERE TO SHOP

Irish Centre   Right near the Third Avenue footbridge, this store features lucky charms, Waterford crystal, and red plaid skirts for kids. 1120 Third Ave. ⌀ **732/449-6650.**

Kate & Company   This cozy gift boutique stocks lots of sweet things to take back home, from candles and photo frames to armoires and wicker couches. 1100 Third Ave. ⌀ **732/449-1633.**

Spring Lake Variety   Browse the large stock of souvenirs, retro toys, beach umbrellas, and surfboards at this five-and-dime store. 1301 Third Ave. ⌀ **732/449-6404.**

Romantic Weekends

NEW ENGLAND HAS MORE THAN ITS FAIR SHARE OF ROMANTIC HIDE-aways. The countryside is filled with old-fashioned inns where you can cozy up in front of fireplaces in the winter or laze about in hammocks in the summer. Historic homes welcome you with an old-fashioned key to your room, just as modern luxury hotels pull out all the stops to lavish your stay with high-end amenities. And the destinations themselves are often as spellbinding as the accommodations: From your bed or balcony, you can take in breathtaking Catskill mountains vistas, savor the briny perfume of fresh sea air, or listen to the crisp sounds of commerce on Main Street, USA.

Whether you're celebrating a special anniversary or simply crave a weekend away from the kids, excellent options await in five different states. Be treated like royalty at the classic Castle on the Hudson or lap up the European-style luxury at the Inn at National Hall. When you book a weekend at Troutbeck, you'll wake up to the sounds of country life—albeit life on a striking manor-style estate.

Updated luxury is yours at the Lefèvre House B&B. Even the notoriously tawdry Atlantic City is seeing the emergence of a number of stylish and romantic lodging choices—and its numerous mass-transit choices make it an incredibly easy place to get to without a car. For something wilder and considerably less glitzy, opt for a stay at an inn and a bike ride on wind-swept Block Island, the quintessential New England seashore retreat. The two-room Saugerties Lighthouse B&B is an ideal Hudson River hideaway for two. And despite its hulking size and room capacity, the painter-perfect Mohonk Mountain House resort makes for a surprisingly private and idyllic Hudson Valley retreat at any stage in the romance game.

Romance doesn't come cheap in these parts, however. That's all the more true when you're using mass transit. These love nests see more traffic than your typical back-road hideaway and tend to be priced accordingly. Still, each one has what most New York couples crave—a good dose of privacy, but with plenty to do right outside the front door.

Romantic Weekends

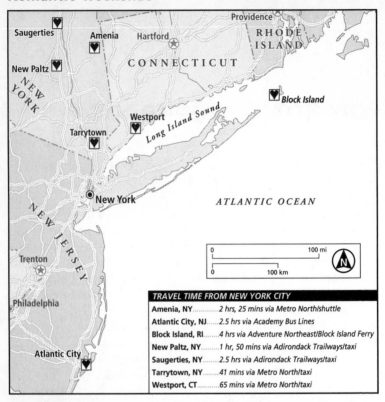

Saugerties
Amenia   Hartford   Providence
RHODE ISLAND
New Paltz
CONNECTICUT
NEW YORK
Block Island
Westport
Tarrytown   Long Island Sound
New York
ATLANTIC OCEAN
NEW JERSEY
Trenton
Philadelphia
Atlantic City

0   100 mi
0   100 km

TRAVEL TIME FROM NEW YORK CITY
Amenia, NY.............2 hrs, 25 mins via Metro North/shuttle
Atlantic City, NJ......2.5 hrs via Academy Bus Lines
Block Island, RI......4 hrs via Adventure Northeast/Block Island Ferry
New Paltz, NY..........1 hr, 50 mins via Adirondack Trailways/taxi
Saugerties, NY........2.5 hrs via Adirondack Trailways/taxi
Tarrytown, NY........41 mins via Metro North/taxi
Westport, CT..........65 mins via Metro North/taxi

Castle on the Hudson

400 Benedict Ave., Tarrytown, NY 10591
⌀ **914/631-1980** · www.castleonthehudson.com

Getting there: Metro-North Hudson line train from Grand Central to Tarrytown, NY, then a 5-min. cab ride from the station to the castle.
Subways: 4, 5, 6, 7, S to 42nd St./Grand Central.
Approximate travel time: 36 min. on the express train, 50 min. on the local.
Schedule: Trains leave Grand Central for Tarrytown about every half-hour on weekends.
Transit costs: Train fare is $15 round-trip off-peak plus about $5 each way for the cab.
Room rates: Doubles $320; suites $395–$650. AE, DC, DISC, MC, V.

Just a half-hour from the city, you can partake of a grandiose four-course feast, spend the night tucked snug between Frette sheets and goose-down comforters, and revel in over-the-top pampering in a romantic stone castle nestled amid 11 forested acres. With its main tower rising majestically above the trees, Castle on the Hudson has yet another singular distinction: It's the highest point in New York's Westchester County.

How did an imposing medieval castle straight out of the pages of *Ivanhood* find itself in Westchester County in the first place? Predictably, a very rich, very imaginative man living during the turn of the 20th century decided to build his family a home. Howard Carroll hired one of the period's most celebrated architects, Henry Killburn, to help him design a house that more resembled a massive Norman fortification from ancient Ireland than the typical Victorians of the period. Massive, indeed: The house would have 45 rooms, medieval-style towers and turrets, and a surrounding stone wall. Construction on the castle began in 1897, and the building served primarily as the Carroll family residence (known as Carrollcliffe) until the 1940s. In 1997 the house became the Castle on the Hudson hotel. Since then it has earned a four-diamond rating from Triple A and a place on *Condé Nast Traveler*'s Top 20 U.S. Small Hotels list. It also became a member of the esteemed Small Luxury Hotels of the World.

For many people, a stay at the Castle marks a special occasion—and management offers plenty of celebratory gestures to wow guests whether the occasion is a milestone or not. Classical music is playing in your room to greet you. Bulgari toiletries are yours to use in the soaking tub or the marble-walled, free-standing shower. The ultimate in luxury, six tower suites feature four-poster beds, wood-burning fireplaces, and marble bathrooms—oh, and from your tower window you can practically yoo-hoo to your buddies slumming in Manhattan. For a real romantic kick, ask to have champagne and chocolate-covered strawberries delivered to the room on a tray adorned with fresh flowers just after you arrive.

GETTING AROUND

Taxis are normally waiting at the train station to pick up passengers. It is common for drivers to group passengers together, even if they are traveling to different destinations.

If you plan to travel to and from the Castle premises, allow 10 to 15 minutes' advance notice for cabs to show up at the Castle or any pickup point in Tarrytown. Most rides cost between $4 and $8; try **Knapp McCarthy Taxi** (✆ 914/631-TAXI).

WHAT TO DO

Fortunately, this castle has taken entertainment a few centuries beyond jesters and jugglers. The heated outdoor pool cozies up to a 25-person hot tub, bocce court, tennis court, and the poolside **Grotto Bar** made of quarried stone. Those who can't skip a workout even when they're on vacation can reserve an in-room massage after a visit to the 24-hour fitness center. If you prefer to order room service and eat in for the evening, you can watch a complimentary DVD movie. Each room has at least one TV with built-in DVD player; the front desk is happy to deliver their two-page list of DVDs—many released in the past year or two.

What to Do Nearby

It's easy to lock yourselves up in your suite and throw away the key (card), but Tarrytown and environs are teeming with things to do. See the related entries in this book on historic **Sunnyside,** Washington Irving's home (chapter 7); **Lyndhurst,** a nearby Gothic Revival–style castle (chapter 7); **Stone Barns Agricultural Center** and **Blue Hill** restaurant (chapter 5); **MYO Wine** (chapter 5), and **Kykuit,** a Rockefeller estate (chapter 7).

WHERE TO EAT

Equus Restaurant   This Zagat-rated, award-winning dining room is everything you could want from a meal at a castle: It's formal and decadent, and its servers have been meticulously trained to wait on you hand and foot. Culinary Institute of America–trained chef David Haviland's seasonal menus feature course after ethereal course—from escargots with garlic parsley butter to hickory bacon–wrapped beef tenderloin. It all arrives at the table with a photo-perfect presentation that could easily wow the *Iron Chef* judges. Best of all, even with waitstaff checking in from all directions and the multitude of courses, the timing is perfect—you're never waiting, but you're never rushed.

Ratchet Up the Romance

Why do the romance thing halfway? Inquire about packages that may include breakfast, a four-course dinner, in-room champagne and strawberries, spa treatments, golf, a rose-petal turndown service, complimentary minibar, a suite with wood-burning fireplace, or grand-tour tickets to nearby Kykuit, the Rockefeller estate.

The grand finale, the Castle Chocolate Cake, never fails to delight—it's served in a chocolate casing that is decorated and sculpted to resemble the castle's stone turrets.

In the summer, make your reservation in the restaurant's **Garden Room,** with its day's-end light, mountain views, and an eclectic collection of potted plants and flowers.

In the winter the stately **Oak Room** is warmed by a roaring fire in the massive stone fireplace. Let the sommelier select a toasty red wine from the 36-page wine list (which has its own table of contents). The restaurant carries 350 labels from around the world—and its wine list won the Award of Excellence from *Wine Spectator* magazine in 2001. By the way, the Oak Room's historic feel has not been fabricated: The room belonged in its entirety to Louis XIV and was brought intact to New York explicitly for the Castle more than a century ago.

> **Getting the Best Room**
>
> Some rooms are much more luxurious than others. To avoid disappointment, ask for a room in the main Castle building if possible.

In any season, the $71 four-course menu (appetizer, salad, entree, and dessert) is worth every penny. The chef even sends diminutive amuse-bouches from the kitchen for tasting. Megafoodies should ask about the six-course chef's tasting menu ($100 per person) and the tasting and wine-pairing menu ($160 per person). Reservations and jackets are required. Call ✆ **914/631-3646** for reservations or book through the hotel's website. You should also reserve a spot for the **Castle High Tea,** held in the restaurant daily from 2:30 to 5pm.

Other choices on-site: For a predinner drink, try the **General's Bar.** Outdoors near the pool, the **Pool Menu** offers oysters on the half shell, chilled lobster, littleneck clams, and other gourmet lunch items. For a quiet evening in, order **room service** (popular faves are the Maryland crab cakes, baked brie, French onion soup, and a Castle-made selection of ice creams and sorbets).

Saugerties Lighthouse Bed & Breakfast

Saugerties, NY 12477
✆ **845/247-0656** · www.saugertieslighthouse.com

Getting there: Adirondack Trailways bus line from Port Authority to Saugerties, NY, plus a cab from the bus station to the lighthouse parking lot.

Subways: A, C, E to Port Authority or N, Q, R, S, W, 1, 2, 3, 7 to Times Sq./42nd St.

Approximate travel time: 2½ hr., plus a 15-min. cab ride.

Schedule: Buses leave Port Authority once in the morning and once in the evening and return from Saugerties on a similar schedule.

Hours: The bed-and-breakfast portion of the lighthouse is open year-round but is often closed Mon–Tues. Tours of the lighthouse are open to the public weekends 2–5pm from Memorial Day through Labor Day.

Cost: Bus fare is $48 round-trip.

Room rates: $160 double, including breakfast.

The Saugerties Lighthouse seems plucked from a turn-of-the-20th-century novel. Set on a massive stone base jutting into the Hudson, this weather-beaten brick building stands watch over the river with the regal bearing of a royal. The lighthouse was built in 1869 to help steer river traffic away from the dangerous shallows and guide boats into the nearby Esopus Creek on the way to Saugerties. Its beacon (restored to operation in 1990) was lit manually for 85 years until its automation in 1954 eliminated the need for a keeper. After being ignored for several decades, the lighthouse was finally recognized for its important role in local history and was added to the National Register of Historic Places in 1978. A major restoration and reconstruction of the building followed, including 10,000 new bricks to replace those that had crumbled.

Rules of the House

Due to a desire to conserve energy, no hair dryers or the like are permitted. No pets are allowed. No smoking is allowed inside the lighthouse. There is no television. The one downstairs bathroom is shared by everyone staying in the lighthouse.

Today the lighthouse looks much as it would have in the early 1900s, both inside and out. By day you can visit the small museum room and take a guided tour, including a climb up to the light tower, which offers breathtaking views of the Hudson and the Catskills in the distance. There is a table for picnic lunches and a long, shallow sandbar for wading and swimming. When the sun sets, though, you may feel as if you've been transported to a bygone era. Bring your own steaks to grill on the barbecue and then adjourn to the picnic area, which is located on its own private island separated from the lighthouse by a wooden bridge. As you dine or sip a glass of wine, the occasional boat meanders up or down the river, fish splash nearby, and the night train muscles its way along the Hudson's opposite bank. If ever there was a time to propose to that special someone, this is it. In fact, the last three lighthouse keepers stepped down from their duties here in pursuit of true love. The former keeper even had his wedding on the lighthouse grounds, the very place where he met his future bride.

The beauty of a stay at the Saugerties Lighthouse Bed & Breakfast is that after your mellow evening picnic by the banks of the Hudson, you don't have to suddenly switch gears and pack up and go home. You can spend the night in one of two guest rooms. If you've come with another couple, it's as if you've rented your own personal inn—and if you've come during the week, you may have the place entirely to yourselves. One room has a sunset view; the bigger, east-facing room sees the sun rise; take

> ### Pitching In
>
> Taking care of the lighthouse and its inn is a one-man job—and that man is busy! To help out, guests make their own beds in the evening and take them down in the morning.
>
> —with Alex Altman

your pick. Creaky wooden floorboards and antique bed frames only add to the historic charm. In the morning, your innkeeper will make you a delicious breakfast on an authentic 1920s gas stove. Refreshed, rested, and well fed, you can spend the day relaxing or exploring the lighthouse. Climb the steep set of stairs and venture up into the actual light tower and out onto its dinky balcony. When it's time to leave, you can take the half-mile walk back to the real world armed with the knowledge that the money you spent on your room goes directly toward preserving this historic gem, thus ensuring that future guests will be able to share experiences as special as yours.

Note: The lighthouse is in high demand most weekends throughout the year and books especially early during the summer season. Even weekdays in the warmer months tend to fill up months in advance. Check the online calendar for availability.

GETTING AROUND

You will need to take a cab from where the bus drops you off. The only cab service in town is **S&K Car Service** at ✆ **845/247-4444.** Call in advance if possible.

Unless you arrive by boat, you will need to carry your belongings along the half-mile trail to the lighthouse—so it's a good idea to travel light. The trail out to the lighthouse from the parking lot can get awfully soggy when the tide starts coming in or when it hasn't finished going out. Check with the keeper about the tide schedule for the days of your reservation so you don't get mired in the mud.

WHAT TO DO

If you take the morning bus and have packed light, consider bumming around town a bit before heading to the lighthouse. Saugerties has some neat antiques shops, galleries, a bookstore, a movie theater, and a Saturday community farmers market with chefs' demos and free tastings (Main and Market sts.; July–Oct 9am–2pm).

WHERE TO EAT

The keeper makes a full breakfast in the morning. During your stay you have access to the grill, a fridge, dishes, glasses, utensils, and even a corkscrew, all of which you can use to prepare a picnic or host your own tiny dinner party on the adjacent island—whether you've packed soy dogs or a grilled rack of lamb.

WHERE TO SHOP

The lighthouse sells souvenir items (shirts, hats, mugs, and the like), the proceeds of which benefit the Saugerties Lighthouse Conservancy and the preservation of the structure itself.

Atlantic City

Atlantic City, NJ 08401
✆ 888/AC-VISIT · www.atlanticcitynj.com

Getting there: Academy Bus Lines from Port Authority's Gate 1 to various Atlantic City casinos.
Subways: A, C, E to Port Authority or N, Q, R, S, W, 1, 2, 3, 7 to Times Sq./42nd St.
Approximate travel time: 2½–3 hr., depending on traffic.
Schedule: Buses leave Port Authority every half-hour. They leave Atlantic City frequently throughout the day and evening.
Cost: $30 round-trip, but you will receive a $20 voucher for the slot machines of the casino where the bus drops you off.

Atlantic City romantic? Absolutely. From great hotel rooms, spas, and nightlife to days spent lounging on the beach, strolling the boardwalk, and riding amusement park rides of yore, the city by the sea offers plenty to do with your honey. Atlantic City is the other city that never sleeps, and at all hours of the day or night it has something exciting to see, eat, or do. Their "Always Turned On" motto has never been more true—and it ventures worlds beyond the lights and sounds of the casino floor.

Back in its pre–World War II heyday, Atlantic City was the biggest seaside resort in the country. People came by the thousands to wade in the water, inhale the salty shore breeze, stay in the glamorous hotels, and promenade along the nation's very first boardwalk. But a postwar decline sent the World's Favorite Playground into a serious tailspin. The city's renaissance began in the 1970s, when casino gambling was approved.

These days, Atlantic City looks like an old friend you haven't seen in years, the once-blowsy sad sack who has lost weight, coiffed her hair, and taken a liking to all things high-style. It's cleaner, brighter, safer, and more exciting than it was even 3 or 4 years ago (but it's still dirt cheap to get to and easy to get around once you do). Change has come fast and furious to a town that's getting a little more Vegas by the day. Everywhere you look, hotels, casinos, restaurants, and stores are all about what's hot and what's new. An open-air outlet shopping complex has taken over downtown, beach clubs compete for the best late-night scene, and cutting-edge chefs are tuning in to the preferences and palates of a more sophisticated clientele. Miss America may be gone, but so, to a large extent, is the tacky, tawdry Atlantic City of recent years.

To many, this transformation has a lot to do with the opening of the ultramodern **Borgata Hotel Casino & Spa** (1 Borgata Way; ✆ **866/ MY-BORGATA;** www.theborgata.com) and its more than 2,000 rooms and suites in 2003. It hit the scene hard as the first new casino to open here in more than a decade. Once the rest of the town saw travelers clamoring for new, more, and better, the resort's once-staid businesses decided to step it up. Hotels underwent wholesale renovations; accommodations services and amenities were improved to meet the demands of travel-savvy customers. The result: The city is prospering, rooms are full, and more and more urbanites are discovering the ease of the instant A.C. vacation just a couple hours down the coast.

A Little History: The Atlantic City Boardwalk

A railroad conductor named Alexander Boardman came up with the idea of building a boardwalk as a means of keeping sand out of the railroad cars and hotels. In June 1870, Atlantic City constructed Boardman's Walk: an 8-foot-wide temporary wooden walkway. Over the years, as the "boardwalk" was expanded and businesses built up around it, it became the beachside stage set of the city, where leisurely after-dinner promenades along the boardwalk became the American equivalent of the Italian *passeggiata*.

Atlantic City

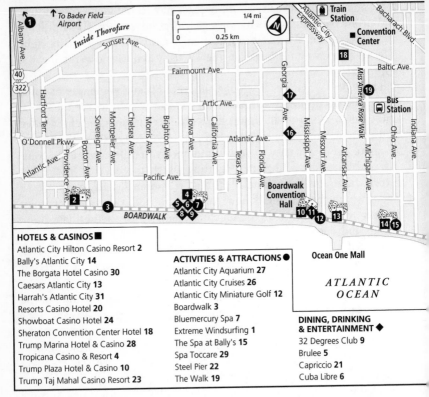

HOTELS & CASINOS ■
Atlantic City Hilton Casino Resort **2**
Bally's Atlantic City **14**
The Borgata Hotel Casino **30**
Caesars Atlantic City **13**
Harrah's Atlantic City **31**
Resorts Casino Hotel **20**
Showboat Casino Hotel **24**
Sheraton Convention Center Hotel **18**
Trump Marina Hotel & Casino **28**
Tropicana Casino & Resort **4**
Trump Plaza Hotel & Casino **10**
Trump Taj Mahal Casino Resort **23**

ACTIVITIES & ATTRACTIONS ●
Atlantic City Aquarium **27**
Atlantic City Cruises **26**
Atlantic City Miniature Golf **12**
Boardwalk **3**
Bluemercury Spa **7**
Extreme Windsurfing **1**
The Spa at Bally's **15**
Spa Toccare **29**
Steel Pier **22**
The Walk **19**

Ocean One Mall

*ATLANTIC
OCEAN*

**DINING, DRINKING
& ENTERTAINMENT** ◆
32 Degrees Club **9**
Brulee **5**
Capriccio **21**
Cuba Libre **6**

Some things don't change, however. The boardwalk—now in its fifth incarnation—is still the heart of Atlantic City. People bike along the ocean's edge from dawn until 10am, those who push wicker rolling chairs call out for riders, and children win stuffed toys at the Steel Pier arcade. Yes, the casinos have become the city's main draw, but there is much more to this ocean-side resort than casinos—much of it plenty romantic.

TRANSIT FACTS

Academy Bus lines rotates its schedule so that different NYC departures drop off at different casinos. It makes sense to take a bus that will drop you off at the casino-hotel closest to the one where you have reservations. Pick up a schedule at the Academy counter in NYC when you buy your ticket so you can plan when and where you need to meet a bus to return home.

Academy services 10 different casinos, but neither Harrah's nor the Borgata are among them. (I guess they figure you're taking a limo to

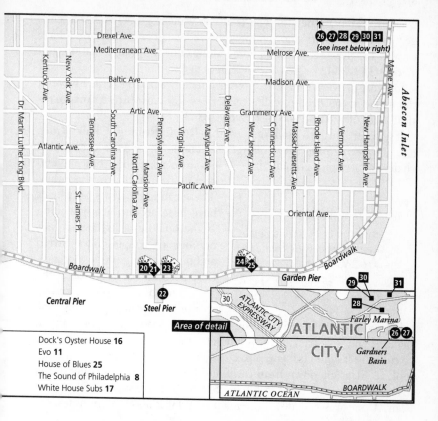

Dock's Oyster House **16**
Evo **11**
House of Blues **25**
The Sound of Philadelphia **8**
White House Subs **17**

get there.) For these hotels, the closest drop-off is at Trump Marina, from which you can catch a cab or take the jitney. (All casinos are a cab or jitney ride apart, if they aren't within walking distance.) *Note:* On the schedule, the "Claridge" stop is the casino at Bally's.

You can also take the Greyhound Bus to Atlantic City, but there is no advantage to this in terms of cost, scheduling, or experience. Really.

GETTING AROUND

The city's favorite transportation since 1915, the light blue, 13-passenger minibuses known as **jitneys** are the subway cars of Atlantic City. They're cheap and easy—fast, too—and everyone takes them. For $1.75 per person (the driver can make change), hop on and reach almost any part of town, 24 hours a day. The main route hits most of the big casinos by running up and down Pacific Avenue—parallel to the boardwalk but a few blocks up. The other three routes loop out to the Borgata/Harrah's/Trump Marina area and to historic Gardner's Basin, among other destinations. Your hotel concierge can tell you where to catch a jitney for wherever you want to go. The only hitch is getting a seat: There's no standing allowed, so occasionally you'll have to wait for the next jitney to come along. For more information, call ✆ **609/344-8642** or go to www.jitneys.net.

Just like in New York City, **taxis** are readily available with a wave of the hand. If you need to call a car service, try **Absolute Transportation** at ✆ **609/625-1965** or 609/641-6363.

It's never hard to find one of the **Royal Rolling Chair Rides** (✆ **609/347-7500;** www.rollingchairs.com), an open wicker-basket chair and a strong-armed "driver" willing to push you from one end of the boardwalk to the other. These canopied chairs on wheels have been around nearly as long as the boardwalk itself, and generations of couples have flirted and floated along inside. A gigantic stuffed lion or bear won at the Steel Pier has even been known to ride along on top. Cruise the full length of the boardwalk and you'll know every stop you want to make as you walk back. Plus, you'll get some welcome shade and a ride so relaxing it could lull you into a catnap—if there weren't so much to look at. Flag one down from early in the morning till all hours of the night. Rates start at $5 for 5 blocks, $25 for a half-hour, and $40 for an hour. A one-way ride down the main strip takes about 30 minutes.

> **Discount Coupons**
>
> Order the *Official Visitor's Guide* at **www.atlanticcitynj.com** and check out the coupons in the online "Great Discounts" section.

WHAT TO DO

Atlantic City is full of action that has nothing to do with slot machines and free drinks brought to the blackjack table by busty women who wink at you when you tip them. . . .

The Beach & the Beach Clubs Anyone can throw down a towel and enjoy the resort's free, lifeguarded beaches. "Beach clubs" for eating, drinking, and live entertainment (oh, how the sounds of karaoke do travel) can be found on the sand in front of Resorts, Bally's, the Hilton, Caesars, and Trump Plaza. Volleyball tournaments and limbo contests are part of the culture, and various clubs will rent you a chair, umbrella, or your own private cabana.

The Steel Pier Rides, games, and fair food all with an ocean breeze. Now gloriously restored, the Steel Pier originally opened in 1898 and was a big player in the big-band era, with the likes of Benny Goodman and Jimmy Dorsey gracing its stages. Charlie Chaplin, Mae West, Bop Hope, and Frank Sinatra performed here, too—as did the famed

Diving Horses, who wowed crowds with their 40- to 60-foot dives into a tank of water from a platform on the pier. Virginia Ave. and Boardwalk. ✆ **609/898-7645.** www.steelpier.com. 35-ride tickets $25. Mon-Fri 3pm-midnight; Sat-Sun noon-1am.

Gardner's Basin & Boat Cruises Once teeming with rumrunners and commercial fishing fleets, historic Gardner's Basin still offers a plethora of boat rides and cruises. **Atlantic City Cruises** offers morning skyline cruises and sunset cruises (Memorial Day to Sept 30), harbor cruises (July 1 to Labor Day), and marine-mammal adventure cruises (Apr 15–Nov 12). 800 N. New Hampshire Ave. ✆ **609/347-7600.** www.atlanticcitycruises.com. Tours $17–$27.

Atlantic City Aquarium This 17-tank aquarium lies right next to the Gardner's Basin dock. 800 N. New Hampshire Ave. ✆ **609/348-2880.** www.atlanticcityaquarium.com. Admission $7 adults, $4 children 4-12, free for children under 3. Daily 10am-5pm.

Extreme Windsurfing This watersports school makes its base on a wide, protected cove of Lakes Bay to offer windsurfing and kite-surfing lessons for beginners and beyond. The pros call it one of the best places on the East Coast to learn; experienced professional instructors provide personal attention in a 2-hour lesson that will have you standing and sailing before it's over. The bay is consistently windy but has little in the way of currents or waves to interfere—and no boats zipping by making waves. And since the water stays fairly shallow for a long way out, you don't have to be a world-class swimmer to take a lesson. If you already windsurf, you can opt for an advanced lesson ($60 per hour) or rent a board ($35 per hour or $70 for 3 hr.) and sail away. Lessons are taught from April to October and start at $75 per person for 2 hours. Bring your own water shoes/aqua socks and sunblock, and it's a good idea to change into your swimsuit before you arrive. *Note:* The school is just outside of town so you'll need to take a cab to get there (less than $20 fare). The school sits right behind the Hampton Inn; the front-desk staff can call a cab for you when you need to get back to town. 7079 Black Horse Pike. ✆ **800/781-8461.** www.extremewind surfing.com.

Spas Lodgings around the globe are beefing up their spa offerings, and Atlantic City's hotels are no exception. Here are a few of the top choices.

You can't buy love, but you can buy the loveliest couples treatments in town at the **Spa Toccare at the Borgata.** What's hotter than your own spa suite with whirlpool and double shower? The "So Happy Together" 80-minute treatments (choose from Swedish massage, deep tissue massage, or glow facials; $475–$555) are followed by 30 minutes of alone time for the couple inside the suite. Men and women each have their own steam room, large sauna, whirlpools with waterfalls, and salon. The men's salon offers sharp haircuts for just $20; their fancy version of a barbershop has a billiards table and refreshments, a shoeshine, and old-fashioned shaves. Borgata Resort. 1 Borgata Way. ∅ 609/317-7555. www.theborgata.com.

Popular with celebs, **Bluemercury Spa at the Tropicana** has an "apothecary" that carries nearly every high-end beauty product on earth. Two popular treatments are the brown-sugar body polish and hydrating massage combo, and a Japanese journey that starts with a rice-and-bamboo scrub followed by a sake bath and 30-minute rice oil massage. The Quarter at the Tropicana, Brighton Ave. and Boardwalk. ∅ **609/ 347-7778.** www.tropicana.net/spa.

The Spa at Bally's offers a day pass for using their pool, seven whirlpools, sauna, and fitness center—all of which are open later than most. 1900 Boardwalk at Park Place. ∅ **609/340-4600.** www.caesars.com/ Ballys/AtlanticCity. Mon-Sat 7am-9pm, until 7pm Sun.

Nightlife   The beach clubs and casino lounges call to young crowds, as do a dozen dance clubs, if you dare. The town hosts an endless stream of stage acts from music to comedy, too, so get tickets far in advance. The Quarter at the Tropicana is an especially lively nightspot. **Cuba Libre** (2801 Pacific Ave.; ∅ **609/348-6700**) is the best place for a tropical predinner drink—late night it's a fiery Latin dance club. Also in the Quarter, **The Sound of Philadelphia (TSOP)** at the Tropicana (∅ **609/887-2200**) and, at the other end of the boardwalk, the **House of Blues** at Showboat (801 Boardwalk; ∅ **609/236-BLUE;** www.hob. com) are top venues for live jazz. The HOB also does a Sunday gospel brunch with seatings at 10am and 1pm ($33 per person). Make reservations in advance.

WHERE TO STAY
To check availability, rates, and discounts for all Atlantic City hotels, call ∅ **877/331-3560** or go to www.acenethotels.com. *Note:* Hotel rates can be up to 50% less on weekdays than the rates quoted for a weekend.

Plenty of people make the mistake of saying they'll just go for the day, stay up all night, and sleep on the bus home when they get tired. A) This is not romantic. B) This is rarely as fun or adventurous as it sounds. And C) If you decide you want to book a room after all, you'll be hard-pressed to find one. Most hotels are either booked for the night already or will pretend to be—no one knows why.

The Rendezvous Tower at Resorts Atlantic City Resorts has an ideal location on the boardwalk, a rooftop indoor-outdoor pool with sun deck and oversize whirlpool, a fitness room, five restaurants, and the largest hotel rooms in the city. Futuristically fast elevators zip to the top of the new Rendezvous Towers, where you can relax in peace and quiet in your room with a view as the city rages on. The lavish king-size bathrooms alone could cause you to forgo other plans—each has a cavernous marble shower, double sinks, a vanity makeup table, and a separate commode room. If you do venture out, the **25 Hours Lounge** in the casino has cozy booths for people-watching or telling secrets. 1133 Boardwalk. ✆ **800/336-6378.** www.resortsac.com. Weekend rates start at $200 (more for the Rendezvous Towers).

WHERE TO EAT

Each casino has its own collection of restaurants, as does the board-walk. Two popular places to stop along your walk are the hip **Evo at Trump Plaza,** for cafe-style outdoor dining, more than a dozen wines by the glass, modern Italian cuisine, and brick-oven pizzas (2998 Boardwalk; ✆ **609/441-6000;** entrees $12–$24), and **Opa Bar & Grille,** for lunch or late-night drinks and snacks (1700 Boardwalk; ✆ **609/344-0094;** www.opa1.com; entrees $15 and up).

Brulee: The Dessert Experience Eat a small dinner—or none at all—and make a reservation for the sweetest three-course menu in town. Here, you don't have to wait until the end of the meal for your sugar fix: It comes as your appetizer, main course, and dessert. "Entrees" are preceded by a chef's choice amuse-bouche—a tiny dessert to get you prepped for the main attraction. Among the mains, the vanilla crème brûlée is made the traditional way here: wide and flat with the ideal ratio of crispy scorched topping to rich cream; a paper cone of orange madeleines sits alongside. A quintet of chocolate desserts on one plate makes the perfect sampler, and a flaming bananas Foster is a harmonious marriage of brown sugar, nutty crunch topping, and fluffy chocolate mousse. Dessert wines, specialty cocktails prepared tableside, and coffee served in its own French press complement the selections. You'll finish with a tiny plate of cookies, candies, or some other sugary confection. Every dessert receives a uniquely glamorous presentation, and you can watch the world-class pastry chefs at work by taking a seat at the bar or following along on the Food Network–style, real-time TV screens. Cowhide booths and 6-foot strands of crystals raining from the ceiling give this spot the feel of a lounge—which is exactly what it becomes at 11:30pm. The sugary waitresses are swapped for spicy ones, and a line of patrons forms out the door, all

clamoring to get into the restaurant's alter ego, the **32 Degrees Club.**
The Quarter at Tropicana, 2801 Pacific Ave. ✆ **609/344-4900.** www.brulee
desserts.com. Dessert "entrees" $18–$22.

Capriccio at Resorts   One dining room looks out over the water,
but if you're coming at night (when the ocean looks like a big black
puddle anyway), the middle dining room is the most romantic. Murals
of high-society folks dressed for a masquerade ball line the walls, and
palm fronds fill dramatic urns. Clouds are painted on a ceiling dripping
with crystal chandeliers. The classic northern and southern Italian cuisine doesn't come cheap, but this Zagat-rated jewel has been a casino
restaurant favorite for years. The traditional *stracciatella* (chicken egg-
drop) soup with spicy meatballs and toasted cheese is a standout starter,
and one of the tastier entrees is the *crostacei e pescatore*—tender lobster,
clams, scallops, shrimp, and mussels over linguine, in a *fra diavolo*
sauce. Save room for one of the classic Italian desserts. 1133 Boardwalk.
✆ **800/932-0734.** Entrees $18–$38.

Cuba Libre   Part restaurant, part rum bar, part Latin dance club, this
stop at Tropicana's Quarter lets you pick your poison. Stop in on your
way to dinner and soak up the old-world Havana plaza design as you
soak in a few frozen tropical drinks. Or dine here yourself among the
lively dinner crowd. Well before midnight the cigar bar lights up and
the dance floor calls to those who take salsa seriously. The Quarter at
Tropicana, 2801 Pacific Ave. ✆ **609/348-6700.** www.cubalibrerestaurant.com.
Entrees $15–$25.

Dock's Oyster House   Seafood fanatics and steak lovers alike should
look no further than Dock's for their most memorable meal in Atlantic
City. It may not have an ocean view or a boardwalk location, but the
original home of beef and reef since 1897 is a dining experience you
shouldn't pass up. Besides, the view doesn't get better than seeing all
those pretty babies on ice—10 varieties of oysters chilling on one
impressive raw bar. After a peek at the smartly organized wine list, start
with a shellfish sampler for two before moving on to something more
substantial, like a 24-ounce porterhouse or grilled yellowfin tuna. Lobster comes steamed, broiled, or stuffed with crab imperial—whether
you order a 2-pounder ($37) or a hungry-man 6½-pounder ($88).
Don't miss the Maine chowder studded with clams still peering out
from their shells, or the ice-cold shrimp cocktail. Service is outstanding and unstuffy. Omar—the finest waiter in old A.C.—loves to make
you laugh. Dock's has been owned by the Dougherty family for four
generations and has been known for Joe's cheese pie ($6) since the

1970s. It's the first and most popular item on the dessert menu, but the last is equally yum: chocolate fondue with seasonal fruits and home-made pound cake—order it with two forks ($12). Reservations strongly recommended. 2405 Atlantic Ave., at Georgia Ave. ✆ **609/345-0092.** www. docksoysterhouse.com. Entrees $19–$38, lobster dishes up to $88.

White House Sub Shop   This 1946 institution is nearly twice as old as the casinos, but it attracts the same melting pot of characters. There's generally a wait whether you want to take out or eat in, so you might as well get in line for one of the orange booths, where you'll dine beneath a wall of 8×10-inch glossies from decades of sub-sated stars—from Tom Jones and the Beatles to Rat Pack singers and multiple Miss Americas. One of the waitresses has been here for 3 decades and will tell you little has changed but the prices. It still takes months to train a sandwich builder, who uses a chef's knife to deftly fold the subs and hoagies in half. Burgers are superb, and the Italian sub is the most popular thing on the menu, but the cheese steaks could run Philly out of business. Everyone claims the neighborhood-baked bread—and the water used to make it—is half the key to the shop's sandwich success. 2301 Arctic Ave., at Mississippi Ave. ✆ **609/345-1564.** Sandwiches $3.15–$15.

WHERE TO SHOP

In an effort to keep any money you might win from ever leaving the premises, most **casinos** offer plenty of in-house shopping. The Quarter at the Tropicana combines some of the nicest upscale shopping with the best atmosphere. The Borgata also has a fancy retail plaza. Slated for completion before the end of 2006, The Pier at Caesars juts out into the ocean to flaunt its enormous acreage of high-end stores (Gucci, Versace—you get the picture), restaurants, and entertainment options—expect the joint to be jumping from opening day on.

Souvenir shops line the **boardwalk,** along with fortune-tellers, taffy and ice cream stores, and Chinese-chair-massage parlors that charge $1 a minute to get your back ready for a few more hours of walking along the boardwalk.

The Walk, Atlantic City Outlets   Brand-new and so successful it's already expanding, The Walk fills several streets with outlet and retail stores, entertainment, and restaurants along Michigan and Arctic avenues. Shop Banana Republic, Gap, Brooks Brothers, Kenneth Cole, Coach, Polo Ralph Lauren, Sunglass Hut, and more. If you like H&M, this place has a huge one—but unlike most other H&Ms everywhere else, it's not crowded and the wait for a dressing room is short. ✆ **609/ 343-0081.** www.acoutlets.com.

The Inn at National Hall

2 Post Rd. W., Westport, CT 06880
✆ 203/221-1351 · www.innatnationalhall.com

Getting there: Metro-North New Haven train line from Grand Central to Westport, CT, and a taxi from the station.
Subways: 4, 5, 6, 7, S to 42nd St./Grand Central.
Approximate travel time: 65 min.
Schedule: Trains leave Grand Central for Westport roughly once an hour on weekends. Trains leave Westport once or twice an hour.
Cost: Train tickets are $22 round-trip off-peak, plus cab fare to the inn.
Room rates: Double rooms start at $325 per night. AE, DC, MC, Visa.

The simple, sturdy-looking, redbrick facade of this luxury hotel looks as if it could house any number of businesses—and it has. Built by a businessman named Horace Staples in 1873, the three-story Italianate structure was constructed to house the First National Bank of Westport (of which Staples was chairman) on the ground floor, along with the local newspaper on the second floor, and an informal town hall of sorts on the third. Over the years the building—dubbed "National Hall"—played a list of dutiful, practical roles: high school, police headquarters, and even a tri-level furniture store.

So unassuming was this Westport harbor stalwart that few Westport residents living at the turn of the 20th century would have guessed that it would one day attract celebrities, diplomats, and hordes of East Coast couples sneaking off for a romantic weekend at a European manor-style inn, which it was carefully transformed into in 1993.

Even today, the building's lobby offers no clue of its jewel-box interior—that is, until the elevator doors open to transport you to the third floor for check-in: All four walls of the elevator are painted as an elaborate *trompe l'oeil* library. Leather-bound books, trinkets from world travels, even a suspicious little kitty are all drawn in fine detail and bathed in the light of a green, glass-shaded banker's lamp. As the doors to the third floor open, you're greeted by a small antique desk with beautifully polished wood—quite possibly the quaintest front desk you'll ever see. You have arrived at National Hall.

Whether you've chosen a two-story suite—where a winding staircase leads to a canopied bed in the loft—or a "standard" room with 12-foot-high windows, towering bookcases, and gleaming chandeliers, you'll immediately find yourself pillowed in layers of luxury.

The inn's designers fashioned it after a European manor house, albeit one designed with a clear sense of *trompe l'oeil* whimsy. The drawing room has an African-safari-meets-French-colonial feel. Look closely at the "Old World" map painted onto the walls: The geographic locales are pure fiction, named after the many people who made the inn first come alive.

In fact, hand-painted murals throughout the rooms and public spaces are the vision and work of 15 local artisans. Each of the 16 rooms and suites is decorated with colonial antiques. An antique billiards table beckons downstairs and the upstairs drawing room has a small bar hidden in an armoire that's open to guests. Both give the place a clubby, exclusive feel. Still, the National Hall manages to feel more like a buddy's mansion than a stuffy hotel. More than a decade since its opening, the inn has settled comfortably into a state of understated opulence, with gold-edged mirrors, swags of rich fabrics, cutglass doorknobs, tassels, tufts, and fringe throughout. It succeeds in being both gorgeously elegant and warmly inviting.

While the Inn at National Hall is a great choice for a quick escape in any season, it's especially cozy on winter weekends when the snow is falling and the four-poster beds are piled high with pillows, duvets, and the finest linens. After a hot bath, grab a fluffy towel from the heated towel barn and bask in the glow of a sun lamp. Armoires in both the sitting room and the bedroom hide televisions with DVD players. Choose a title from the hotel library at the front desk. Or order a bottle of port from a local wine shop and plant yourselves in front of the drawing room's stately fireplace. You'll find tables for playing Scrabble or chess and plenty of seating options for sinking into a good book. In the morning, the *New York Times* is delivered outside your door.

Name-droppers might mention that the Clintons have stayed here. Some of the cast and crew of *Stepford Wives* stayed here when the movie was being filmed nearby. Artists, actors, philanthropists, and socialites have their favorite handpicked suites at this waterfront refuge. But don't worry, you won't have to resort to showbiz strutting to stay here: For a hotel that's lavished with adornments and dripping with drama (in a good way, of course), it is also a remarkably quiet and private retreat.

Note: There is a 2-night minimum on weekends from June through November.

GETTING AROUND

The **Westport Star** taxi service (✆ **203/227-5157**) has its office at the station, so taxis should be waiting at the station upon the train's arrival.

The Inn at National Hall is well situated for walking to nearby shops and restaurants. Depending on the season and your mood, however, you may want a cab even for short trips—some of the roads see few walkers.

WHAT TO DO

A walk along the curving, wooden-plank boardwalk, with its old-fashioned, globe-topped street lamps, is in order any season. In the 1800s, working sloops and majestic schooners would dock along the waterfront in front of National Hall to load local crops to be sold in New York City and beyond.

What to Do Nearby

Campo Beach and Marina   This 29-acre community park with a long curl of sandy beach on Long Island Sound is just a few minutes' cab ride from the inn. Facilities include picnic tables, a bathhouse, and a concession stand. ⌀ **203/341-5090.**

Westport Country Playhouse   Paul Newman and Joanne Woodward, whose friends often book rooms at the inn, have both had a hand in ensuring that this newly renovated performing-arts center snags professional touring companies. Shows are new, modern, and evocative, with a few revivals and children's shows thrown in throughout the year. Westporters beam with pride with the fact that Joanne chooses plays and directs, while Paul, at an energetic 80 years of age, just opened the theater's new restaurant. The Playhouse is a half-mile down the road from the inn. 25 Powers Court. ⌀ **203/227-4177.** www. westportplayhouse.org.

WHERE TO EAT

A continental breakfast is laid out sweetly in the inn's **Drawing Room** from 7 to 10am, with glass pitchers of juice, baskets of flaky croissants, cereals, fresh fruit, and plenty of strong coffee. At lunch, make the stroll to the **River House Tavern** (299 Riverside Ave.; ⌀ **203/226-5537;** www.riverhousetavern.com; entrees $12–$28) and have conch fritters with Key lime aioli or a pulled-pork or tilapia sandwich on the patio overlooking the river's edge. For dinner, consider the following choices:

Acqua   The Mediterranean menu and romantic look and feel of this place make it a winner—and a chef trained at Lutèce doesn't hurt. The centerpiece, a wood-fired oven, bakes lusty thin-crust pizzas. But the seafood creations involving roasted skate, house-cured salmon, and yellowfin tuna are the dishes that smack of true love. 43 Main St. ⌀ **203/222-8899. Entrees $16-$38.**

Da Pietro's   It's small and crowded, and you may have a merciless wait, all because word has been out for more than 15 years that this is the best Italian fare in the entire state of Connecticut. Its "Best Restaurant for Wine Lovers" award from *Wine Spectator* is a worthy testament to its wine list and such menu items as grilled rack of venison and black-truffle risotto—the food is beyond outstanding. Reservations recommended. 36 Riverside Ave. ∅ 203/454-1213. Entrees $12–$25.

Tavern on Main Snugly set inside a colonial home from 1810, the Tavern welcomes diners with its beamed ceilings, wide-planked

> **A Fitness Perk**
>
> The inn's guests are permitted to use the extensive health and fitness facilities of the Westport YMCA.

floors, and the glow and warmth from three fireplaces. A chef with serious Big Apple restaurant chops (he cooked with Alfred Portale at Gotham Bar & Grill) serves local favorites like roast duckling with mulled wine reduction and a New England lobster stew. 146 Main St. ∅ 203/221-7222. www.tavernonmain.com. Entrees $20–$33.

WHERE TO SHOP
Cross the bridge over the Saugatuck River and explore the downtown Westport shopping along Main Street and the Post Road shops along the water. Apropos of a wealthy suburb, the cutesy boutiques are styled and priced accordingly.

Lefèvre House Bed & Breakfast

14 Southside Ave., New Paltz, NY 12561
∅ **845/255-4747** • www.lefevrehouse.com

Getting there: Adirondack Trailways bus line from Port Authority to New Paltz, then cab to inn.

Subways: A, C, E to Port Authority or N, Q, R, S, W, 1, 2, 3, 7 to Times Sq./42nd St.

Approximate travel time: 1 hr., 45 min., plus 5-min. cab ride.

Schedule: Buses leave Port Authority about once an hour and return from New Paltz on a similar schedule.

Cost: Bus fare is $38 round-trip.

Room rates: Doubles start at $150 per night. AE, DISC, MC, Visa.

New Paltz may have a reputation for being a granola-crunchy college town, but it has a subdued side for grown-ups as well, starting with this delightfully mature and romantic getaway.

Judging by the exterior of this pink "painted lady," you might expect the inside to be top-to-bottom teddy bears, dollhouses, and gilt-edged floral teacups. For those who are allergic to frilly B&B overkill, relax. The few select antiques in this boutique B&B merely finish rooms that have been tastefully and unostentatiously drenched in colors, textures, and furniture worthy of a cover story for *Metropolitan Home*. And a professional staff trained in high-end hospitality makes Lefèvre House run like the Ritz.

The Lefèvre House was built as a farmhouse in 1870 by Peter Lefèvre, who likely never envisioned its classic Victorian bones outfitted in highly modern European furnishings. But the combination gels beautifully. In the communal living room, dark-chocolate walls are neatly complemented by fern-green accents, a marble fireplace, shag fur pillows, and a crystal chandelier. (The modern artwork displayed throughout the house was picked up on the owners' world travels, and most is for sale.) Upstairs, beds are dressed in Versace linens and down comforters. Three rooms have four-poster beds. The "Purple Rain" room features Asian flourishes and makes up for its detached bathroom with what must be the biggest, deepest tub in town.

Check Out More Photos

In addition to what's on the hotel's own website, additional photos that really exude the flavor of this resort can be seen at www.besthotelsresorts.com.

When you're feeling ready to unwind, Lefèvre house brings the spa to you with a full-service menu of in-room facials, massage, body treatments, and reflexology. Afterward, take a seat in the steam room.

In the evenings, many guests scurry back to the B&B after dinner in town to avoid the college bar scene. Stop by **In Good Taste** (45 Main St.; ✆ **845/255-0110**) and pick up a bottle of champagne to pop open while you soak away in the bubbling hot tub on the backyard stone terrace. With tiki torches and candelabras flickering in the breeze and the crickets humming away, Lefèvre House turns into your own private country escape.

"Breakfast" here is more like a hearty brunch, served as a three-course meal in a stylized formal dining room with leather dining chairs, spotlights, and a love seat decked out in faux mink. The presentation alone is enough to wake you up. A typical morning might include a soft-boiled egg with truffle oil and caviar, two wedges of French toast balanced artfully and drizzled in ginger maple syrup, and a pear poached in pink champagne with a dollop of Grand Marnier–laced whipped cream.

This Victorian beauty has come a long way since 1870. Future plans for the inn include a sauna and a duo of two-story suites in the barn out back. But its original owners would be proud to see that the old covered porch still warmly envelops the house, and the original pine boards still creak softly underfoot.

GETTING AROUND

You can get a cab at the bus station, where **New Paltz Taxi** (📞 **845/ 255-1550**) has its headquarters. Call ahead with your arrival time so they'll have a taxi waiting.

New Paltz is made for walkers, and the Lefèvre House is just a 10-minute walk up the hill from downtown. Cabs are available for the weary or for any side trips. It's probably a good idea to take one when you first arrive, since you'll be carrying your bags. As far as New Paltz goes, the farther away from the bus station (and the hostel next door) you go, the less SUNY hippie it gets.

WHAT TO DO

Fuel the romantic fires by booking one of the **inn packages** that mix and match spa services and gourmet picnics with champagne and truffles. Or add them on to your room reservation a la carte. Chocolate-covered strawberries, a bouquet of flowers, rose petals, or an herbal bubble bath adds some snazz to any weekend escape. The talented chefs at Lefèvre House can customize lunches, picnics, afternoon teas, and gourmet dinners on the porch, in the formal dining room, or wherever you'd like.

Here are some other ways to pass the time during your stay in the area.

Huguenot Street   Daily walking tours wind through the oldest continually occupied street in the U.S. and its stone houses dating to 1692. French Huguenots settled here to escape religious persecution, and the stories of how they lived out each season will move you. You'll need to take a tour to get inside the French Church and several of the stone houses—with walls 2 feet thick and held together with mud and straw. Tours cost $7 to $10 and run several times a day Tuesday to Sunday from May through October. 8 Broadhead Ave. 📞 **845/255-1660.** www. hhs-newpaltz.org.

Wallkill Valley Rail Trail   Rent a bike at **Bicycle Depot** and roll on down this easy-does-it 12.2-mile path that stretches leisurely from New Paltz through Gardiner. Catch it right off Main Street. Rentals start at $25 for a half-day (after 2pm) to $35 for a full day; helmets cost extra. The trail is open 10am to 6pm Saturday and Sunday. Reservations are encouraged on weekends. (The more adventurous can head out to the 22 miles of trails in Minnewaska State Park, where the carriage trails get a little rougher and helmets are required.) 15 Main St. ∅ **845/255-3859.** www.bicycledepot.com.

Samuel Dorsky Museum of Art at SUNY New Paltz Just down the street, this museum specializes in 20th-century works, plus Asian and pre-Columbian art and artifacts. 75 S. Manheim Blvd. ∅ **845/257-3844.** www.newpaltz.edu/museum.

What to Do Nearby

Skydive the Ranch The romance factor in falling 13,000 feet from the sky is questionable, but you'll be kissing the ground when you land safely. (See also chapter 3, "Outdoor Activities.") 45 Sandhill Rd., Gardiner, NY. ∅ **845/255-4033.** www.skydivetheranch.com.

EMS Climbing School Many would think it a sin to leave New Paltz without getting your sweaty paws on some Gunks rock. Spend a day learning the ropes at a rock-climbing clinic tailored to your ability. (See also chapter 3, "Outdoor Activities.") 3124 Routes 44/55, Gardiner, NY. ∅ **800/310-4504.** www.emsclimb.com.

Mohonk Preserve You can get a day pass to hike the hilly trails here, many with breathtaking views. (See also the entry for Mohonk Mountain House later in this chapter.) 3197 Rte. 44/55, Gardiner, NY. ∅ **845/255-0919.** www.mohonkpreserve.org.

WHERE TO EAT

The Bakery Skip the basic delis on Main Street and head for this 25-year-old New Paltz institution inside a former barn. Loaves of sourdough and Kalamata-olive bread share the shelf with pastries, bagels, and giant cookies. Order a sandwich on English-muffin bread with a side of roasted-butternut-squash soup and take it out to the garden. (Be sure to pick up the bakery's brochure, which has a walking tour of town.) 13a N. Front St. ∅ **845/255-8840.** www.ilovethebakery.com. Sandwiches $5.95–$7.50.

The Cheese Plate Part gourmet gift shop and part artisanal cheese boutique, this cafe with outdoor seating on the plaza creates sampling plates made just for two. Choose from several cases of imported and domestic cheeses (a handful are produced locally), then add bread, olives, fruit, chocolates, or even fig cake to make it a meal. It's open Monday to Saturday from 11am to 7pm, Sunday 11am to 6pm. Water Street Market, 10 Main St. ∅ **845/255-2444.** Cheese plates $7–$12, plus $3 per additional person.

Cookies & Cream By the end of summer, every New Paltz parent has taken their kids here more times than they can count. Unusual ice-cream flavors like Purple Cow (blackberry ice cream with white and dark chocolate chunks) and mango sherbet appeal to kids big and small. Organic teas, herbal iced tea, and coffee drinks are also served, and it's open late on weekends. 48 Main St. Ø **845/255-8780.**

Gilded Otter Restaurant and Brewery Inside this big stone building with a lodgey feel, upscale pub food is served downstairs while the brews ferment upstairs. More than a half-dozen homemade beers are on tap, including a pale ale, brown ale, red lager, blueberry lager, Hefeweizen, and stout; order one of four sizes. Live music takes the stage on weekends. 3 Main St. Ø **845/256-1700.** www.gildedotter.com. Entrees $13–$30; sandwiches $6.95–$8.95.

Harvest Café Seasonal American and vegetarian fare with indoor and outdoor seating, lunch and dinner, Saturday-night jazz, and Sunday-afternoon folk guitar. Water Street Market, 10 Main St. (2nd level). Ø **845/255-4205.** www.harvestcafenp.com. Entrees $15–$21; sandwiches $7.95–$8.95.

The Village TeaRoom In addition to a daily afternoon tea ($18 per person) with scones and clotted cream, this secluded side-street cafe serves casual lunches and dinners and has a walk-up coffee bar with homemade baked goods. 10 Plattekill Ave. Ø **845/255-3434.** www.thevillagetearoom.com. Entrees $6.75–$16.

WHERE TO SHOP

Intriguing finds from French country antiques to exotic collectibles from countries across the world can be found in **antiques stores on Main and Church streets.** Some stores (like Asian treasures–filled Medusa Antiques at 2 Church St.) will deliver to the city.

Cocoon Silk pillows, sleek barware, and earth-friendly dog toys mingle with candles, soaps, and must-haves for the urban baby and her nest-driven parents. 69 Main St. Ø **845/255-6862.**

Events: Sunday Farmers Market

A Sunday-afternoon farmers market sets up in the Elting Memorial Library parking lot (at the corner of Church and N. Front sts.; Ø **845/728-1103;** 10am–3pm) from the end of June through October. Browse the tent-covered tables brimming with fruits, vegetables, jams, eggs, soaps, syrups, meats, herbs, plants, cheese, honey, fudge, hand-spun yarn, artisan breads, and assorted baked goods, plus New York State wines.

Pegasus Footwear Outlet   A retail and outlet shoe store with more than 50 brands of shoes for city streets and the great outdoors. 27 N. Chestnut St. ⌀ 845/256-0788. www.pegasusshoes.com.

Rock & Snow   Outdoors enthusiasts (and those who dress the part) love this store, with its clothing and gear for hikers, climbers, and skiers. Great sales and an entertaining staff of handsome young fellas. 44 Main St. ⌀ 845/255-1311. www.rocksnow.com.

Water Street Market   Antiques, handcrafted gifts, and galleries fill the shops of this two-story, open-air strolling complex. 10 Main St. ⌀ 845/255-1403. www.waterstreetmarket.com.

Block Island

Block Island, RI, 02807
⌀ **401/466-5200** · www.blockisland.com, www.blockislandinfo.com, or www.blockislandguide.com

Getting there: Adventure Northeast bus line from NYC (2 stops in the city) to New London, CT; transfer to the Block Island Ferry. See details under "Transit Facts," below.
Subway: 4, 5, 6 to Second Ave./85th St. or 1 to 79th St./Broadway.
Approximate travel time: 3 hr. to New London, CT, plus 1-hr. ferry ride to the island.
Schedule: Buses leave the city at 8:15 and 11am Sun–Fri, with only 1 departure on Sat, at 8am. They depart New London at 2:30 or 5:45pm Sun–Fri, leaving at 2pm on Sat. Ferries run every 3 hr., 4 times a day.
Season: Both Adventure Northeast and the Block Island Ferry run during the summer months only. Peak vacation time on the island runs mid-June to mid-Sept.
Cost: $99 round-trip bus fare plus $32 round-trip for ferry tickets.

Block Island, 12 miles off the coast of Rhode Island, is the ultimate destination for those seeking a true island getaway. Named for Dutch navigator Adrian Block, who happened to stumble across the 7-mile-long island in 1641, the island is home to approximately 900 year-round residents, many of whom are descendants of the original English settlers of 1661. Bluffs overlook sandy beaches, and hundreds of freshwater ponds nurture the flora and fauna that inhabit the inner island. Among the natives are so many species of birds that it's considered one of the best bird-watching locales in the country.

Clean, wind-swept beaches are one of the island's major attractions, and it's not hard to find a near-deserted stretch of sand for a leisurely

Block Island

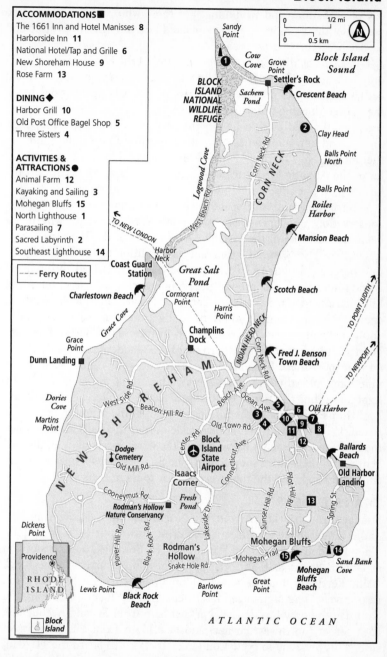

ACCOMMODATIONS ■
The 1661 Inn and Hotel Manisses **8**
Harborside Inn **11**
National Hotel/Tap and Grille **6**
New Shoreham House **9**
Rose Farm **13**

DINING ◆
Harbor Grill **10**
Old Post Office Bagel Shop **5**
Three Sisters **4**

ACTIVITIES & ATTRACTIONS ●
Animal Farm **12**
Kayaking and Sailing **3**
Mohegan Bluffs **15**
North Lighthouse **1**
Parasailing **7**
Sacred Labyrinth **2**
Southeast Lighthouse **14**

--- Ferry Routes

0   1/2 mi
0   0.5 km

Sandy Point
Cow Cove
Grove Point
Block Island Sound
Settler's Rock
Crescent Beach
BLOCK ISLAND NATIONAL WILDLIFE REFUGE
Sachem Pond
Clay Head
Balls Point North
CORN NECK
Balls Point
Roiles Harbor
Logwood Cove
West Beach Rd.
Corn Neck Rd.
Mansion Beach
TO NEW LONDON
Harbor Neck
Coast Guard Station
Charlestown Beach
Great Salt Pond
Cormorant Point
Harris Point
Scotch Beach
Grace Cove
Grace Point
Champlins Dock
INDIAN HEAD NECK
Corn Neck Rd.
TO POINT JUDITH
Dunn Landing
Fred J. Benson Town Beach
TO NEWPORT
Dories Cove
West Side Rd.
Beacon Hill Rd.
Beach Ave.
Ocean Ave.
Old Harbor
Martins Point
Old Town Rd.
Ballards Beach
NEW SHOREHAM
Center Rd.
Block Island State Airport
Isaacs Corner
Connecticut Ave.
Old Harbor Landing
Dodge Cemetery
Old Mill Rd.
Cooneymus Rd.
Fresh Pond
Rodman's Hollow Nature Conservancy
Lakeside Dr.
Sunset Hill Rd.
Pilot Hill Rd.
Spring St.
Dickens Point
Plover Hill Rd.
Black Rock Rd.
Rodman's Hollow
Snake Hole Rd.
Mohegan Bluffs
Mohegan Trail
Sand Bank Cove
Providence
RHODE ISLAND
Block Island
Lewis Point
Black Rock Beach
Barlows Point
Great Point
Mohegan Bluffs Beach
ATLANTIC OCEAN

day of sunbathing and swimming. For those who prefer to see and be seen, the island's more heavily populated beaches offer live music and all-day beach bars.

The island is divided into two "regions": **Old Harbor,** the island's only village, and **New Harbor.** In the Old Harbor, timeless inns and bed-and-breakfasts offer sunrise views of the Atlantic. Besides being the seaside docking point for the Block Island Ferry and most private seafarers, the Old Harbor houses the island's main strip for shopping, dining, and entertainment. Away from bustling Old Harbor and farther inland, New Harbor, on the Great Salt Pond, offers a narrow outlet to the Atlantic for a trickle of commercial boat traffic. It's off the beaten path but close enough for an easy stroll into town.

Most of the island is dedicated to environmental protection, wildlife conservation, and open-space preservation. Maybe that's why it has been named "One of the Last 12 Great Places in the Western Hemisphere" by The Nature Conservancy. In addition to the miles of pristine beaches, dozens of hiking and bicycling trails lead through the island's interior. A ride around the perimeter offers a varied terrain of hills, farmland, lakes, classic Cape Cod vacation homes—and, of course, the ocean surf. If you're noodling around the island on a bike, you may want to seek out one of two historic lighthouses. The first, **North Light,** sits at the northern tip of the island, out on Sandy Point. (*A note of caution:* Even after your ride out, you will be faced with a mile-long hike through deep sand.) There is a museum inside the lighthouse, but the tower is not open to the public. The **Southeast Lighthouse** rises above the Mohegan Bluffs at the southern end of the island. Wild tomatoes and honeysuckle border the trails leading down the bluffs to the beaches below, where the water is crystal clear, the surf gentle, and the sunsets spectacular. The Southeast has a small museum and a gift shop, and the tower is open for tours in the summer.

TRANSIT FACTS

Sunday through Friday **Adventure Northeast** buses depart from Second Avenue and 85th Street (northwest corner) at 8:15 and 11am. They also depart from 79th Street between Broadway and Amsterdam at Dublin Bar at 8:30 and 11:15am. These buses arrive at the Block Island Ferry Terminal in New London, Connecticut, at 11am or 2pm, respectively. The high-speed ferry departs at 11:20am or 2:30pm. On Saturday the only bus departs NYC at 8am from Second Avenue and 85th Street (northwest corner) and at 8:15am from the 79th Street stop. This puts you in New London at 10:45am to board the 11:20am ferry. Ferries leave the island bound for New London at 12:50pm daily (and at 4:10pm Sun–Fri). For details on Adventure Northeast bus lines, visit www.adventurenortheast.com or call ✆ **718/601-4707.** For a Block Island Ferry schedule, go to **www.goblockisland.com**.

Alternate Transit

Most ferries only run during the busier summer months. For year-round service to the island, **Interstate Navigation** (✆ **866/783-7340;** www.blockislandferry.com) departs from the Port of Galilee in Rhode Island. From Montauk on Long Island, accessible by the LIRR, **Viking Star** (✆ **631/668-5700;** www.vikingfleet.com) offers passenger service to and from Block Island.

For an alternative way to reach the high-speed ferry at New London, **Amtrak** (✆ **800/872-7245;** www.amtrak.com) stops directly across from the ferry dock several times a day, and **Bonanza Bus Lines** (✆ **888/751-8800;** www.bonanzabus.com) also makes the NYC–to–New London, CT, route.

GETTING AROUND

Walking and **biking** are the way to go, but that doesn't mean you can't call a cab. Try **Mig's Rig Taxi** (✆ **401/480-0493** or 401/466-2892), **McGoverns' Cab** (✆ **401/862-6087**), **A. Ernst Cab Co.** (✆ **401/742-1446**), or **Monica's Taxi** (✆ **401/742-0000**).

If you really want to get that breeze-through-your-hair feeling, **rent a moped** from **Island Bike & Moped** (✆ **401/466-2700**) on Chapel Street in Old Harbor behind the Harborside Inn. Just remember that you can't use them after dusk or on any dirt roads. Rates can run about $70 to $85 for half and full days.

WHAT TO DO

A Block Island vacation wouldn't be complete without **renting a bike.** There's no destination that's too far to reach on two wheels, and the views as you round a corner and catch sight of the Atlantic sparkling in the distance make breaking a sweat worthwhile. Among the cool places to take your newfound wheels, seek out: **Animal Farm,** between Spring and High streets in Old Harbor, where goats, emus, sheep, llamas, and other farm animals can be found grazing on a meadow; the **Sacred Labyrinth,** near the northern tip of the island, a centuries-old stone path reported to heal both body and soul; and the **island cemetery**—with some settlers' headstones from the late 1600s—where you can take in views of New Harbor. For bikes (about $20/day), stop by **Island Bike & Moped,** Chapel Street (✆ **401/466-2700**), or **Block Island Bike & Car Rental,** Ocean Avenue (✆ **401/466-2297**).

Who Needs Addresses?

Notice anything funny about Block Island—even on paper? The town is not into using actual numerical addresses. A few places list them, but many don't. In fact, technically, there are no street addresses here, so what you may see listed is actually a "fire number" used by the fire department when responding to calls. The islanders' habit of telling you where something is located by supplying the street name—or just describing the general vicinity—is guaranteed to send any Type-A personality into straitjacket mode. Hey, it's a small island, and any number of people will be more than willing to help point you in the right direction. Besides, no matter which way you go, you will eventually end up back in town.

Beach bumming   Block Island offers beaches staffed with lifeguards and all the paraphernalia you'll need for a day of sunbathing and body surfing, as well as private stretches of sand for quiet relaxation. **Town Beach,** offering showers, lockers, rental chairs, and umbrellas, and **Ballard's Beach,** right by Old Harbor and with a well-stocked oceanfront bar and volleyball nets, are both manned by lifeguards. **Black Rock Beach,** named for a huge boulder lurking beneath the water, is accessible only by bike or car. **Vaill Beach** requires a careful climb down Snake Hollow, a rocky hike over some uneven terrain; your efforts, however, will be rewarded by what seems like miles of uninhabited beachfront.

Hiking   Twenty-five miles of trails on one small island? No wonder hiking is one of the town's most popular activities. No, this isn't strenuous, kill-your-calves hiking, but some trails have steep slopes and tricky footing and nearly all have pretty views. For a complete list of trails, go to **www.blockislandguide.com/nature.html**.

Kayaking   There's no rough stuff here, but there's lots of scenery in Great Salt Pond and it's a nice little workout for the arms. Rental kayaks ($30 single, $40 double for a half-day) are available at **Oceans and Ponds.** Ocean Ave. (corner of Connecticut Ave.). ✆ **401/466-5131.**

Nightlife   There are more than two dozen bars on the island. **Captain Nick's Rock & Roll Bar** (69 Ocean Ave.; ✆ **401/466-5670;** www.captainnicks.com) is the island's biggest club, with two bars, two floors, and live music every weekend. Also located in the downtown section of Ocean Avenue, **Albion Pub** (✆ **401/466-9990**) offers more than 40 varieties of beer, a large-screen TV, and a pool table. The historic **Empire Theatre** (Water St.; ✆ **401/466-2555**) has one screen and alternates between new releases each night. The theater was erected in 1882 and has housed vaudeville acts and a roller-skating rink, and is the oldest existing theater in Rhode Island.

Parasailing The best and breeziest way to take in the spectacular island views. Rates are $70 for the 500-foot sail and $80 for the 800-foot sail. Rentals and lessons at Block Island Parasail & Water Sports, on the Old Harbor dock, next to Ballard's restaurant. ✆ **401/864-2474.**

Sailing While in New Harbor, lovebirds should consider a 2-hour sail on *Ruling Passion*, appropriately crewed by a husband-wife duo. The 45-foot trimaran leaves the harbor three times daily with a small crowd of 29, and serves wine and cheese on the sunset cruise ($45 per person). Those already skilled can rent Hobie Cats and other craft, and those who aren't can reserve a lesson. ✆ **401/741-1926.**

WHERE TO STAY

Apartments, cottages, and hotel rooms are available for rent on the island. The **Block Island Chamber of Commerce** can help you out with availability (✆ **401/466-2474;** www.blockislandchamber. com). Block Island can be a pricey place to go once you add up the transportation, meals, and lodging. Going during the week helps cut down on costs, as does renting an apartment or a house so you don't have to eat every meal out. Choose one of the weekly and long-term rentals available at www.blockislandhotel.com. A complete list of accommodations can also be found on **www.blockisland.com**.

> **Foghorn Alert**
>
> Some people find the sounds of the foghorns hard to sleep by, while others love it. If you're in the former category, choose a hotel off the main harbor.
>
> —Sarah Baker

The Harborside Inn Listed on the National Register of Historic Places, the Harborside has 36 small rooms for rent, some with air-conditioning and many with ocean views. Water St. ✆ **800/892-2022.** Doubles $49–$279.

The National Hotel It's celebrating 118 years of welcoming travelers, with 45 rooms in the heart of historic Old Harbor. The porch, and some rooms, have great views of the water. Water St. ✆ **800/225-2449.** www.blockislandhotels.com. Doubles $99–$209; suites $169–$339.

The New Shoreham House Located in front of Old Harbor at the ferry landing, this B&B offers economical rooms with shared baths for those who don't plan to spend a lot of time inside. ✆ **401/466-2651.** Doubles $95–$175.

Rose Farm Inn   A working farm until 1963, this simple white inn serves breakfast in the porch dining room and rents bikes right on the property, a short walk from the village. Roslyn Rd. ∅ **401/466-2034.** Doubles $99–$250.

WHERE TO EAT

Many of the Old Harbor inns offer dining on large wraparound porches that overlook the Atlantic. You'll find a number of both informal and formal (sundress and sandals or a crisp shirt and nice shorts will do) restaurant choices scattered about the main tourist areas.

The Harbor Grill   A popular spot for breakfast, lunch, and dinner, it serves a mean lobster quesadilla and orders of deep-fried brie. Across from the ferry on Water St. ∅ **401/466-2828.** Entrees $15–$35.

Old Post Office Bagel Shop   Satisfy your inner New Yorker at the only place on the island where you can get fresh bagels, lox, and cream cheese. Corn Neck Rd. ∅ **401/466-5959.**

The 1661 Inn   An enormous daily breakfast buffet ($16) includes an omelet station, homemade muffins and pastries, fresh fruit, and baked bluefish. Spring St. ∅ **401/466-2421.**

Romantic Dining

The **1661 Inn and Hotel Manisses** (1 Spring St.; ∅ **401/466-2421;** www.blockislandresorts.com) offers a fully catered romantic dinner for two, served on the beach or in your room and prepared tableside with a full complement of linens, china, and fresh flowers. The $325 tab includes gratuity and transportation to and from the beach.

Tap and Grille   Inside the National Hotel (the first hotel on the island, dating back to 1888), this ocean-side restaurant is known for its steak but also serves local seafood, a slammin' fish and chips, and award-winning chowder. Water St. ∅ **401/466-2901.** Entrees $13–$32.

Three Sisters   Comfort food (meatloaf, mac-n-cheese) and creative salads and sandwiches are served weekdays 11am to 2pm. Eat inside or stake out the hammock or an Adirondack chair. Old Town Rd. near Bridgegate Sq. ∅ **401/466-9661.** Most entrees around $7.50.

WHERE TO SHOP

The Old Harbor houses several quaint island gift shops that sell handmade jewelry, ceramics, and souvenirs. The **Glass Onion** (∅ **401/466-5161**) devotes space to island-crafted jewelry, nautical charts, and one-of-a-kind gift items. For the trendy consumer, **Bonnie and Clyde** on Water Street (∅ **401/466-8895**) sells Seven jeans, C&C California tees, and Lilly Pulitzer along with accessories created from sea glass and shells. For Block Island tees, sweatshirts, and last-minute sand-castle supplies, there's the **Star Department Store** on Water Street (✆ **401/466-5541**). Fudge and candy stores dot the area, offering amazing varieties of fudge and just about anything you can imagine coated in chocolate. Try **Blocks of Fudge** (✆ **401/466-5196**) or **Old Salt Taffy Co.** on Chapel Street (✆ **401/466-5005**) to satisfy your sweet tooth. For 20 years running, **Littlefield Bee Farm** (✆ **888/ 466-5364;** www.blockislandhoney.com) has sold honey produced by generations of bees that flock to Block Island wildflowers.

Troutbeck

515 Leedsville Rd., Amenia, NY 12501
✆ **845/373-9681** · www.troutbeck.com

Getting there: Metro-North Harlem train line from Grand Central to Was-saic, NY, then shuttle ride to the inn.
Subways: 4, 5, 6, 7, S to 42nd St./Grand Central.
Approximate travel time: 2 hr., 15 min., plus 10-min. shuttle ride.
Schedule: Trains leave Grand Central about every 2 hr. on weekends and return from Wassaic on a similar schedule.
Cost: Train fare is $27 round-trip.
Room rates: Doubles $250–$400 per night. AE, DC, DISC, MC, V.

Set on a verdant patch of land that also holds 200-foot-high sycamore trees, a pond with a gazebo, and a stream that's stocked with trout each spring is this 1920s stone English Tudor cottage. As you make your way up the lane, you may feel as if you've been transported to the English countryside, where a formal garden is tucked behind a garden wall, and smoke curls from the manor's chimney. Inside, fires burn warmly for arriving guests who have discovered this slice of genteel country living up near the New York–Connecticut border. Celebrities have also discovered the area and love to make discreet pilgrimages here (you may even spot one at brunch).

Tucked in the foothills of the Berkshire Mountains, the original Troutbeck farm was settled in 1765. Emerson, Thoreau, Teddy Roosevelt, and Hemingway were all guests. It's an inspiring setting: The idea for the NAACP was formed around one of its stately tables. The first Troutbeck house succumbed to a fire, and this one was built in its place in the 1920s, when it became a gathering place for many of the celebrated literati, liberals, and revolutionary thinkers of its time.

The days of glittering literary powwows gradually faded over time, and by the time the present owners found the property in 1978, the house and grounds were in a tragic state of disrepair. The house and grounds were given a fastidious and loving restoration, and Troutbeck opened to guests in 1978.

Troutbeck's radiant warmth is the perfect antidote for the stressed-out city dweller. It's important to know, however, that if you come to Troutbeck by train, you're pretty much stuck at Troutbeck. Out here in the country, little is within walking distance, and cabs need to be arranged in advance. So plan to settle in—and know that there are many worse places to do so. In the warmer months, guests use the jogging and walking trails that curl through the property, which totals 600 acres once you include the adjacent community of 40 private homes. An outdoor pool; tennis, basketball, and volleyball courts; and fly-fishing are all available on the grounds. Come the first snow, Troutbeck becomes the best place in New England to settle into a comfy chair by a wood fire with a cup of coffee to read the entire Sunday *Times*. There's also an indoor pool with a glass atrium, an exercise room, and a pool table in the basement.

The house itself wears its original slate roof and leaded windows and houses more than 12,000 books—endless shelves of poetry, religion, politics, and fiction. The general manager has picked one up from time to time only to have a 1920s postcard or ticket stub fall right into his lap.

If you've ever longed to spend the weekend at a real country estate—with history, hospitality, and space to spread out—Troutbeck won't leave you disappointed. Couples who can't get away from ruffles and lace fast enough will be happy to find that the main house has a distinguished, almost masculine feel. Much of the interior has been divided into small rooms with dark woods and wood-beam ceilings, nooks of books and more books, stone floors, and stone fireplaces with real firewood crackling, hissing, and popping all winter long. There's a television in the library-den and an antique poker table in the game room, where board games are stored in a former owner's gun cabinet. If you're feeling particularly Hemingwayesque, you can belly up to the bar in the Red Room and order a single-malt scotch, a vintage port, or a martini.

Of Troutbeck's accommodations choices, which should you request? Here's a rundown of the types of rooms guests have to choose from. Keep in mind that Troutbeck is listed in the *New York Times* Wedding Directory and is a popular pick for brides in the region year-round, so you should reserve well in advance to get the type of room you prefer.

Manor House: The hallways of this building are lined with bookshelves. Here are some of Troutbeck's largest rooms. A few have a wood fireplace or a sunny sitting-room porch with wicker furniture. High-speed Internet service is available in all rooms. *Note:* Bathrooms in the Manor House may be private or shared.

Garden House: This section comprises five rooms overlooking the walled formal English gardens. Two have wood fireplaces, two have a private deck, and two have a balcony. Room no. 4 has a great view and a steam shower.

Century House: This quiet, modern-looking building is just a short stroll from the main inn. There's a television in the lobby and several common areas. Many of the rooms have sun porches, fireplaces, and four-poster or canopy beds.

GETTING AROUND

Be sure to mention that you're coming by train when you make your reservation; a member of the Troutbeck staff can arrange to pick you up at the station. If they're unable to get you, they can arrange to have a taxi waiting to pick you up; otherwise, none will be waiting at the station unless you arrange a pickup yourself.

You'll need to arrange taxis in advance for any side trips. Try **Lakeville Taxi** (⌀ 860/435-8000), **DeLango Taxi** (⌀ 845/877-9000), or **Tony's Taxi & Limo** (⌀ 845/677-5560).

WHAT TO DO NEARBY

Marlene Weber Moroccan-Inspired SalonSpa   This spa offers a large treatment menu of massage, facials, body treatments, six pedicures, and a full salon. The "Spa Journeys" packages are a great value and are 3 hours ($160) or 5 hours ($235) long. 2647 Rte. 44, Millbrook, NY. ⌀ 845/677-1772. www.marleneweber.com.

Bike to Troutbeck!

Bring your bike on the train and hit the nearby **Harlem Valley Rail Trail** (www.hvrt.org). The trailhead is right next to the train station at Wassaic. From there, it's about a 10-minute ride to Troutbeck (which is in Amenia). Riders need to purchase a $5 lifetime bike permit, which is issued immediately at window no. 27 at Grand Central Station. Space is available on a first-come, first-served basis and some restrictions apply for certain dates and times. Specifics are outlined on the permit application.

Events: Holiday Dinners

Troutbeck's chefs prepare full-course holiday dinners, leaving you and your family time to relax and catch up without having to cook, clear the table, or do the dishes. Reserve for Thanksgiving, Christmas, and Easter dinners well in advance. Other events throughout the year include evenings with live music and dancing, wine dinners, jazz brunches, and other performing arts, photography, and poetry events.

Millbrook Antiques stores   Five within a 2-block stretch, including the Millbrook Antiques Mall, which holds 40 vendors under one roof. 3301 Franklin Ave., Millbrook. ✆ 845/677-9311. www.millbrookantiquesmall.com.

Cascade Mountain Winery   Open Thursday through Sunday for wine tastings and lunch on the terrace. Reservations required. Flint Hill Rd., Amenia. ✆ 845/373-9021.

Silo Ridge Golf   Eighteen holes of hillside golf. Rte. 22, Amenia. ✆ 845/ 373-7000.

WHERE TO EAT

Troutbeck's chef was trained at the Culinary Institute of America (CIA), and the food has received numerous awards. Locals have made this a popular destination for dinner and come for specialties like miso-glazed Chilean sea bass, Black Angus NY strip steak, and lobster bisque (dinner entrees $16–$25). Daily meals include a continental breakfast, lunch, and dinner, plus a full breakfast on Saturday and a Sunday brunch with live jazz ($35 per person, including cocktail). Room service is available upon request. For something really special, a private dinner can be arranged for two in one of the main house's smaller rooms. In the summer, have your lunch by the pool and take your cocktails out on the lawn. You can make reservations by calling ✆ 845/373-9681.

Mohonk Mountain House

Lake Mohonk, New Paltz, NY 12561
Information ✆ 845/255-1000; reservations 800/772-6646 ·
www.mohonk.com

Getting there: Adirondack Trailways bus line from Port Authority to New Paltz, then a free shuttle to the resort.
Subways: A, C, E to Port Authority or N, Q, R, S, W, 1, 2, 3, 7 to Times Sq./ 42nd St.

Alternate transit: Take a Metro-North Hudson line train from Grand Central to Poughkeepsie, NY ($26 round-trip off-peak). Mohonk can arrange a shuttle to pick you up and bring you to the resort with a few days' notice. The cost is $50 one-way for tow passengers. (It's a lot more expensive to choose this option over the Trailways bus—around $70 more per couple.)
Approximate travel time: 1 hr., 45 min., plus 7-min. shuttle ride.
Schedule: Buses leave Port Authority about once an hour and return from New Paltz on a similar schedule.
Cost: Bus fare is $38 round-trip.
Room rates: Doubles start at $416 per night and include 3 meals per person. AE, MC, V.

I have treated this property as a landscape artist does his canvas.
—Mohonk Mountain House cofounder Albert Smiley in 1907

If you splurge on one special-occasion getaway this year, I recommend you make it to Mohonk Mountain House—a retreat in every sense of the word. When twin brothers Albert and Alfred Smiley stumbled upon this serene setting in the 1860s—Alfred, a Poughkeepsie farmer, first visited on a picnic outing—it held a tiny clapboard tavern surrounded on all sides by majestic mountain views. From 1879 to 1910, the Quaker brothers worked tirelessly constructing their idyllic resort high on the ridge of the Shawangunk Mountains, taking their design inspiration from the natural scenery. Even after the building was completed, they continued to expand upon and add enhancements to the hotel until 1923. The result is a rambling structure that exudes the jumbled whimsy and elegance of an old-time carousel.

Rising above the lake where that old tavern used to stand, Mohonk Mountain House is one of the last of the great 19th-century mountain

---

Events: Theme Weekends

Throughout the year on most weekends, a theme guides a portion of the programming on the activities schedule. (Lots of other activities are offered as well that don't touch on the theme.) Many guests choose a weekend specifically for the theme, even if they only plan to attend one or two of the related activities. There is no extra charge for participating in the weekend's themed activities. Themes have included: Hikers Holiday, Mystery Weekend, Swing Dance Weekend, Holistic Way, Mohonk Sampler, Jazz on the Mountain, Scottish Weekend, Ballroom Dancing, Garden Holiday, Stargazing, and a Celebration of Readers and Their Favorite Authors, with a lineup of notable writers leading the weekend's workshops and readings.

resorts—a turreted Victorian castle with fanciful flourishes. The magnificent house and its polished-wood dining room, 261 rooms, plus lounges, porches, and fire-lit parlors span a full ⅛ mile along the lake. The stone portion of the house's facade was hand-cut from the Shawangunk Mountains just across the way, and cedar shingles give its roof a gingerbread-house look. Named for the Lenape Indian word for "lake in the sky," Mohonk remains under the ownership of the founding family after 130-plus years—a full four generations of hands-on hospitality.

The Scoop on Mohonk

Tripadvisor.com has a heap of honest reviews about Mohonk, many from people who have been going there for years. It's a great website to get a well-rounded picture from the peanut gallery.

Set past a road entrance sign that reads SLOWLY AND QUIETLY PLEASE, Mohonk exudes a sweet, old-fashioned atmosphere that a newer resort can only try to replicate. The rooms are warm and cozy, and the pastimes are simple—horseshoes are still played on the lawn, lemonade is served on the veranda, and après-ski Earl Grey tea can be sipped by a roaring fire.

If money is no object, reserve one of Mohonk's largest and most luxurious accommodations: the **Tower Rooms.** A balcony, wood-burning fireplace, and a pair of plush robes are all you need to get the romance under way—if you haven't already. Antiques—not televisions—furnish the rooms at this tranquil old hotel, as do beautiful views from the rocking chairs on the balcony. Three other room categories work their way down to the simplest Traditional Rooms—small but still cute and mountain-retreat quaint. (The website has photos and room descriptions of the different styles and floor plans.) When you're booking a room, remember that this old house is a National Historic Landmark. Floors are creaky, hallways remain endearingly uneven in parts, and rooms are not uniformly outfitted—they may be decorated in Victorian, Mission, or Adirondack twig furniture. It's all part of the place's unique charm.

Mohonk has a Full American Plan, meaning the price you pay for your room includes your meals, most activities, access to the gorgeous grounds, and the privilege of being welcomed like family into a house of old-time grandeur and grace.

Note: Most weekends have a 2-night minimum. Look into packages when making a reservation. The "Midweek Rejuvenation Package," for example, adds the spa experience to your stay.

Kids' Programs & Discounts

If you caved in and are bringing the kids along, there are several times of the year when they can stay for free (certain weekends in Apr) or half-price (certain midweek dates in Dec). **Mohonk's Kids Club** leads age-specific programming morning to evening for ages 2 to 12. Mohonk also has a small game room, family-friendly activities, and the option of babysitting services. The **Mohonk Teen Club** has hiking, rock scrambling, and other cool activities designed for ages 13 to 17.

GETTING AROUND

Transportation to and from the New Paltz bus station is complimentary for overnight guests. Gratuity is not expected, however the driver will certainly appreciate it.

If you're living large, let Mohonk send a private sedan for door-to-door car service. The cost is $199 one-way (Manhattan to Mohonk) for two people. You could probably fly for that much—if only there were an airport.

While there is plenty to see and do in the area—the FDR home and library in Hyde Park; West Point; shopping at Woodbury Commons; or a day spent tasting at the Hudson Valley wineries—Mohonk is a hard place to leave. If you insist, however, the hotel's transportation department can customize a trip for you to these or other attractions with a few days' advance notice (✆ **845/256-2016**).

WHAT TO DO AT MOHONK

All told there are 85 miles of **hiking, walking,** and **running trails** for all levels of exertion. Wind your way up Sky Top Path to the tower for a closer-to-heaven view of six states. Spring Path across the lake makes another nice hike. If you were to count, you'd find nearly 130 gazebos on the grounds (the Smileys call them "summerhouses"). And for ambitious roamers, Mohonk's 2,200 acres adjoin another 6,400 that belong to its neighbor—the meandering Mohonk Preserve.

In warm weather, visit the **formal gardens,** take **trail rides** on horseback, use the **tennis courts,** go golfing on a **9-hole mountain course,** or go **swimming** in that pretty bowl of water, Lake Mohonk. It's ½-mile long, 60 feet deep, and full of fish for those who like to catch them.

In winter Mohonk looks as lovely covered in a new blanket of snow as it does decked out in spring blossoms or bright autumn foliage. **Snow tubing, snowshoeing, cross-country skiing,** and **broomball**

games are all a part of the Mohonk winter landscape. Don't leave without trekking up to the Pavilion to lace on a pair of ice skates and go **ice-skating.** This open-air rink has a view of the grounds, a 39-foot-tall stone fireplace, and plenty of hot chocolate. Sit snug under a blanket on a **carriage ride** over the mountain's trails (extra charge) or stay inside for the **daily workshops, readings,** or **tours,** or find a quiet nook to sit back with a book. You can even raid the cabinet full of **board games.**

House History Tours, offered daily, are led by rotating members of the hotel's staff and the Smiley family. This is the best way to learn about the house's quirky design and hear anecdotes about its history, guests, traditions, and the family who grew up here.

Barn Museum   SHOD IN THESE THEY TROD THE MOHONK TRAILS TO PLACE reads a sign above an entire wall of retired horseshoes from beloved animals who've gone on to greener pastures. Trix, Harry, Queenie, Doll, and many others are remembered in this museum devoted to Mohonk's century-old past. Wander through the old yellow barn—one of the largest still standing in the northeastern U.S.—and marvel at the farm machinery and cooking tools of the resort's earliest years—some of which is for sale. Blacksmithing demos are on view in season. It's open Saturday and Sunday.

The Greenhouse   Take a tour on Saturday morning at 9:45am to see how the Mohonk gardens get their start—or wander through on your own some afternoon.

The Spa   Not yet a year old, the spa has blended right in with the old-world charm of the resort while adding its own version of rustic luxury. Book one of the signature treatments using indigenous witch hazel and finely ground quartz crystals quarried from the Gunks' own cliffs. Then enjoy the solarium with stone fireplace, a heated outdoor mineral pool, and coed relaxation verandas for lounging around in your robes. The locker rooms each have a steam room and sauna; the women's has a tea bar, the men's a TV lounge. For couple's facials or massages, reserve the intimate fireplace suite ($220 for 50 min., $330

Must-See TV

Mohonk has no TVs in its guest rooms, but there are places where guests can watch television, including a comfy lounge with Mission furniture and leather club chairs. A room has also been added for guests to use the Internet and check e-mail.

Mohonk for a Day

Forgot to put Mohonk in the budget this year? You can get a **day-guest pass** when you buy a 1-day grounds pass for the trails ($10 midweek, $15 on weekends and holidays). For an extra charge, you can also go ice-skating or rent cross-country skis. Or make reservations in advance for a meal, which will give you access to the grounds and a glimpse inside the house. Another day-guest package combines a massage with a pass to the grounds. If you want to spend the night nearby, stay at Lefèvre House in New Paltz and cab it to Mohonk and back—all the beauty for a fraction of the price. (See the "Lefèvre House" entry in this chapter and the "Rock Climbing in the Gunks with the Eastern Mountain Sports School" entry in the "Outdoor Activities" chapter for more details.) Go to the Mohonk website for more on day passes and packages.

for 80 min.). Just want to learn? Try 80 minutes of couples massage instruction ($170) so you can practice your moves back at home.

Fitness Center & Classes   The indoor pool with floor-to-ceiling windows and timber beams, along with a full fitness center and a roster of free fitness classes, is open to overnight guests even without a spa appointment. Choose a class in yoga, Qi Gong, Pilates, meditation, aqua aerobics, and more. Some classes are held outdoors on the "green roof" or as a brisk hike up the side of the mountain. Several private classes intensify your workout, including a Cardio Mountain Trek, and Peace in the Pool with tai chi, aromatherapy, and "singing bowl" meditation.

What to Do Nearby

Why you'd want to stray from Mohonk is unclear, but New Paltz has some attractions (see "Lefèvre House" in this chapter and "EMS Climbing School" in the "Outdoor Activities" chapter). Also nearby is Skydive the Ranch—for romance on cloud nine; see p. 33.

WHERE TO EAT

Go ahead and splurge on that bottle of cab sauv at dinner—the rest of the meal has already been included in your nightly lodging cost, so you might as well live a little. Afternoon tea and cookies are also part of the meal-inclusive plan at Mohonk. You'll need reservations for dinner in **one of three dining rooms;** it's a good idea to make your dinner reservations when you check in. Gentlemen will need to wear a jacket, and women are asked to dress up for the evening meal. Dieters can look for "Sound Choices" on the menu at the buffet breakfast and lunch or the table service for more formal dinners. In the summer **The Granary** hosts a lunchtime barbecue and lobster bakes 3 nights a week for dinner—all overlooking Lake Mohonk. The **Picnic Lodge** serves stacked sandwiches and wood-fired pizzas on the big wooden porch. And any time of day, you can stop into the old-fashioned **Soda Fountain** (ca. 1910) to purchase snacks, coffee concoctions, or ice cream to tide you over. Floats, malteds, and egg creams? You betcha.

WHERE TO SHOP

Mohonk has three equally sweet gift shops. The spa also sells several lines of beauty products. In addition, the Barn Museum (see above) sells various farmhouse antiques and Mohonk artifacts, once used but not forgotten.

The Mohonk Gift Shop sells all things Mohonk—from sweatshirts to coffee mugs—and then some. Once a post office and barbershop, this area off the lobby now brims with cookbooks, candles, bath products, journals, and women's wear. Attached is the **Soda Fountain,** which stockpiles its shelves with gourmet goodies (jams, sauces, oils, spreads, and candies) to eat there or take home.

The Greenhouse Garden Shop sells garden supplies and housewares. Gardeners will go for the red rubber clogs, decorative pots (and plants to put in them), stylish birdfeeders, and soothing hand cream. Handcrafted housewares with the same theme are blessed by angelic statues made of stone.

Far beyond a traditional gift shop, the **Gazebo Shop,** a prim and dainty Victorian-style boutique, carefully displays its high-end clothing, jewelry, scarves, and collector's-quality antiques, especially glassware.

Food & Wine Adventures

THE BIG APPLE DINING SCENE IS JUSTIFIABLY CELEBRATED, BUT sometimes you have to get out of town to experience something truly unique. A soul-satisfying culinary adventure has as much to do with the setting as what's on the plate. Sitting down to a meal prepared amid a pastoral landscape on a community farm, sampling dishes on-site at the remarkable chef-making laboratory known as the Culinary Institute of America, or dining aboard the world's largest four-masted sailing ship still afloat can flavor a meal immeasurably.

New Yorkers enjoy an embarrassment of riches when it comes to spirits as well. New York State has four major wine-producing regions—none with vineyards in Manhattan. Of the two wine regions closest to the city, the Hudson Valley vineyards reap the benefits of river-moderated temperatures and swift breezes that are pushed through the Palisades. But the wine-trail maps for the area's 20-some wineries only work if you have a car (and a designated driver). That leaves the sunny Long Island wine region, with its ever-ripening reputation for a long growing season that yields full-bodied merlots and chardonnays. If a trip to Long Island's wine country is on your list of fun things to do, it's time to head out for a tasting. Some visitors love the experience so much they sign themselves up for Wine Camp (or a winemaking school upstate) for a chance to concoct their own unique blends.

A few entries in this chapter focus on beer instead, what some like to call the poor man's bordeaux. Not everyone boards a Metro-North train in search of the perfect cold brew, but after a trip to atmospheric Guinan's pub, they may feel they should.

Food & Wine Adventures

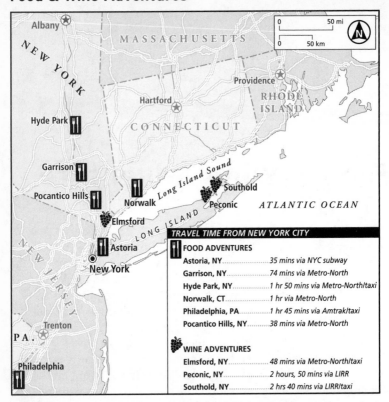

TRAVEL TIME FROM NEW YORK CITY

FOOD ADVENTURES

Astoria, NY .... 35 mins via NYC subway
Garrison, NY .... 74 mins via Metro-North
Hyde Park, NY .... 1 hr 50 mins via Metro-North/taxi
Norwalk, CT .... 1 hr via Metro-North
Philadelphia, PA .... 1 hr 45 mins via Amtrak/taxi
Pocantico Hills, NY ..... 38 mins via Metro-North

WINE ADVENTURES

Elmsford, NY .... 48 mins via Metro-North/taxi
Peconic, NY .... 2 hours, 50 mins via LIRR
Southold, NY .... 2 hrs 40 mins via LIRR/taxi

Culinary Institute of America (CIA)

1946 Campus Dr. (Rte. 9), Hyde Park, NY 12538
Information ☎ **845/452-9430;** restaurant reservations
845/471-6608 · www.ciachef.edu

Getting there: Metro-North Hudson line train from Grand Central to Poughkeepsie, NY, then a cab from the station.
Subways: 4, 5, 6, 7, S to Grand Central/42nd St.
Approximate travel time: 1 hr., 50 min.
Schedule: Trains leave Grand Central about once an hour and return from Poughkeepsie on a similar schedule.
Hours: Lunch 11:30am–1pm; dinner 6–8:30pm. Restaurants closed Sun, major holidays, and most of July.
Transit cost: $26 round-trip off-peak.

Rocco studied here, renegade chef and author Anthony Bourdain attended, and Todd English worked his magic right here in CIA's kitchens. The founder and CEO of Chipotle Grill, Steve Ells, has a degree, and if you're a fan of Gotham Bar & Grill, know that celebrated executive chef/owner Alfred Portale did his time up in Hyde Park as well.

You might say that CIA is the Harvard of American cooking schools. It's certainly going strong, recently celebrating its 60th year of educating talented chefs. Say what you will about snobbery and egos and lenient admissions requirements, but when a cook has the Culinary Institute of America on his resume, people pay attention. The proof is in the pudding: More than 300 companies recruit chefs on campus each year.

Come for a visit to poke around, eat lunch or dinner, or buy some baked goods and a cookbook to take home. Anyone can sign up for one of the public tours given on Monday, Wednesday, and Friday when school is in session ($5 per person). A CIA student will lead you through kitchens, classrooms, and the school's restaurants, with running commentary. The glass cases lining the hallways of the main building, Roth Hall, are filled with trophies, awards, and antique baking equipment. You can get lost in the massive food library (feel free to photocopy recipes from the cookbooks).

You can even take demonstration or hands-on classes, generally taught on Saturday from 9am to 3pm ($165 per class). A 1-day demo class in food-and-wine pairing, for example, or a 1-day hands-on program in artisan breads, classical French cuisine, Asian noodles, or smokin' and grillin' methods is tailor-made for visitors without a car. Classes are held in one of the school's kitchens, the bake shop, or the dining room, depending on the theme. If you want to make a full day of it, you can take a cab to a nearby attraction after class, then come back for dinner at one of the restaurants before taking the train back home. If you plan to take one of the longer 2- and 3-day classes or the week-long intensive Boot Camp program, check out "Where to Stay," below.

Before it became part of the CIA, the impressive main building (Roth Hall) was St. Andrew-on-Hudson, a former Jesuit seminary. The CIA purchased the five-story, 150-room building and its 80 acres overlooking the Hudson River back in 1970. Students take their meals in the former chapel, complete with stained glass and a platform for the altar.

The oldest culinary school in the country, CIA was founded in 1946 in New Haven, Connecticut. Today, between this campus and its Californian sister (the CIA at Greystone) in Napa Valley, the college employs more than 130 chef-instructors and faculty members representing 16 countries.

TRANSIT FACTS

Poughkeepsie is the last stop on the Hudson line (the most scenic of the Metro-North train lines), so there are plenty of cabs waiting outside the station. All will know where the CIA is—just a few miles up the road—and the fare should be about $5.

Alternate transit: There's no real advantage to this alternative except a slight time savings, but Amtrak trains do run from Penn Station to Poughkeepsie, New York. You will arrive at the same station as the Metro-North trains do, and you'll still need to take a cab. The cost is $56 round-trip (more than twice as much as Metro-North) and takes about 1 hour, 25 minutes.

GETTING AROUND

For those without cars, cabs are pretty much the only game in town. Although there are other highly recommended attractions in the CIA vicinity, none are within walking distance. Three companies to try are **Hyde Park Taxi** (✆ 845/229-8402), **Delroy Taxi** (✆ 845/452-1222), and **Poughkeepsie Taxi** (✆ 845/471-1100).

WHERE TO EAT

This will be your biggest decision, one you need to make before you arrive. Reservations are strongly recommended for every restaurant except the Apple Pie Bakery Café, and can be made on the CIA website or by calling ✆ 845/471-6608. Be sure to ask about each restaurant's dress code; the more upscale places ask that diners wear business or country-club casual (collared shirt and dress or chino-style slacks)— "no jeans or sneakers, please." On days when students do not have class, all restaurants are closed and no public tours are given. Because different restaurants are open on different days, check the website or call for dates. All restaurants are open on Wednesday.

Unlike the discount you might receive when an apprentice instead of the salon's master stylist cuts your hair, the CIA doesn't slice their restaurant prices just because students are manning the sauté pan. In fact, that's a big part of the draw—these award-winning restaurants

> **Tip**
>
> Although you should book up to 3 months in advance for Friday or Saturday restaurant reservations, same-day reservations are often available for lunch and dinner on weekdays. January through April are the least busy months.

often have a budding superstar at the stove. If a few should rise to stardom, you can say you ate their smoked sea scallops first.

Menus for all of the following CIA restaurants, and even their wine lists, are available on their websites. Reservations can be made by calling ⊘ **845/471-6608** or reserving online.

American Bounty   New American and Hudson Valley regional cuisine using fresh, local ingredients. Entrees $21-$26.

Apple Pie Bakery Café   Baking and pastry arts students turn out all the sandwiches, soups, salads, pizzas, pastries, and outrageous desserts here. Closed on weekends. Salads $1.95-$5.75; sandwiches and pizza $5.75-$6.50.

Escoffier   Classic French fare with a light touch, delicate sauces, and tableside preparations. Entrees $27-$58.

Ristorante Caterina de'Medici   A Tuscan-style villa sets the tone for an authentic Italian meal. Entrees $17-$25.

St. Andrews Café   A casual place for items high in nutrition and low in fat and cholesterol. An excellent choice for lunch. Entrees $8-$20.

WHAT TO DO NEARBY

Home of Franklin D. Roosevelt National Historic Site   The four-term president's birthplace and summer home. 4097 Albany Post Rd. ⊘ 800/FDR-VISIT. www.nps.gov/hofr. Admission $14 adults, free for children 16 and under (combination ticket includes admission to FDR Presidential Library and Museum). Daily 9am-5pm.

Franklin D. Roosevelt Presidential Library and Museum   America's first library with exhibits on the Roosevelts, the Great Depression, and World War II. 4079 Albany Post Rd. ⊘ 800/FDR-VISIT. www. fdrlibrary.marist.edu. Admission $14 adults, free for children 16 and under (combination ticket includes admission to FDR Home). Daily 9am-5pm Nov-Apr; daily 9am-6pm May-Oct.

Vanderbilt Mansion National Historic Site   The famed family's 54-room Gilded Age mansion and formal gardens is open to the public. 4097 Albany Post Rd. ⊘ 845/229-9115. www.nps.gov/vama. Admission $8 adults, free for children 16 and under. Daily 9am-5pm.

Events: Classes for Parent & Child in the Kitchen

On select Saturdays throughout the year, you can team up with your little chef in a CIA kitchen where together you'll prepare and enjoy a four-course meal. One child age 8 to 15 per parent; cost is $165 per person (www.ciachef.edu).

Val-Kill, Eleanor Roosevelt National Historic Site Mrs. Roosevelt's restored home commemorates her humanitarian ideals. *Note:* Val-Kill was undergoing a renovation at press time but was expected to open by spring 2006; call ahead. Violet Ave. ⌀ **800/FDR-VISIT.** www.nps.gov/elro. Admission $8 adults, free for children 16 and under. Thurs-Mon 9am-5pm.

> **Tip**
>
> If you don't have time for a class, learn at home with one of the CIA's training DVDs on specific cooking and baking topics (www.ciachef.edu).

Rhinebeck A scenic village just 15 miles up the road, Rhinebeck has homes dating back to the 1800s, great restaurants, antiques stores, an old Aerodome, and the country's oldest inn, the Beekman Arms, built in 1766. See more at **www.escapemaker.com/ny**.

WHERE TO STAY

Holiday Inn Express, Poughkeepsie The CIA lists eight hotels and B&Bs on its website that are within 5 miles of the school, but this is the only one that offers a *free shuttle* to the CIA. They'll pick you up at the train station, bring you back to check in, then you can take the CIA shuttle at your leisure. It's an ideal arrangement if you want to take multiday adult-ed classes. The hotel boasts updated rooms, an outdoor pool, a fitness center, and complimentary continental breakfast. ⌀ **845/473-1151.** www.poughkeepsiehi.com. Doubles $99-$119.

WHERE TO SHOP

CIA Barnes & Noble Bookstore The front of the store has your typical college logo stuff, though it's weird to spy a baggy gray sweatshirt that you normally see from OSU or USC emblazoned with "CIA". In back, peruse kitchen tools and cooking gadgets, aprons and oven mitts, and cookbooks of every sort—including many that are authored by graduates of the school.

Vintage Tours–Long Island Wine Country Tours

Peconic, NY 11958
⌀ **631/765-4689** • www.northfork.com/tours

Getting there: LIRR from Penn Station to a designated station between Riverhead East and Greenport, depending on your tour's itinerary.
Subways: 1, 2, 3 to 34th St./Penn Station or A, C, E to 34th St./Eighth Ave.
Approximate travel time: 2 hr., 50 min.

Schedule: Tour will meet between 11:30am and noon. You'll likely take the 5:47pm train back from Greenport, which gets back into the city around 8:37pm.

Season: Year-round.

Cost: Fare to Greenport $29 round-trip off-peak (less to closer stations). Cost of tour is $65 per person Sat–Sun, $58 per person weekdays, plus each winery's $2–$5 fee for optional tastings.

A great way for anyone without a car to explore the North Fork wineries of Long Island is by guided van tour with a knowledgeable and fun-loving expert. Few do it better than owner and tour operator Jo-Ann Perry, whose immaculate midnight-purple van with plushy bucket seats has been affectionately dubbed the "Big Grape." All you have to do is sit back, take in the scenery, and listen as Jo-Ann whisks your group from vineyard to vineyard, wine tasting to wine tasting, remarking on the history, culture, and local color of the area in between.

Between the Big Grape and Jo-Ann's occasional renting of a bus, the company can accommodate up to 14 people per tour—which only really happens during the couple weeks of autumn's color explosion or by special request from a larger group. On a regular weekend, the tour is generally a very manageable 4 to 10 people.

There's no canned script here, and no two tours are alike. Each journey to the North Fork offers a different mix of vineyards, from the immensely popular giants to little-known ventures, from the oldest (Costello Di Borghese) to the newest additions (like Roanoke). When you make a reservation, Jo-Ann will ask about anything particular you'd like to experience. An affinity for sparkling wines, an interest in bold reds, or a desire to get behind the scenes on an in-depth tour in addition to a few tastings will help her develop a plan for the day based on guests' suggestions. In the summer or fall, your group might want to pick up a strawberry-rhubarb pie at one of the farmers markets that dot the main highways. Or you might ask

Tip

Reserve early if you've set your sights on the fall. And remember that once the leaves turn, the wineries will be jammed with like-minded tasters.

to take a quick but scenic detour to gape at a few of the grander houses that look out across Peconic Bay (not unlike the one on the South Fork with three ponds, a golf course, and an asking price of $75 million in Bridgehampton, for example). Generally speaking, the tour includes stops for tastings at three or four wineries, or tastings at three wineries with a tour of one.

Most wineries charge a tasting fee of $2 to $5—a bargain considering the number and scope of wines they'll let you choose. If you taste at every vineyard on the tour, you'll still spend less than $20. (Couples sometimes share tastings if they have already sampled at previous vineyards or are each only interested in trying one or two on a vineyard's wine list.)

If you want to try a regional varietal, cabernet franc is big out on the North Fork. It's known for being full-bodied, floral, and peppery. Long Island produces many chardonnays and merlots, but give the sauvignon blancs and late-harvest wines a try as well.

Lunch is included in the tour fee, a spread put together by a local chef with a chicken, fish, or vegetarian option. Depending on the weather and which winery Jo-Ann chooses for the lunch stop that day, some groups have picnicked outdoors, while others have used the winery's cafe-style seating indoors. With a background of more than 20 years in the travel industry, Jo-Ann makes a warm and personable hostess. She's more than a chauffeur, too—she works in historical information, interesting facts, and anecdotes about the area. (Did you know, for example, that nearby Cutchogue is rumored to be the sunniest place in New York State?)

Some guests like to work tours into an extended weekend in Greenport, and Jo-Ann will happily do hotel pickups. The Harborfront Inn (www.theharborfrontinn.com) is a popular option; it has an outdoor pool as well as attractions and restaurants within walking distance.

Guests on Vintage Tours have come from all over the world. Travelers from Japan to Norway on a trip to NYC have added the tour as a kick to their otherwise Manhattan-heavy itinerary. Jo-Ann is also in

---

Visiting Brotherhood Winery

Wine lovers might also be interested in visiting Brotherhood Winery in Washingtonville, New York, the oldest winery in America. Shortline/Coach USA offers a package trip daily that includes round-trip transportation from Penn Station, wine tastings, and a tour ($50 per person). You'll see the original buildings and the underground cellars with enormous oak barrels while you learn about barrel-aging and taste the juicy results. On fall weekends the winery hosts live music and grape-stomping contests. Other events on the winery's calendar include wine and food fests, cheese sampling, photo exhibits, dancing in the courtyard, a clambake, and a cooking-with-wine fair. For winery information, call ✆ **845/496-3661** or go to www.brotherhoodwinery.net. For Shortline package details, call ✆ **800/631-8405** or go to www.shortlinebus.com.

The Limo Alternative

There is another way to see the Long Island vineyards. **Metro Limousine** (✆ **516/LIMO-SERVICE;** www.metrolimousineservice.com/winetours; rates start around $125 per person) is skilled at taking groups round-trip from Manhattan out to the vineyards for the day and back. They will even arrange a picnic lunch for your group, a tour of one of the wineries, or a farmers-market detour for donuts and cider on your way home.

---

demand among yachters who dock at the local marinas and want to visit the wineries and see some of the area before climbing back aboard.

TRANSIT FACTS

Brooklynites might find it more convenient to leave from the Flatbush Avenue LIRR station at the Atlantic Avenue/Pacific Avenue subway station in Brooklyn. Either way, you will need to transfer trains at the Ronkonkoma station just less than an hour and a half into the trip. *A fair warning:* Do not miss your train and do not miss your transfer. These trains run only a few times daily; the next one won't be soon enough to let you catch up with the tour, not even for the tail end of it. Allow plenty of time and pay attention to announcements from the conductor about transferring so you know when and where to catch your connecting train.

Stone Barns Center for Food & Agriculture

630 Bedford Rd., Pocantico Hills, NY 10591
✆ **914/366-6200** • www.stonebarnscenter.org

Getting there: Metro-North Hudson line train from Grand Central to Tarrytown, plus cab from station.
Subways: 4, 5, 6, 7, S to 42nd St./Grand Central.
Approximate travel time: 38 min. for express trains, 50 min. for local.
Schedule: Trains leave Grand Central about every half-hour on weekends and return from Tarrytown on a similar schedule.
Hours: Wed-Sun 10am-5pm.
Transit cost: $15 round-trip off-peak, plus about $7 in cab fare. Free to enter grounds; tours are $5-$9.

Pull on your wellies for an off-road walk up, down, and around this picturesque model of the agrarian life. Gardeners, gourmands, artists, photographers, nature lovers, flower fanatics, bird enthusiasts, and anyone with a taste for a Hudson Valley farm-to-table meal are sure to be thrilled with a visit to Stone Barns.

Guests who make the trip to this former Rockefeller estate can explore the more than 80 peaceful acres on foot (on a guided or self-guided tour). The property has a greenhouse with retracting roof panels, crop fields brimming with vegetables and berries, and livestock and other farm animals living as nature intended—plus a restaurant, a cafe, and an educational center hosting programs, classes, and tours.

The hills and fields at Stone Barns were farmed by the Rockefeller family during the 1920s, brought back to life in the 1970s by Peggy Rockefeller with a herd of beef cattle, then renovated a few years ago as an homage to her memory with the help of David Rockefeller. It is already one of Westchester's—and the greater Hudson Valley's—most compelling attractions: a living, working, breathing center for eating, growing, and learning. Adding to its day-trip appeal, it adjoins the 50 miles of hiking trails in Rockefeller State Park Preserve.

In case you're wondering, the distinguished-looking, Normandy-style stone hay barns that now house the visitor center were built by John D. in the 1930s. Hay was pitched on the ground floor, then tossed up for storage on the second. These massive structures were key elements of his dream to have a self-sufficient estate for his family. Across the way, you can curl up inside the silo for a quiet moment or two—it's the best-kept secret on the property.

Take a tour and receive a crash course in the "natural systems" agriculture practiced here, based on a responsible partnership with the environment. Food is grown without chemical fertilizers, pesticides, or herbicides, and a compost heap is maintained for the restaurant and cafe. As you're led through lush fields, your guide explains the time-honored process of rotating the crops in the greenhouse and fields, and the rotational grazing that benefits the animals, who roam free in a clean, nearly idyllic environment. Pigs root happily in the dirt; piglets grow up with their mothers. Sheep have a guardian sheepdog named Stella who sleeps beside them in the fields.

Tip

Pets on a leash are welcome on the roads, trails, and in the courtyard of Stone Barns—but not in the greenhouse, fields, or buildings.

At once, Stone Barns becomes an exhibit, a classroom, a laboratory, and a garden. There's even harmony among the staff. Chefs slap on work boots and help out with the farm chores, while farmers are in and out of the kitchens to make sure the cooks have everything they need. (At harvest time, dedicated volunteers file into the fields.) Staff members have found their calling here from all different places: The livestock manager is an eighth-generation New York farmer, while a younger colleague did a short stint on an organic farm abroad before arriving in West-chester. Regardless of back-ground or position, Stone Barns staff will tell you this: "We manage our farm in a symbiotic relation-ship, attempting to mimic nature's own methods."

> **Tip**
>
> No bikes are permitted at Stone Barns or the on the trails at Rock-efeller State Park. And please don't pick the plants.

GETTING AROUND

Taxis are usually waiting to meet trains at the station. To get back to the station or to any other Tarrytown attractions, try the following cab companies: **Knapp McCarthy** (✆ 914/631-TAXI) or **Tarrytown Taxi** (✆ 914/631-8100). The wait is about 10 minutes, and fares generally range from $5 to $8.

WHERE TO EAT

Menu items—often seasonal and grown on the grounds or nearby—are designed with an eye toward self-sufficiency. Much of what is served at Stone Barns comes from these productive rolling acres, keeping outside "imports" to a minimum.

For reservations at Blue Hill Café or Blue Hill at Stone Barns, call ✆ **914/366-9600.**

Blue Hill at Stone Barns This clean-lined, modern restaurant reverts to nature for the decor: wood floors, steel beams, pussy willows, sunflowers, and, of course, lots of stone. Farm-fresh seasonal menus for dinner and brunch draw such crowds that it's recommended that reservations are made 2 months in advance. Here, quality is not to be compromised: The chef has been known to inspect the plates coming back into the kitchen to make sure each dish has been met with approval. Dinners are billed as multicourse menus; a three-course dinner is $62; a four-course dinner is $75; and the Farmers Feast is $95 (Blue Hill also has another location at 75 Washington Place in NYC.) *Tip:* Cancellations do occur, so call the day before if you're interested in a last-minute reservation at Blue Hill restaurant. Or do like other savvy New Yorkers do and dine at one of the seats at the bar.

Blue Hill Café Throughout the day (10:30am–5pm), a regular stream of hikers comes off the trails to fuel up here with a latte or homemade trail mix. Stake out a panini, roasted vegetables sold by the pound, or a huge sandwich wedge built with crusty bread.

WHAT TO DO

Between the farm and the state park's trails, you'll find plenty of acreage for **walking** or **hiking.** For those with energy to burn, the trek to **Union Church of Pocantico Hills** (555 Bedford Rd., off Rte. 9; ✆ **914/631-8200;** open Wed–Fri 1–4pm, Sun 2–5pm) is worth it. The church, built by the Rockefellers, dates from 1921 and is illuminated with stained glass designed by Marc Chagall and Henri Matisse. Finding himself bedridden at the time of this commission, Matisse developed a way to design large compositions from a bed in his studio. Matisse completed his design for the church's Rose Window just 2 days before his death on November 3, 1954.

Stone Barns has a year-round calendar full of periodic and one-time events (like **Harvest Festival** in Oct), including lectures, workshops, special tours, tastings, cooking classes, film screenings, and musical performances. A **Friday farmers market** is open in season from noon to 5pm (get there early for the best stuff). **Family programs** are also a big part of the center's education efforts—such as the Sunday-afternoon Family Farm Chores & Stories ($5), a hit with kids ages 4 to 8, who are put to work collecting eggs, feeding chickens, or repairing fences. *Note:* Most events require advance online enrollment.

You can also take one of the farm's **guided tours.** In-depth 1-hour Insider's Tours are led on Friday from 11am to 12:30pm ($9). Docent-led farm tours (45 min. long) leave from the visitor center on Saturday and Sunday at 11:30am, 1pm, 2:30pm, and 4pm ($5). *Note:* Tour frequency decreases in inclement weather, so be sure to check the schedule. Wear shoes you can muddy, and be ready to walk. Only the Insider's Tour requires advance enrollment, which you can do online.

The historic homes of **Sunnyside** and **Lyndhurst** are a quick cab ride away, as are **Kykuit** and **Philipsburg Manor.** See details on each in chapter 7.

WHERE TO STAY

Hotels including the **Tarrytown House Estate** (✆ **800/553-8118;** www.tarrytownhouseestate.com) and **Castle on the Hudson** (✆ **914/ 631-1980;** www.castleonthehudson.com; see chapter 4) are both a short cab ride away.

WHERE TO SHOP

In addition to the wares sold at the Stone Barns shops below, you can also purchase a **Thanksgiving turkey** from the farm. You'll need to place an order as early as September to get dibs on one of the farm's

Events: Vacation Farm Camp

Enroll your child in the farm's 1-week day camp for kids ages 5 to 10 on their winter or spring school break. In addition to hands-on farm chores, children may help out in the greenhouse or take walks on nature trails (⌀ **914/366-6200,** ext. 111; $70 per day or $180 for 3 days).

Bourbon Red or Broad Breasted White turkeys, which are pasture-raised on certified organic grain. (The Reds sell out fast!) The turkeys will be fresh and available for pickup a day or two before turkey day.

Blue Hill Café   In addition to selling seasonal gourmet lunch foods and snacks, the cafe stocks its shelves with jams, honey, homemade granola, Blue Hill seasonings, and Stone Barns cow-logo T-shirts. The cafe also sells delicious farm-fresh eggs laid right outside by Rhode Island Red hens. These eggs have bright yellow yolks that hold together and more omega 3s than the ones in the supermarket.

Visitor Center Farm Store   Both adults and kids will delight in this shop full of adorable impulse buys. Farm- and nature-themed merch includes books, cards, pottery, and educational toys.

Bohemian Hall & Beer Garden

29-19 24th Ave. (btwn. 29th and 31st aves.), Astoria, NY 11102
⌀ **718/274-4925** • www.bohemianhall.com

Getting there: N subway line.
Subways: N to Astoria Blvd. in Queens. At the Astoria Blvd. stop, exit near Astoria Blvd. and 31st St. Start walking down 31st St. toward Hoyt Ave. South. Make a left onto 24th Ave. The Bohemian Hall is on 24th Ave. between 29th and 31st sts., closer to 29th.
Approximate travel time: 35 min. from Times Sq.
Schedule: Subways run on a frequent basis.
Hours: Garden portion open Mon-Fri 5pm-2am; Sat-Sun noon-2am in warm weather.
Cost: $2 MetroCard fare.

What looks like your basic Queens pub in front gives way to a full-fledged, European-style beer garden out back with a gargantuan cement garden where wooden picnic tables are scattered under a grove of tall trees. People are everywhere—drinking, laughing, eating charred-to-perfection sausages. The "decor" consists of a few lampposts, plastic ashtrays on the tables, a small band shell for live music events, and strings of plastic beer flags that go flapping in the breeze. When there isn't a breeze, however, this place can get hot. So people order more beer. And get a little tipsy. And that's pretty much it for ambience.

Bohemian has a full bar, but this is a traditional beer hall, after all. Several Czech and German beers spill from the taps (Pilsner Urquell, Starapromen, and Spaten dark), and many more come in bottle form. Some rather obscure Czech brews are in the mix; ask the bartender inside to make a recommendation. Groups order by the pitcher, which comes with a set of tall mugs. For the price, you can afford to drink until you actually think you're in the Czech Republic. It's been done many times with great success.

The indoor bar is open year-round, with a maze of rooms to hide out in off the main room. But the beer garden is what sets this place apart—and brings people to this stop off the N train in Astoria from every subway line in the city. For many urbanites, this *is* New York City in the summer.

On a weekday in nice weather, the garden fills up fast after work—and even faster on a weekend. It's every man or woman for themselves, so line up at either of the bars (inside or out) and place your order. If you're really lucky, live polka music will be playing in the background.

Bohemian Hall is not just a boozy backyard: It's the last remaining outdoor beer garden in all of New York City. At one time the five boroughs boasted *more than 800* outdoor beer gardens—three in Astoria alone. In 1892 the Bohemian Citizens' Benevolent Society was formed, and in 1910 the society purchased two adjacent lots, part of a farm. The cornerstone of Bohemian Hall was laid that October. So, drink up: Each beer served goes a long way toward preserving this piece of urban history.

WHERE TO EAT

You've got two choices: from the menu or from the big smokin' grill. *Hint:* The grill is faster. (When the garden is packed, food may take a while; especially if the outdoor grills are not going yet and the tiny kitchen is flooded with orders.) Czech specialties are featured in both options, with more home cooking on the menu and more sausages and

---

Events: Annual Czech/Slovak Festival

Held over Memorial Day weekend for more than 20 years as the official garden season kickoff. The schedule plans for folk dancing, a brass band, other entertainment, and lots of beer and food ($10).

BBQ-style delights on the grill. *Note:* They take credit cards only if you're eating, not if you're here just to drink.

Silvermine Tavern

194 Perry Ave., Norwalk, CT 18229

✆ **203/847-4558** · www.silverminetavern.com

Getting there: Metro-North New Haven train line from Grand Central to South Norwalk, CT.
Subways: 4, 5, 6, 7, S to 42nd St./Grand Central.
Approximate travel time: 1 hr.
Schedule: Trains leave Grand Central once or twice an hour and return from South Norwalk on a similar schedule.
Season: Open year-round; closed Tues.
Transit cost: Train $20 round-trip off-peak.
Room rates: Doubles start at $120 per night including continental breakfast.

For 75 years, this gathering place has been hosting guests in true New England tavern spirit: as an inviting refuge for good food, good music, and rest and refueling. A member of American Historic Inns, the property has a unique history. The tavern's five buildings have stood on this land for more than 2 centuries, housing over the years a speakeasy; a grocery and post office accidentally blown up by a drunk reveler on a turn-of-the-20th-century Fourth of July; and an old mill, one of whose owners died trying to replace the rocks that washed out of the dam in 1924.

Decades later the current innkeeper, Frank Whitman, Jr., visited the Silvermine Tavern as a boy with his family. His father, Francis, who like his son had graduated from Cornell University's School of Hotel Administration, loved the old inn so much he told the owner, "If you ever want to sell this place, let me know." Lo and behold, the call came, and the Whitmans bought the tavern in 1955. The family's two-generation dedication both to welcoming guests and to maintaining the tavern's historic integrity has earned the property numerous accolades along the way.

The tavern's colonial decor, sloping ceilings, post-and-beam construction, and rippled window glass all date from the mid-1800s. Five fireplaces glow in the winter to warm the meandering dining rooms. Much of what you'll see is left from when the inn had its own antiques business. Handcrafted farm tools, local antiques, portraits of people forever unknown. On one wall hangs a map from 1836, hand-copied by a young schoolgirl.

The river and area are called Silvermine, or Silver Mines on very old maps of the area, but Frank says no silver has ever been found. As he tells it, water-powered mills, agriculture, an artist colony, and suburban homes are all part of the Silvermine community that overlaps parts of three towns: Norwalk, New Canaan, and Wilton, Connecticut.

In addition to its historic ambience, Silvermine Tavern offers serious food and serious jazz entertainment (see "What to Eat" and "What to Do," below). But the tavern is not just about savory eats, convivial spirits, and good music. Unlocking the door to your room upstairs after a hearty dinner, you'll feel as if you got the best bedroom for a weekend stay at your aunt and uncle's country house. Before you notice the lack of phone or TV, you'll probably spy the jar of "birdie bits" on the dresser for feeding the ducks down by the water. Floral wallpaper, duck prints, creaky wide-plank floors, a canopy bed, and antique lamps complete the atmospheric picture. A couple of rooms even have their own back porch. For added privacy, book the Mill Pond Suite—a separate cottage with a deck on the water. *Note:* Ask about packages that include a jazz dinner and 1 or 2 nights' lodging.

GETTING AROUND

You'll need to take a cab from the station to the tavern; a few are usually waiting to meet the trains. To get downtown, call **Yellow Cab** (∅ **203/853-1267**). Public phones are in the hallways of the inn.

WHERE TO EAT

The Silvermine Tavern serves a continental breakfast, lunch, and dinner, and a Sunday brunch. At dinner start with sweet corn soup with lump crabmeat and a red-pepper-puree side or a bowl of comforting clam chowder. New England entrees include a chicken potpie with shiitake mushrooms, a braised lamb shank with red-wine reduction, and a pecan-crusted filet of brook trout. Go whole hog and add a side of the creamy, apple-wood-smoked-bacon risotto (entrees $19–$31).

The complementary continental breakfast features the tavern's famous honey buns, baked daily in the ovens here for the past 50 years.

Events: Wine Dinners

Make reservations in advance for these five-course meals paired with eight spectacular wines. Themes range from "Wines of Tuscany, Liguria & Piedmont," and "Wines of the Alexander Valley," to the "Annual Fall Harvest Zinfandel Dinner," and the annual "Mondavi Opus One Dinner."

In the mix: plenty of cinnamon, Georgia pecans, and New England clover honey. And one of the state's favorite Sunday brunch buffets is loaded down with made-to-order pancakes, corned beef hash, broccoli-cheddar soufflé, blintzes, eggs Benedict, fresh fruit, and champagne.

WHAT TO DO

A highly respected **jazz venue,** the Silvermine Tavern is blessed with an innkeeper who has been a serious buff for years—one look at the music calendar and it's obvious that Frank has far-reaching connections in the industry. The weekly jazz musicians who take center stage are mostly local, with new talent showcased monthly. Thursday is reserved for Dixieland; on Friday and Saturday the "Inn Late Jazz' schedule books piano jazz, swing, standards, steamy vocalists, and a quintet with marimbas for a Latin flavor. One group is known for its Cuban and Brazilian rhythms; another takes cues from funk, Afro-Cuban, and world music influences.

Note: While the Dixieland jazz on Thursday goes from 6:30 to 9:30pm and attracts locals and families, the weekend music doesn't start until 9pm—which

> **Tip**
>
> If you are coming up for jazz, dinner, and a night or two at the inn, be sure to tell your waitress that you are an overnight guest so she will waive the cover charge for the evening's music.

leaves just enough time for you to take the train after work on a Friday evening, check into your room, then come downstairs for dinner and some great tunes—miles away from Midtown.

Silvermine Tavern's website provides printable details for a 2-mile **walking tour** straight from the inn past the river, a converted barn, flower gardens, a glass A-frame house, a waterfall and a bridge, artists' studios, a cemetery, and what's left of an old water-powered sawmill.

WHAT TO DO NEARBY

Downtown SoNo and Historic Seaport   Shop, snack, see a movie, then take a cruise to Sheffield Island or a spin through the Maritime Aquarium all along the Norwalk Harbor, just a short cab ride from the tavern and within walking distance of the train station. Visit **www. southnorwalk.com** for more information.

WHERE TO SHOP

The Country Store   Across the street from Silvermine is this tavern-owned store with such New England–style gifts as pottery, pewter, candy, candles, and toys. Since the 1880s, it has been a store, a church meeting room, a blacksmith shop, and a dance hall.

Make Your Own Wine

105 Fairview Park Dr., Elmsford, NY 10523
✆ **914/741-5425** · www.myowine.com

Getting there: Metro-North Hudson line train to Tarrytown then a cab to the school.
Subways: 4, 5, 6, 7, S to 42nd St./Grand Central.
Approximate travel time: 38 min. for express train, 50 min. for local, plus 10-min. cab ride.
Schedule: Trains leave Grand Central for Tarrytown twice an hour on weekends and return with similar frequency.
Season: Four class sessions are spread out between mid-Aug of one year and July of the next year. The first 3 workshops are 1½ hr. long; the final workshop lasts 3 hr.
Transit cost: $15 round-trip off-peak, plus $10 cab ride.
Program cost: Starting at $350 up to $2,400 to make a whole barrel of your own stuff—call for details.

Some have served it at weddings or dinner parties, and others have given it away as gifts. Still others have hoarded every last bottle for themselves. Whatever they choose to do with it, the instant winemakers who follow the wine trail from grape to gulp have MYO Wine to thank for helping them create their own personal blends.

Billed as "Westchester's Winemaking School," MYO Wine was started by local resident Rich Mattina, who dreamed up this 5,100-square-foot, climate-controlled, wine-crafting facility and opened it in 2004.

Before you even begin the workshop, it's your job to select and order the grapes you plan to use for your private label reserve. The California grapes you order—whether cabernet sauvignon, merlot, sangiovese, syrah, zinfandel, chardonnay, pinot grigio, Riesling, or a blend—arrive at the school within 5 days of harvesting, and your first of four group winemaking sessions is timed so you can greet them when they do.

An intense winemaking program ensues, with four workshops scheduled at specific times throughout the winemaking year. In these sessions, you'll master the four phases of winemaking: crushing/de-stemming, pressing, racking, and bottling. By the end of the last session, you and your fellow vintners will not only have learned a great deal about winemaking (and tasted) fine wines, you also will have produced, oak barrel-aged, bottled, and custom-labeled your very own wine.

The process begins anywhere from mid-August to early November. Equipment, yeasts, fermentation, and maceration are all part of Phase

One. Sometime between late August and early November you'll return for Phase Two, where the techniques and methods of turning grapes to wine are reviewed before you press your precious grapes and pump them into an oak barrel, where they will begin to settle and age. In February the wine is ready to be racked—a process that entails removing your wine's sediment, cleaning the barrel, and pouring the wine back into the barrel to finish finding its flavor. This is also the class in which you'll choose and print personalized wine labels.

Nearly a year later, in July or August, your wine is ready to be bottled. Bottles, corks, wineglasses, and storage are covered during your final session. Then you'll head to the bottling station to sterilize your bottles, fill 'em up, pop in the cork, and add the labels. Your wine is finally ready to go home.

The four trips to Tarrytown for the classes will actually be five if you decide to attend one of Rich's open houses before you commit. He encourages anyone interested to come and sample the wines, tour the state-of-the-art facility, scope out the workstations, admire the oak barrels, and ask any questions. Rich accepts solo participants and winemaking groups. The advantage of the latter, of course, is splitting the costs—but also sharing the fun with friends.

"Fine," you say. "Sounds like a good time. But what does wine made by a novice like me really *taste* like?" Pretty darn good, actually. Rich compares the finished products to liquor-store quality wine that would sell for $12 to $22 a bottle.

Not sure if winemaking school is for you? Attend one of MYO's free **open houses** to decide for yourself. You can tour the facility, sample wines made, see the equipment you'll work with, and hear an overview of how the entire process works. Open houses are held periodically on weekends throughout the year—call or e-mail to check the dates and reserve a space (www.myowine.com).

GETTING AROUND
Taxis are generally waiting at the station in Tarrytown. If not, try **Knapp McCarthy Taxi** (✆ 914/631-TAXI), and give 10 to 15 minutes' advance notice for a cab to show up for pickup. Most rides cost between $4 and $8. *Note:* It's common practice for the taxi drivers at the Tarrytown station to group passengers together, even if they are traveling to different destinations.

WHERE TO EAT
Each class begins with appetizers served in a wine-cellar-themed presentation room. After a 20- to 30-minute lecture, the class moves to snazzy workstations for the more exciting, get-your-hands-purple activities.

Events: Wine Appreciation Seminars

From an intro workshop ("wine is made from grapes . . .") to advanced appreciation where you'll learn about buying "Bordeaux futures" as an investment, the school skillfully blends learning with tasting (www. myowine.com).

WHERE TO SHOP

The Wine Enthusiast Conveniently located (I'll say!) right next door to the facility, the Wine Enthusiast Retail Outlet and Showroom offers stemware, barware, corkscrews, storage units, and other countless wine accessories. Among the gear for the urban wine hound are edible Gummy Shot Glasses—which come with instructions suggesting imbibers "take a swing and take a bite." 103 Fairview Park Dr. ∅ 800/648-6058. www.wineenthusiast.com.

WHAT TO DO NEARBY

Other Tarrytown attractions include the **Stone Barns Center for Food & Agriculture** (see earlier in this chapter) and historic homes **Sunnyside & Lyndhurst** (see chapter 7).

The *Moshulu*

401 S. Columbus Blvd., Penn's Landing, Philadelphia, PA 19106
∅ **215/923-2500** • www.moshulu.com

Getting there: Amtrak from Penn Station to Philadelphia's 30th St. Station, then a cab from station.
Subways: A, C, E to 42nd St./Port Authority or N, Q, R, S, W, 1, 2, 3, 7 to 42nd St./Times Sq.
Approximate travel time: 1 hr., 45 min., plus a short cab ride.
Schedule: Trains leave Penn Station several times an hour and return from Philadelphia on a similar schedule.
Cost: Train fare starts at $106 round-trip, plus cab fare.
Alternate Transit: Budget-conscious travelers can hop a NJ Transit train south to Trenton then transfer there for a SEPTA (Southeastern Pennsylvania Transit Authority) R7 train line to Philadelphia's 30th St. station. The trip will take about 2½ hr. and cost less than $30. For New Jersey Transit information, call ∅ **800/772-2222** or 973/762-5100; for SEPTA, call ∅ **215/580-7800.**

Zipping down to Philly for the weekend is easy and affordable. Like New York, Philadelphia is a city brimming with culture and top attractions. It's also brimming with great food. You can find plenty of classic Pennsylvania culinary pleasures here—we're talking scrapple, shoofly pie, chow chow, and chipped ham—but the city also has its fair share of sophisticated restaurants, celebrated chefs, and menus meant to make even NYC-based mouths water. And then there's the Philly cheese steak (more about that later). But one particular dining experience sets Philadelphia apart from New York—dinner and drinks aboard the *Moshulu*, the world's largest four-masted sailing ship still afloat, a completely restored 1904 beauty that recently garnered AAA's Four Diamond Award for excellence in food and service.

Having traveled the world and nearly the seven seas in her working years, the *Moshulu* now lights up the harbor at Penn's Landing with glorious views of the Philadelphia skyline and waterfront. Sip a cocktail at the Bongo Bar toward the boat's stern and take in the glittering views. Then head below for a memorable meal where, naturally, seafood is the house specialty. Herb-crusted Jail Island salmon is bathed in bouillabaisse jus, while dry-boat halibut perches on corn and mushroom ravioli. Steak, duck, and lamb dishes are equally well prepared. Desserts like Tahitian vanilla crème brûlée and a coconut tart with mango coulis are not to be missed.

Here's the suggested weekend itinerary: Leave work on Friday afternoon and arrive just in time for dinner on the *Moshulu*. Wind down with dessert or a nightcap at the bar at the Penn's View Hotel before retiring to your room upstairs. Tour the city the next morning, with Philly cheese steaks lined up for lunch. On Saturday night, dinner reservations at one of chef Steven Starr's restaurants (see below) completes the culinary picture.

GETTING AROUND

Just like New Yorkers, Philadelphians rely on flagging down cabs and using their own two feet to get around town. Once you've arrived, you'll have no trouble getting a taxi at the taxi stand outside Philadelphia's 30th Street Station. Or hop on the big, purple **Phlash Trolley** (www.phillyphlash.com; $1 per ride or $4 per day; May 1–Nov 30), which starts its loop outside the hotel at Penn's Landing and makes 17 other stops including the Rodin Museum, Reading Terminal Market (a gourmet farmers market), City Hall, the Shops at Liberty Place (favorite mall stores), the Franklin Institute Science Museum (Ben Franklin, IMAX, and more), and, at the far end, the Philadelphia Museum of Art.

WHERE TO EAT

After your dining experience on the *Moshulu*, try the following home-town favorites.

And keep an eye out for street vendors selling **water ice,** another time-honored Philly treat.

The Franklin Fountain   An old-fashioned throwback serving egg creams, sundaes, banana splits, and a double-decker waffle ice cream sandwich. 116 Market St. ∅ 215/627-1899. www.franklinfountain.com. Sundaes $5–$8. Closed Mon.

Philly Cheesesteaks   Jim's Steaks, Geno's Steaks, and Pat's King of Steaks are regarded by many as the only proper places to dig in to the city's most indulgent institution. The rivalry between Geno's and Pat's, who duel it out across the street from one another, is intense—as are the lines out their doors. Whether you eat these hoagies with Cheez Whiz or provolone, with onions and peppers or plain as day, the thinly sliced grilled meat on a fresh roll has addictive properties known to foodies the world over. **Jim's Steaks:** South St. at 4th St.; ∅ 215/928-1911; www.jimssteaks.com. **Geno's Steaks:** 1219 S. 9th St.; ∅ 215/389-0659; www.genosteaks.com. **Pat's King of Steaks:** 9th St. at Wharton and Passyunk Ave.; ∅ 215/468-1546; www.patskingofsteaks.com. Philly cheese steaks $6–$7.

Ristorante Panorama and il bar   Locals love the warm, villa-style atmosphere with a mural of the Italian countryside and superb dishes to match. If you can't choose from the 120 wines available by the tasting portion, bottle, or glass, order one of the flights of wine. The Penn's View Hotel, I 14 N. Front St. ∅ 215/922-7600. www.pennsview hotel.com. Entrees $20–$27.

> **Tip**
>
> The **Independence Visitors Center** across from the Liberty Bell at 6th and Market streets has maps, brochures, and answers to all of your questions about what to see, do, and eat during your visit.

Steven Starr restaurants   The biggest name on Philly's cuisine circuit, Starr is about high concept, high fashion, and (how shocking!) high prices. But everyone wants to dine in one of his dozen trendy establishments. **Buddakan** dishes modern Asian against a waterfall wall while a 10-foot golden Buddha blesses the scene (325 Chestnut St.; ∅ 215/574-9440). At the chic, Mediterranean-themed **Tangerine** (232 Market St.; ∅ 215/627-5116; www.tangerine restaurant.com), the food is spiced with flavors from France, Spain, Italy, and Morocco. Both are in the Old City within walking distance, as is **Continental,** Starr's first and most affordable restaurant venture

Events: Concerts at Festival Piers

From November through March, the RiverRink here provides ice skaters with views of the skyline and Ben Franklin Bridge. In the summer, however, concerts and festivals pump up the jams. Columbus Boulevard and Chestnut Street (✆ **215/LOVE-222;** www.pennslandingcorp.com).

(138 Market St.; ✆ **215/923-6069**). Other faves are **Alma de Cuba** for Havana soul (1623 Walnut St.; ✆ **215/988-1799**), **Striped Bass** for seafood (1500 Walnut St.; ✆ **215/732-4444**), and the futuristic sushi at **Pod** (3636 Sansom St.; ✆ **215/413-9070**). Reservations are a must for all (www.starr-restaurant.com).

WHAT TO DO
Adjacent to the Penn's Landing area is the scenic and richly cultural **Old City,** brimming with galleries, museums, shops, small theaters, and restaurants. Pick up a brochure in the hotel lobby (✆ **800/555-5191;** www.oldcityarts.org).

Also see the "Getting Around" section (above) for attractions on the **Phlash Trolley** loop.

Independence National Historical Park (including Independence Hall and the Liberty Bell)   In the heart of historic Philly, visit the very ground where the Constitution was written and the Declaration of Independence was signed. Visitor center at 6th and Market sts. ✆ **800/537-7676.** www.nps.gov/inde. Free admission. Daily 9am–5pm.

Ride the Ducks   Yes, it's a little cheesy that you're asked to sport a duck-bill-shaped "quacker" around your neck. But if you're short on time, this 80-minute ride is a fast way to see some of the highlights of the "City of Brotherly Love." With a fast-talking historian at the helm, you'll glimpse historic landmarks and colonial architecture as you bump along the cobbled streets—all before your amphibious vehicle makes a splash right into the Delaware River. Purchase tickets in advance (6th and Chestnut sts.) or that morning for trips anytime that day. Tours depart every half-hour mid-Mar through Nov. 437 Chestnut St. ✆ **215/227-DUCK.** www.ridetheducks.com.

WHERE TO STAY
The Penn's View Hotel   Just down the street from the *Moshulu* and Penn's Landing and in the heart of the Old City, this romantic hotel pulls off history, charm, and the intimacy of an inn with all the smoothness of a top hotel. Tuscan-touched rooms may have exposed brick walls, marble bathrooms, river views, a Jacuzzi tub, or a fireplace. This

family-owned hotel, built in 1828, has a fitness room, Wi-Fi, and an award-winning restaurant and wine bar downstairs. If you can snag 1 of the 51 rooms, your weekend is already off to a great start. **14 N. Front St., at Market St.** ✆ **215/922-7600. www.pennsviewhotel.com. Doubles start at $165 per night including continental breakfast.**

Guinan's Pub and Country Store

7 Garrison's Landing, Garrison, NY 10524
✆ 845/424-3440

Getting there: Metro-North Hudson line train from Grand Central to Garrison, NY.
Subways: 4, 5, 6, 7, S to 42nd St./Grand Central.
Approximate travel time: 74 min. on train.
Schedule: Trains leave Grand Central about once an hour and return from Garrison on a similar schedule. *Note:* After 11:30pm you won't find a train out of Garrison until the morning commute begins at around 5am.
Hours: 6am to early evening, depending on business.
Cost: Train fare $20 round-trip off-peak.

Destination: dive bar. But not just any old dive bar. This place, with its vintage general store, Hudson River views, and location just steps from the train platform, has a storied history and quirky personality worthy of a work of nonfiction.

Guinan's (pronounced *Guy*-nanz) has stood like a port in a storm on the edge of the Hudson since 1959. Across the water is West Point Military Academy—another long-standing establishment with a storied heritage.

Just as many people have a daytime persona and a nighttime alter ego, so, too, does Guinan's. As the sun rises, Guinan's stretches and opens its front door to a stream of Manhattan-bound morning commuters. Coffee on the warming burners, bagels wrapped in cellophane, packs of sugarless gum—the place is stocked with things people use to jumpstart their day. Commuters waiting for trains spread newspapers out on the waterside picnic tables to skim the headlines.

But come evening, the newspapers are in the trash bins and the coffee pots are cool. Tacked on to the back of the bustling general store is the Guinan family's Irish watering hole—where vinyl-topped stools await their regulars, and beers are plucked from an old metal Coca-Cola cooler. In the winter a fire from an old stone fireplace warms the pub.

It was the nightlife at Guinan's that inspired the *Wall Street Journal* columnist Wendy Bounds to pen the highly lauded *Little Chapel on the River: A Pub, a Town, and the Search for What Matters Most* (William Morrow, 2005), much of which is set inside this very back room. Actually, it was the *people* who come to life at night—the owner, 79-year-old Jim Guinan, and his extended family (biological and otherwise)—who led Bounds to tell her post-9/11 tale. Wendy and her partner, who had lived and worked near the World Trade Center, found the peace they were looking for here in Garrison, New York. They also ultimately found a home here, starting with the tavern that sits beside the town's tracks.

The two-story white box that is Guinan's looks like a house—and it is. Jim lives here, just feet from the bar. The truth is that *many* people think of it as home—a place where they spend those last few minutes of tranquillity before their commute officially begins, or where they drop in after work. Bounds heard one of the regulars liken the place to his form of church, and, looking around this shrine to beer, you can't help but nod in agreement. It's all here—confession, forgiveness, love, and community.

Guinan's closing time is hit-or-miss, which adds to its gritty charm. Wendy says folks arriving by train in the summer on a Friday night can safely expect to get a beer until 8pm—though the pub has been known to buzz along until 11pm or so if enough people are still around. That's why she advises getting to Guinan's in the late afternoon in the warmer months to enjoy the local color outside on the patio by the river and talk with the proprietor, Jim Guinan, and his children John and Margaret.

There's more to say about Guinan's—every dive has its dirt—but unless you're Wendy Bounds, words don't seem to do it justice. The beers are cold and the train ride scenic. So, as Wendy writes in her Author's Note:

"To anyone who has ever known a spot like this, a spot that feels more at home sometimes than home itself, I'd just like to add, go there if you still can. Be there. And don't wait for tomorrow. Go today."

The end.

GETTING AROUND

As Hudson River towns go, Garrison is a little light on the taxicab scene. Only one company, **Highland Transit** (⊘ **845/265-TAXI**), serves the town and appreciates as much notice as possible—you may have a 15-minute wait before it arrives. Guinan's patrons are also quick to offer a ride to a new friend.

WHERE TO STAY

Garrison has a hotel and at least one B&B, though not within walking distance of the bar. (See "The Garrison: A Riverview Resort," below.) Nearby Cold Spring also has the cozy Pig Hill Inn (✆ 845/265-9247; www.pighillinn.com).

WHAT TO DO NEARBY

If you want to see something besides your pile of shredded Bud labels, the following are recommended.

Boscobel Restoration   This early-19th-century mansion just 3 miles up the road contains one of the country's top collections of furnishings from the Federal period. Daily tours are given, and you can explore the rose garden, herb garden, orangery, and trails on your own. 1601 Rte. 9D. ✆ 845/265-3638. www.boscobel.org. Admission $10 adults, $7 children 6-14, free for children 5 and under. Apr-Oct 31 Wed-Mon 9:30am-5pm; Nov 1-Dec 31 Wed-Mon 9:30am-4pm. Closed Jan-Mar.

The Garrison: A Riverview Resort   This 300-acre resort has a challenging 18-hole golf course, rolling grounds, and spectacular views—a lovely private-club-caliber experience that's blessedly accessible to the public (18 holes $65 Mon–Thurs, $90 Fri–Sun). You can stay here in one of the four luxury rooms, dine well in an acclaimed restaurant, and de-stress in the day salon/spa. The World's End Bar has a terrace with a view, and the Valley Restaurant is known for its chic interior and Hudson Valley foie gras. 2015 Rte. 9. ✆ 845/424-2339. www. thegarrison.com. Doubles start at $225 a night.

Manitoga: The Russel Wright Design Center   Daily tours of this home of the famous designer make this one of the few 20th-century modern homesites open to the public in New York. 584 Rte. 9D. ✆ 845/ 424-3812. www.russelwrightcenter.org. Admission $15 adults, $5 children 13 and under. Office hours Mon-Fri 9am-5pm. House and landscape tours Apr-Oct 11am weekdays, 11am and 1:30pm weekends.

Events: The Rising of the Moon

Every Thursday night after a full moon, musicians from around the region head to Guinan's Pub, where improvised Irish music is the entertainment for anyone who drops by. The evening starts around 8pm and offers reels, jigs, and hornpipes until midnight or later. There are few better venues in New York to take in a traditional Irish session—a jam session featuring seasoned musicians playing the tunes by memory and instinct. No cover, either. Note that the last train back to NYC leaves around 11:28pm (check the schedule, as times change).

Long Island Wine Country's Wine Camp

Southold, NY 18229
✆ **631/495-9744** · www.winecamp.org

Getting there: LIRR from Penn Station to Southhold or Greenport, depending on your inn choice.

Subways: 1, 2, 3 to 34th St./Penn Station or A, C, E to 34th St./Eighth Ave.

Approximate travel time: 2 hr., 40 min. on train, plus cab to inn.

Schedule: Trains leave Penn Station 2-4 times daily and return from Southold on a similar schedule.

Season: Wine Camp is offered periodically throughout the year, and the experience changes with the season.

Transit cost: $29 for round-trip off-peak train fare.

Alternate Transit: Take the **Sunrise Express** (✆ **800/527-7709;** www.sunrisecoach.com) bus from the southwest corner of 44th St. and Third Ave. in NYC to either the Southold or Greenport stop, depending on your inn's location. There are several departures and return trips daily. The cost is $35 round-trip and takes about 2½ hr. each way. You'll need to make reservations in advance. (Pay the driver in cash on board.) For details, visit the Sunrise Express website.

Camp cost: All-inclusive: $1,350 per couple per standard room; $1,470 per premium room. A "transportation included" option can be added to your tour for $75, which will cover all costs of getting you to and from the wineries, the restaurants for dinner, and the like.

If you've ever dreamed of quitting your 9-to-5 job, moving out to Long Island's glorious wine country, and making your very own wine with your very own hands, you can now get a real-life taste of the vintner's life as a member of a 4-day, 3-night wine camp.

At Long Island Wine Country's Wine Camp, you'll learn not only how to blend wines and taste them, but you'll actually get your hands dirty in the vineyards of the North Fork. The camp is led by passionate professionals steeped in the island's winemaking culture, who draw from their hard work and experience and use layperson's language to demystify the culture surrounding wine. By camp's end, you will be better equipped at detecting the differences between varietals, deciphering subtle flavors, and buying wine with confidence—but you'll also understand the knuckle-bleeding labor that's buried deep within that hard-earned glass of wine with dinner.

The first wine camp raised its glasses in March 2005, and demand for the opportunity to play wine magnate has been growing ever since. The camp has drawn participants ranging from restaurant owners and culinary students to party planners, schoolteachers, and retirees.

From tasting room to laboratory to vineyard, you'll be engaged in the actual work of making wine. Depending on where your camp falls within the winemaking calendar, you might be pruning or planting or helping with the fall harvest. In any season, you'll meet with vineyard owners and winemakers who offer solid insider advice on what it takes to make an excellent Long Island wine.

Long Island's North Fork is home to more than 30 wineries and an impressive range of award-winning wines. Wineries included in the program are Bedell Cellars, Castello di Borghese, Corey Creek Vineyards, The Lenz Winery, Peconic Bay, The Old Field Vineyards, Paumanok Vineyards, and The Tasting Room.

> **Tip**
>
> Once you have a reservation at one of the B&Bs and know which train or bus you'll be arriving on, ask if the inn offers pickups from the station. Some inns are even close enough to walk to from the train: The Stirling House B&B, for one, is just 6 blocks from the LIRR Greenport station.

Sure, it's pricey, ringing in at $675 per person for a standard room if you're attending as a couple. But Wine Camp's price includes your accommodations, meals, activities, schooling from the names behind the wines, Wine Camp souvenirs, and plenty of tastings. The "sleep-away camp" of your childhood was never this elegant: You'll stay in one of seven amenity-laden B&Bs, plus, you'll graduate with a full mixed case of Long Island wines to take home with you—care of the winery owners who hosted you.

TRANSIT FACTS

If you're taking the LIRR, remember that you need to transfer trains in Ronkonkoma about an hour and a half into the trip. Listen for the conductor's instructions as you near so you know which train to board.

GETTING AROUND

Most of the B&Bs are within walking distance of the wineries and/or other activities—always ask about the proximity of the inn to the camp's activities when you book. If you need to escape from your fellow campers for a bit, **Vintage Tours** (✆ **631/905-2461**) is available to provide transportation or local expeditions while you're out on the island. Taxis are also available; check with your innkeeper for phone numbers.

WHERE TO EAT

You start your day with a hearty breakfast at your B&B. Lunch is served alfresco at the wineries, where a picnic spread is laid out by a professional caterer. Lunch choices have included chicken salad, eggplant roll-ups, a fresh caprese salad, or anything featuring Long Island's seasonal bounty. But the real reward after a day of hard work and focused learning are the wine-paired dinners at the region's best restaurants. The first night kicks off with "farm to table" cuisine at the Fifth Season in Greenport, known for its slow-food approach. The culinary grand finale comes in the form of a lavish six-course dinner at Castello di Borghese Vineyard, to the accompaniment of a live pianist.

WHERE TO STAY

The Long Island Wine Country Bed & Breakfast Group is comprised of seven charming B&Bs: **Acorn Hollow, Blue Iris, Ellis House, Harvest Inn, Home Port, Shorecrest,** and **Stirling House.** Descriptions, photos, and links to each can be found at **www.winecamp.org**. Some offer down comforters, fireplaces, or Jacuzzi tubs, while others have free beach passes, wraparound porches, tennis courts, and water views. (Your choice of rooms is subject to availability, of course.)

6

Spas & Spiritual Retreats

YOU CAN FIND ALMOST ANY KIND OF SPA OR SPIRITUAL RETREAT you're looking for just a couple of hours from the city. The scenic area around Woodstock, New York, in particular, is a natural magnet for one-stop rejuvenation shops. While some spots are essentially bare-bones retreats whose goal is to help you pare down or lose the wretched excess of stress and noise and urban dissonance, many full-service spas pull out all the stops and props to ensure a decadently indulgent weekend. Look for lounges with designer teas, fresh juices, and lemon water, glossy travel mags, flickering fireplaces, and armchairs that embrace.

The spas in this chapter have a proven record of exceptional service, care, and professionalism.

Ananda Ashram Weekend Program

13 Sapphire Rd., Monroe NY 10950
✆ 845/782-5575 • www.anandaashram.org

Getting there: Shortline/Coach USA (✆ 800/631-8405; www.shortline bus.com) bus from Port Authority to Monroe, NY/Mill Pond Pkwy. Stop, then a cab to the ashram.
Subways: A, C, E to 42nd St./Port Authority or N, Q, R, S, W, 1, 2, 3, 7 to 42nd St./Times Sq.
Approximate travel time: 1 hr., 20 min. bus ride, plus 10-min. cab ride.
Schedule: Buses leave Port Authority several times throughout the day and return from Monroe on a similar schedule.
Alternate Transit: Take NJ Transit's North Bergen line train from NY's Penn Station to Harriman, then a cab to the ashram. It only costs $22 round-trip (plus cab fare) but the schedule is limited and you'll need to transfer trains. See www.njtransit.com or call ✆ 800/772-2222 for details.

Spas & Spiritual Retreats

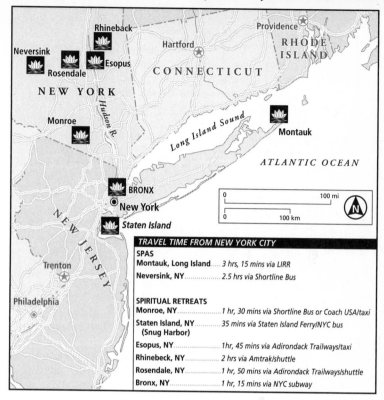

TRAVEL TIME FROM NEW YORK CITY

SPAS
Montauk, Long Island.....3 hrs, 15 mins via LIRR
Neversink, NY.................2.5 hrs via Shortline Bus

SPIRITUAL RETREATS
Monroe, NY....................1 hr, 30 mins via Shortline Bus or Coach USA/taxi
Staten Island, NY.........35 mins via Staten Island Ferry/NYC bus
 (Snug Harbor)
Esopus, NY.....................1hr, 45 mins via Adirondack Trailways/taxi
Rhinebeck, NY...............2 hrs via Amtrak/shuttle
Rosendale, NY...............1 hr, 50 mins via Adirondack Trailways/shuttle
Bronx, NY.......................1 hr, 15 mins via NYC subway

Season: Open year-round but with limited meal options in the winter months.

Transit cost: $49 round-trip bus fare.

Ashram cost: About $160 per person for the weekend.

Your first and foremost duty is to know who you are.
Without knowing oneself, real life does not begin.
—Ananda Ashram founder Shri Brahmananda Sarasvati

If you like ritual, come to the Catskills. Every weekend the Ananda Ashram yoga and spiritual retreat center offers the same set program. And it's pretty intense. The first of five hatha yoga classes starts Friday evening at 6pm followed by meditation, a fire ceremony, chanting, and some sort of nighttime lecture or event. More meditation, yoga, fire, reading from the masters, and evening events—along with a daily open Sanskrit class once a day—rounds out the rest of the schedule. If you stay late on Sunday, a *kirtan* (interactive devotional singing and music—bring your instrument) starts at 8:30pm.

Tips for the Happy, Healthy Spa Visit

◆ Staff at the region's many renowned spas and retreats are generally happy to demystify the process and make you feel comfortable. Few treatments have a mandatory level of undress, if that's a concern. Feel free to ask a lot of questions when making an appointment—and speak up during a treatment if it's not what you expected or it makes you uncomfortable.

◆ Although a stay at a spa usually includes a goody bag of product samples, product is what many of these businesses are pushing. Don't feel pressured to buy everything that's used on you. Only purchase what you think you'll need.

◆ Extend your pampering by booking longer treatments—many regret a short treatment that's over as soon as they're really getting into it. Or, tack on smaller "maintenance" services that you might book back in the city—like a haircut, pedicure, eyebrow wax, or personal training session—to get the full experience.

◆ Almost every spa offers package deals that combine lodging, spa services, and sometimes meals. In the winter, spa resorts tend to slash their prices, especially on accommodations. It's the perfect time for a rubdown on a heated massage table or for sitting a spell in an oak sauna.

◆ Make sure to note whether a gratuity was included on your bill—or simply ask. Many spas tack on a service charge of 18% to 20%.

◆ For most spa treatments, you won't need to bring much more than your clean, showered self. Spa slippers, a robe, and a locker are generally provided—and at the full-service spots, the changing rooms often have much more: showers, basic toiletries, hair dryers, even perfumes. Put your hair up to avoid contact with massage oil.

◆ If you don't have time for an overnight escape, arrive early (having booked a treatment or two) and spend the rest of the day having a spa-cuisine lunch and making use of the facilities that come complimentary to spa guests: the pool, fitness center, hot tub, sometimes even fitness classes or tennis courts.

The ashram looks out on a lake with an island and is tucked inside 85 forested acres of upstate New York charm. Three vegan-friendly meals are served each day. If you want to cut out of a particular session, you can always sit by the lake, take a walk in the woods, swim in the outdoor pool, or book a reflexology treatment or massage with a sit in

Events: Workshops

In addition to the regular weekend program, workshops are offered periodically on classical Kathak dance and Indian music, the yoga of voice, Sanskrit, and ayurveda.

the eucalyptus steam room. Though the schedule is a full one, it's not compulsory. You're always free to take a walk with a friend or find a quiet place to work on that sweater you're still knitting.

Ashrams have existed in the East for thousands of years as centers for meditation, learning, cultural exchanges, and spiritual practice. This one was founded on the universal principles of yoga and vedanta and dedicated to East-West cultural exchange. It has been welcoming individuals of all faiths and cultural backgrounds since 1964, priding itself on a strong community of members who work together to keep it going.

One of the best things about the ashram is its simplicity. The feel here is very focused on the ritual. Meals and rooms are functional, and the natural setting makes it an inspiring place to spend an introspective weekend.

> ### Tip
> Bring comfortable clothing for meditation, yoga, or other exercise; warm clothing and sneakers for walking outdoors; a flashlight; alarm clock; toiletries; bug repellent; notebook; and a mat or blanket for outdoor use.

In keeping things simple, they have also kept the price down. It's less than $200 for the regular weekend program, which includes daily meditation programs, cultural events, and ongoing yoga and Sanskrit classes, meals, and lodging.

To reserve your weekend, call as early as possible, especially if you prefer a semiprivate room. A 10% discount is extended to students with photo ID.

GETTING AROUND

You will need to take a taxi from the bus stop for the 10-minute ride to the ashram. It's wise to call from the bus and give the cab company some notice before you arrive. Try **Monroe Taxi** (∅ 845/782-8141), **Village Taxi** (∅ 845/783-6112), or **Beam's Taxi** (∅ 845/783-4444).

WHERE TO STAY

Accommodations are spread among three guesthouses. Dormitories have bunk beds for up to six people per room, while semiprivate rooms with two beds are best for friends or couples who come together. All bathrooms are shared. In nice weather, you can also bring your tent and camp out on the lawn. (The lodging rate is discounted 20% for tent campers.)

WHERE TO EAT

The menu here is soy-centric, comprised of lacto-vegetarian and vegan meals in a variety of cuisines that incorporate fresh, natural foods. Water comes from the center's spring-fed wells. On weekends and during the summer, meals are served three times daily. At other times, only dinner is served, with breakfast and lunch available informally.

WHERE TO SHOP

The gift shop is teeming with books and CDs on Eastern teachings (many by the center's founder), Indian music, meditation rugs, mala beads, clothing, greeting cards, hand-painted prints, and essential oils.

Chinese Scholar's Garden at Snug Harbor Cultural Center

1000 Richmond Terrace, Staten Island, NY 10301
✆ **718/273-8200** • www.sibg.org or www.snug-harbor.org

Getting there: Staten Island Ferry to Staten Island then a quick bus ride on the S40 from Ramp D along Richmond Terrace to Snug Harbor's entrance on the left.
Subways: 1 to South Ferry or 4, 5, 6 to Bowling Green.
Approximate travel time: Ferry ride is 25 min.; bus ride is less than 10 min.
Schedule: Ferries leave the Manhattan and Staten Island terminals every half-hour on weekend days.
Transit cost: $4 MetroCard round-trip; ferry is free.
Alternate Transit: New York Water Taxi leaves Manhattan's Pier 17 at 11:30am and makes a B-line to Snug Harbor's dock on Sun during summer. The $25 ($15 for age 12 or under) 5-hr. getaway package geared toward families includes a guided tour of the grounds, Chinese Scholar's Garden, The Newhouse Center for Contemporary Art, Staten Island Maritime Art exhibits, and a family admission to the Children's Museum. On select Sundays, you may also catch a free outdoor concert. Purchase tickets for the package at Pier 17 or www.nywatertaxi.com.
Hours: Tues-Sun 10am-5pm.
Admission cost: Entry to the Chinese Scholar's Garden is $5 (admission can be paid in the Scholar's Garden gift shop).

If you think the Staten Island experience begins and ends with the free ferry, this refreshing little jaunt will change your mind. As the sacred treasure of the Staten Island Botanical Garden, the New York Chinese Scholar's Garden is the first authentic classical Chinese garden to be built on U.S. soil. It is a magnificent cultural gem, all the more so when you consider the labor required to make it happen.

Traditional Chinese scholar's gardens have been around for almost 2,000 years and were built by scholars or administrators retiring from the emperor's court. The traditional scholar's garden was designed to demonstrate a harmony and connectedness to its adjacent house, symbolizing the link between structure and landscape. The Staten Island garden—the joint effort of organizations and individuals literally from here to the Great Wall—has no house. It was built by the Landscape Architecture Corporation of China in 1999 solely to be a beautiful and educational free-standing garden.

Now here comes the fascinating part: Each of its architectural components—from the roof, doors, windows, floor tiles, columns, bridges, even the hand-placed river rocks laid out in remarkable patterns underfoot—were designed and prefabricated in Suzhou, China, then loaded on a cargo ship and sent to Staten Island. Upon the garden's arrival, 40 Chinese artists and artisans spent 6 months re-creating it to exacting specifications—one beam, one tile, one stone at a time.

The striking result is an entire walled-in acre of exceptional Ming design. The peaceful structure and its lush landscaping succeed in bringing the inside out and the outside in as only a Chinese garden can. Walkways and bridges link courtyards to pavilions, and each doorway—some shaped like moons or banana leaves—opens to another surprise. Wooden 18th- and 19th-century furniture and unusual rooflines share the garden with flowering trees, waterfalls, Japanese maples, persimmons, jasmine, magnolia, bamboo varietals, and lightly scented flora native to China. The tiers and levels throughout the garden create views that trick the eye into thinking the space is bigger than it is.

A staff member hangs out in the garden to answer visitors' questions. (He'll tell you that the interesting zigzagging bridge is meant to lengthen your journey, allowing more time for contemplation.) But you can answer most questions yourself if you grab the oversize "take

Events: Tai Chi in the Scholar's Garden

Move gracefully into your week with a garden tai chi class. Classes are held Monday from 10:30 to 11:30am ($65 for six classes). Call ✆ **718/362-1007** for more information.

along and return" garden guide cards near the entrance. The cards are slightly heavy and bulky to carry around, but definitely worth the trouble. Each themed card has detailed photos from the garden with an explanation of some of the elements' significance. The "Rivers & Mountains" card reveals that the "One-Step Bridge" is made of stairs that are purposefully difficult to ascend quickly—the scholar should stop to take in the different view from each step. On the "Plants & Flowers" card, poke around the garden to find the Three Friends of Winter as pictured: The plum blossom is planted for good luck; the pine stands for longevity, solitude, and loyalty in hard times; while the yellow bamboo represents humility and the valuable trait of being flexible but strong. The "Calligraphy" card is the most fun. Find the characters painted here and there, as the card waxes poetic about how to live and what we ultimately learn from nature.

While the Brooklyn Botanic Garden's Japanese Hill and Pond crawls with crowds most weekends, there are plenty of Saturdays and Sundays here in Staten Island in which the modest stream of visitors flows as unencumbered through the garden as the goldfish that meander through the ponds below.

Included in your admission to the Scholar's Garden is admission to the smaller **Connie Gretz's Secret Garden** (modeled after Frances Hodgson Burnett's children's classic). Its stocky walls of shrubbery create a maze of brick-lined paths with a small, walled-in garden at the center. Children love to run through the garden, shrieking and chasing each other.

The rest of the botanical garden—including the rose gardens, herb garden, dogwoods, peonies, Italian garden, Garden of Healing, Lion's Sensory Garden, butterfly garden, and White Garden (only gray-green foliage and pure, white blossoms) do not carry an admission charge. Wander at will.

The Chinese Scholar's Garden, the Secret Garden, and the Staten Island Botanical Garden as a whole are part of a larger, 83-acre complex known as the Snug Harbor Cultural Center. The center opened in the mid-1970s after its historic buildings—once the first U.S. home for retired sailors—were purchased by the city for use as an oasis of local culture. Other parts of the cultural center are the **Staten Island Children's Museum,** the **Staten Island Museum,** the **Newhouse Center for Contemporary Art,** and the **Noble Maritime Collection.** Information for these attractions is available at the main visitor center just past the main entrance.

Ninety-minute "walk-in" tours run on Saturday from June through October at 11:15am and 1:30pm; the cost is $10. Your guide provides insight into the history of the grounds, galleries, and gardens. Admission to the Center for Contemporary Art, the Maritime Collection, and Chinese Scholar's Garden are included in the tour price.

GETTING AROUND

If you're in a big hurry to get from the ferry terminal to Snug Harbor or vice versa, you can take a cab from the terminal or ask the gift-shop staff to call one to pick you up. It doesn't make much sense though, since the buses and ferries are timed to work together: The bus ride to the cultural center is less than 10 minutes long, and on the way back, the ferry won't be leaving before the bus would have dropped you off.

WHERE TO EAT

Café Botanica   Housed in Cottage no. 4 in the botanical garden, the building is one in a row of five cottages that date back to 1895 (the others house artists in residence). Enjoy fresh and creative restaurant-quality lunch fare on the wide porch or at an umbrella-shaded table on the lawn. The menu is so good that locals come here for lunch, even if they don't plan to visit the gardens. A meatloaf sandwich with broccoli rabe and fresh mozzarella is just as tasty as the Cuban panini and the Asian-chicken sandwich. Wash it all down with an iced peach nectar tea, and don't leave without succumbing to a mountain of strawberry shortcake. (For breakfast, try the eggs in a broiled grapefruit, and a side of scones with spreadables.) Tues-Fri 10am-5pm; Sat-Sun 10am-6pm.

WHERE TO SHOP

Both the visitor center and the Chinese Scholar's Garden have gift shops inside their entrances. The Scholar's Garden shop has a boutique atmosphere and specializes in Asian-influenced decorative housewares with a whimsical twist.

Another Staten Island Treasure

If you like the Chinese Scholar's Garden, you may also appreciate another Asian-influenced Staten Island treasure—the **Jacques Marchais Museum of Tibetan Art.** Wander among the museum's collections of paintings, sculpture, ritual objects, and musical instruments from Tibet and its neighboring countries, then head outside to take in the hilltop garden. From the Staten Island Ferry terminal, catch the S74 bus to Lighthouse Avenue and walk up Lighthouse Hill to the site (338 Lighthouse Ave.; ⊘ **718/987-3500;** www.tibetanmuseum.com).

Gurney's Inn Resort & Spa

290 Old Montauk Hwy., Montauk, Long Island, NY 11954
∅ **631/668-2345** • www.gurneys-inn.com

Getting there: LIRR from Penn Station to Montauk, then free shuttle to the resort.

Subways: 1, 2, 3 to 34th St./Penn Station or A, C, E to 34th St.

Approximate travel time: 3 hr., 15 min. on the train, plus a quick ride to resort.

Schedule: Trains leave Penn Station several times a day. They leave Montauk for NYC on a similar schedule. Times change, so check schedule.

Season: Year-round.

Cost: Train fare is $30 round-trip off-peak.

Alternate Transit: Instead of the LIRR, some prefer to hop on the Hampton Jitney—a bus line that passes out a small bottle of water and a bag of chips or pretzels to each passenger. That's the upside. However, the seats may or may not recline, the bathroom is tiny, and the bus gets very full as it makes periodic stops on its way to the city. The bus is likely to be late getting in due to traffic, you can't exactly get up and walk around, and you need to reserve a seat in advance (exact change or credit cards are accepted on board for payment). So why bother? Because the Jitney has more arrivals and departures than via the LIRR. The bus picks up at several spots on Lexington Ave. between 40th and 86th sts. and drop offs along Third Ave. in the same vicinity. Cost is $28 one-way or $49 round-trip; call ∅ **212/362-8400** or go to www.hamptonjitney.com.

Room rates: Doubles $218–$1,535 per night. All room rates include a Modified American Plan, which gives you a $15 breakfast credit and $25 dinner credit per person. Credits cannot be applied toward alcohol or soft drinks.

For some reason, this seaside hotel and spa on the tip of Long Island seems to generate a wild mix of opinion—from those who swear it's the best spa resort in New York State to those who swear they'll never go back. Those who fall into the latter group, however, often harbor complaints that sound as ridiculous as, "The four glasses of wine they sold me got me very drunk." I've heard such negatives as:

"It's expensive." Yes, it is. It also happens to be an oceanfront resort and spa, with a private beach, an indoor pool, and a fitness center, all on possibly the most desirable location on Long Island. (The price of your room does include meal credits toward breakfast and dinner that can even be applied toward room service.) The steep price tends to set an expectation that the inn doesn't quite fulfill, however. Gurney's offers a world-class location, but it does not deliver the exclusive five-star

luxury of Frette linens and leather club chairs that some guests, rightly or wrongly, expect to find for these prices. It prefers to take its design cues from the beach itself, maintaining a casual, comfortable setting for families and couples of all ages and tastes. No, not everyone can comfortably afford a Gurney's vacation. But those who can return again and again.

"It's old." Yes, Gurney's has been around since 1926 and this year celebrates its 80th anniversary. And yes, if you look closely, you can find some minor but cheesy design remnants left over from

> **Tip**
>
> Because Gurney's includes a timeshare element, no rooms are guaranteed to be nonsmoking—so you won't know until you get here if it's an issue. If it is, simply request another room.

other eras. However, renovations begun in 2005 included nearly every part of the resort. The spa, restaurant, pool, and some of the rooms were revamped. Whether all of this will be enough to please the naysayers and keep up with guests who demand the best remains to be seen.

"The rooms could be better." Some could, but others are amazing. Gurney's is in the process of upgrading all the rooms, starting with the beachfront units first. (Now, *why* would you go to Gurney's and not splurge on a beachfront room in the first place?) Just steps from the sand, a two-bedroom, two-bath suite has a private lido deck, a kitchenette, a sunning balcony, and a sliding glass door off the larger of the two bedrooms that can be cracked open so you can sleep to the sound of the crashing surf. Lower-priced rooms right over the parking lot make a few nights at Gurney's a little more affordable, but to me the tradeoff isn't worth it. You're at the beach! When requesting rooms, get the best room you can afford—if not in one of the oceanfront cottages, then a room in the oceanfront Foredeck building that houses the Captain's Quarters. These two-bedroom suites (room nos. 561, 568, 571, and 578) afford far-reaching ocean views. And request the nightly turndown service, too.

"It's tacky." Fans counter by saying it's cute or kitschy or aging gracefully. For example, some foes turn their noses up at the green Astroturf on the room's outdoor decks. Sure, there are better options in the deck-coverings department. But this is a casual family resort where sand gets tracked in and out of these rooms every month of the year. You want cashmere carpet? You won't get it here. Ocean views, sea breezes, a private beach—that's what you get at Gurney's.

TRANSIT FACTS

The trip on the LIRR is on a double-decker train once you make the transfer at Jamaica. (Listen for the conductor's instructions before the stop so you know which train is yours.) You'll pass through town after suburban town before you finally near Montauk and patches of sand start to peek through the vegetation before giving way to the small Montauk dunes.

Brooklynites may find it more convenient to catch the LIRR at the Flatbush Avenue station near the Atlantic Avenue/Pacific Avenue subway stop.

GETTING AROUND

Several taxi services are available in Montauk if you want to visit the lighthouse, eat out at the casual restaurants in Montauk Village, or do any other activities in town. Try **Montauk Taxi** (✆ **631/668-2468**) or **Lindy's Taxi** (✆ **631/668-4747**). The **Pink Tuna taxi** (✆ **631/668-3838**) is a big pink station wagon that holds six to eight people. The concierge can help you plan excursions, with the average cab costing about $7 into town, $15 out to the lighthouse.

WHAT TO DO

Just steps from your door, a long, pristine **beach** for strolling awaits. Towels, umbrellas, and lounges are provided, and a beach service menu of snacks, lunch, and tropical drinks is available from 9am to 5pm in season. (It doesn't take too many of those 16-ounce frozen piñas to make you forget you ever have to get back on that train.)

The Sea Water Spa and Salon The spa is half the draw of Gurney's—the service and treatments really are wonderful—so book your pleasure well in advance to ensure availability. Although the treatments are bliss, they're a little pricey—but no worse than those you find in the city. And out here, your $45 pedicure comes with a hypnotic view of the rolling surf. After a 60-minute massage ($100) or 25-minute sea mineral scrub ($55), wrap yourself up in your spa robe and collapse in a lounge chair on the adjacent sun deck to bask in the summer sun. Seawater's therapeutic properties are captured in the products and feel great on the skin—especially noticeable with the facials. *Note:* For some unknown reason, payment for spa treatments is due upfront.

> **Tip**
>
> An 18% service charge is automatically added to all charges signed to your room. Purchases and services paid for in cash or by credit card leave the tip to your discretion.

The Sea Water Indoor Pool and Ship-Shape Fitness Center Get wet in the enormous heated seawater pool and the Roman baths with Jacuzzi jets, or kick back in the sauna or steam room. The cardio fitness center looks right out over the ocean—somehow those miles on the bike don't seem quite as long and arduous with that view. Many of the daily fitness classes ($9–$18) are held outside on an oceanview deck. The day's schedule might include hatha yoga, Pilates, medicine-ball exercise, meditation, cardio blast, aqua jog, beach walk, basic sculpt, or "yogua" in the pool. The morning spinning class is perfect for up-n-at-'em types, but those who can hear the music during breakfast like to grumble that it's too early for that much moving around. Personal training appointments are also available.

> **Tip**
>
> Cellphone service is spotty out here on the edge of the ocean. Leave the hotel number with friends and family, in case they need to reach you.

WHAT TO DO NEARBY

Montauk Lighthouse and Museum The oldest lighthouse in New York State was completed in 1796! It's usually open for tours on weekends from April to November and weekdays in good weather, but hours vary so call ahead ($6). Montauk Point. ∅ **631/668-2544.** www. montauklighthouse.com.

Deep Hollow Ranch Western-style horseback rides along trails or the beach. Rte. 27. ∅ **631/668-2744.** www.deephollowranch.com.

Flying Cloud Fishing Full- and half-day fishing charters have been offered for more than 40 years with Capt. Fred E. Bird. ∅ **631/668-2026.** www.montaukflyingcloud.com.

Montauk Downs State Park Golf Course An 18-hole championship public golf course. S. Fairview Ave. ∅ **516/668-1100.**

WHERE TO EAT

Gurney's has several in-house options, among them **room service,** offered beginning at 7:30am. **Caffe Monte,** named for the family who has owned and operated the resort for decades, serves a casual breakfast and lunch menu. **La Pasticceria Café** serves excellent sandwiches, salads, smoothies, ice cream, pastries, and Starbucks coffee. The **Sea Grille Restaurant** is open for dinner, serving seafood and sea views. The seafood isn't always its strong point, but the food is improving.

Events: Nightlife at Gurney's

In an effort to kick up the nightlife scene at Gurney's, the Port o' Call lounge hosts karaoke, comedy, DJs, live music, and dancing. Other seasonal events include beach volleyball, a lobster bake and BBQ, and outdoor dinner theater. They might be trying to please too many with too much, but at least they're aiming to please.

WHERE TO SHOP

A small boutique carries souvenir sportswear, designer bikinis, and toiletries you may have left at home. The spa sells European beauty products as well as Gurney's own line of sea kelp shampoo, conditioner, lotions, and potions.

Mount Saint Alphonsus Retreat Center

Rte. 9W, Esopus, NY 12429
✆ 845/384-8000 • www.msaretreat.org

Getting there: Adirondack Trailways bus from Port Authority to New Paltz, then a cab from station.
Subways: A, C, E to 42nd St./Port Authority or N, Q, R, S, W, 1, 2, 3, 7 to 42nd St./Times Sq.
Approximate travel time: 1 hr., 45 min., plus short cab ride.
Schedule: Seven or so buses throughout the day leave NYC for New Paltz and return on a similar schedule.
Transit cost: Bus fare $38 round-trip, plus cab fare.
Alternate Transit: Take Metro-North's Hudson line train from Grand Central to Poughkeepsie, then a taxi from the station. Travel time is 1½-2 hr. and the train costs $26 round-trip off-peak.
Season: Year-round.
Retreat rate: Weekend retreats start at $140 including room and board.

A striking building with a rich history, Mount Saint Alphonsus rests on a gorgeous plot of countryside with plentiful river views—an ideal spot for those seeking serenity on periodic weekend retreats. This 400-acre Hudson River retreat is hunkered around a huge old seminary building and can sleep up to 136 guests in 92 bedrooms.

Something happens when people enter the gates and approach this majestic brick building. It served as a Redemptorist seminary for nearly 80 years after its completion in 1907. Wine used at Mass was made right on the property, and the library formerly used by thousands of young priests who studied there remains intact to this day. Generous donors gave up sections of neighboring land to the Redemptorists, and the land has grown abundant with hiking trails, Stations of the Cross, and quiet places for personal reflection.

With the departure of the last seminarians in 1985, this magnificent stone building and its long-standing tranquil atmosphere became a retreat center for "seekers of a deeper spiritual experience."

Those who find the main building impressive should find the Romanesque chapel even more so. A half-dome of stained-glass windows above the altar is the jewel in the church's crown. Seating up to 250, this architecturally magnificent church is filled with knee-bending Catholic adornment in its many forms. Guests are welcome to enter for prayer and meditation throughout their stay.

Mt. St. Alphonsus is one of the largest retreat centers in the Northeast, but if you're looking for quiet and contemplative, you'll find it here. Thematic retreats range from 3 to 6 days and include one for church musicians, one for women, and seasonal weekends marking and celebrating the holiest times of the year, among other retreats. The Eucharist is a part of most retreats, and spiritual directors are usually on hand to offer suggestions and guidance. In addition to the retreats, Mt. St. Alphonsus offers 1- to 2-day workshops (such as an "Intensive Journal Workshop").

GETTING AROUND

New Paltz Taxi, New Paltz's only taxi service, is stationed at the bus depot. Call ahead to ensure a prompt ride when you arrive (∅ **845/255-1550**).

A Monastery Retreat

If this retreat center sounds like your scene, you may also want to check out the scheduled and individual retreat weekends at **Holy Cross Monastery** in West Park, New York. Retreats at this monastic community—such as a laid-back fall-foliage weekend, a 12-step weekend, and a 5-day silent prayer retreat—range from $200 to $400, including room and board. Meals are taken with the brothers, and guest rooms are single-occupancy monk's cells. Guests are also asked to participate in shared periods of silence. Call ∅ **845/384-6660,** ext. 3002, or visit www.holycrossmonastery.com for details. To get to Holy Cross, take Metro-North's Hudson-line train from Grand Central to Poughkeepsie, then a taxi from the station. Travel time is 1½ to 2 hours and the train costs $26 round-trip off-peak.

WHERE TO STAY

The 92 simple rooms here are double or single occupancy with shared bathrooms. Many look out over the Hudson, and all provide a quiet peacefulness that's tough to come by back in the big city. *Note:* Reservations should be made by sending a check for $25, plus a note describing the program you're signing up for as well as your contact information, to Mount St. Alphonsus, P.O. Box 219, Esopus, NY 12429-0219.

WHERE TO EAT

Feeling much like a school cafeteria for grown-ups, the convivial dining room is hosted by trained and certified chefs who aim to please with spice and variety. The cost of a retreat includes five meals, beginning with breakfast on Saturday and ending with lunch on Sunday. An optional dinner at 6pm is served during weekend retreats and costs an additional $10 (prepaid).

WHERE TO SHOP

Gift Shop You'll find music, books, note cards and greeting cards, jewelry, Bibles, wedding gifts, rosaries, religious figurines, and spiritual gifts in this shop, which is open daily for browsing.

New Age Health Spa

Rte. 55, Neversink, NY 12765
∅ **800/682-4348** • www.newagehealthspa.com

Getting there: Shortline bus from Port Authority to Liberty (Village), NY, plus cab to spa.
Subways: A, C, E to Port Authority or N, Q, R, S, W, 1, 2, 3, 7 to 42nd St.
Approximate travel time: 2½ hr., plus 10-min. cab ride.
Schedule: Several buses leave Port Authority each morning and afternoon and return on a similar schedule.
Transit cost: Bus costs approximately $55 round-trip.
Spa cost: Lodging starts at $194 per night (meals included) with a 2-night minimum. Activities and classes are included; spa treatments are extra ($55-$180). Check for 2-for-1 specials in the off season (Oct-Apr) and package deals year-round. A miniweek package—including 5 nights (Sun-Thurs) and 2 free qualifying treatments—starts at $970 per person based on double occupancy.

The name of this spa will either turn you on or turn you off. But not so fast. If it turns you on, you're in for a treat. But if it turns you off, keep this in mind: This compound of simple white buildings tucked high up in the Catskills is only as New Age as you want to make it.

Though it hosts just 75 guests at a time, this all-inclusive retreat offers more than 12 hours a day of outdoor activities, classes, lectures, demonstrations, and introspective ways to unwind. Combined with a full array of spa treatments, 5 miles of nature trails, and a menu designed by chefs, nutritionists, and gardeners from the on-site greenhouses, it's less a touchy-feely place to relax than a dynamic spot to rejuvenate.

In the New Age arena, meet with a personal reiki healer, attend a seminar on past-life regression, or book a private consultation to chart your astrological place in the universe. Not your bag? Pick up a racket and play tennis, swim, take a hike, get a massage, or lounge in the steam room or sauna. Before you leave, be sure to get rubbed to a pearly shine with a 50-minute maple-sugar body-polish treatment.

It's hard not to get motivated to make a fresh start at NAHS—whatever kind of start that may be. People come here to work on themselves. Hard-core self-reformers can sign on for a juice-fasting program, holistic weight-loss program, or a hydro-colon cleansing. And who doesn't benefit from a walk in the woods, a spa cuisine demo, or a stretch class? Just know that while New Age Health Spa qualifies as a "destination spa"—and the word "spa" tends to imply luxury—that is not the major focus here. Some aspects of the place may feel luxurious; others are downright bare-bones. But overall, this is a functional and relaxing place to recharge, chill out, or reprogram.

The literature suggests you leave your "drugs, candy, and cigarettes in the trash bin at the gate." You won't find ashtrays, alcohol, or even caffeine here (save for what's in the green tea) during your stay. The rooms lack televisions, phones, and desks for the computer you should probably leave at home. And you can't get a cellphone signal in these mountains or a second piece of cake at dessert.

While some might think of NAHS as the poor man's Canyon Ranch, the New Age Health Spa is not trying to achieve the same goals. Here, simplicity is inherent, even welcomed. You needn't dress up for dinner or put on lipstick before you head down the path to breakfast. New Age Health Spa has created a budget that puts its money where it matters. Yes, some rooms are aging and in need of an upgrade, but the pools, Jacuzzi, and solarium are lovely places to while away the hours. The food is wholesome, abundant, and pretty tasty considering it's good for you. Staff in the spa are professional and highly skilled. And the Cayuga building, which hosts all of the yoga classes, is absolutely breathtaking. If your own priorities gel with theirs, you will enjoy your stay immensely.

The spa draws more women than men, but plenty of couples come, too. Men will not feel out of place.

GETTING AROUND

A taxi stand for **Sureway Taxi** (Ø **845/292-8805**) is across the street from the bus stop in Liberty. (Make sure you buy a ticket for and get off at the Liberty Village and not Liberty [Routes 72 and 15]). It's a 9-mile trip from the station to the center. Call Shortline at Ø **800/631-8405** for details.

The entire property is highly secured with a guard at the gate who has a list of guests and those checking in each day. Leaving the property during your stay can detract from the experience and is highly discouraged.

WHAT TO DO

The Spa   In colder months, try the Hot Stone Therapy Massage ($175 for 100 min.), in which river rocks are heated to 220 degrees, then used with essential oils as part of a soothing massage technique. Or go for a Full-Body Paraffin Wrap ($155 for 100 min.), in which skin is exfoliated, moisturized, then wrapped in warm wax to melt away tension and leave you silky smooth. Aromatherapy massages with oils of fennel, juniper, cypress, and grapefruit are popular year-round.

Daily Classes   A combination of fitness classes and spiritual classes run from a silent meditation at 6:30am to close to dinner at 6pm. Varying levels of ability are accommodated. A given day may include classes in ai chi (water tai chi), Pilates on the ball, hatha yoga, tantric aerobics, and dance. In the winter, snowshoeing is offered daily, and cross-country skiing 3 days a week. Once the weather warms up, the outdoor pool opens, as does the labyrinth, the tennis courts, and the five-story Alpine Climb Tower you can scale more than 20 ways. In-season excursions off-property to check out mountain waterfalls or bald eagles are also an option at no extra charge.

> **Tip**
>
> Quiet hours are nightly from 9pm to 7am. There is one television in each of the two lounges located in the main building. The smaller downstairs lounge also has books, a collection of movies on VHS, and a computer with high-speed Internet access for guest use. Each residential building has a house phone that can be used to call the front desk; several pay phones are also available.

Open Programs   For early risers, each day begins at 7am with a 50-minute countryside walk. If that's all the exercise you want for the day, you can opt to take part in lectures, workshops, or demos—usually three each day. Topics are chosen to appeal to a number of tastes—from

Events: Theme Weekends

Special theme weekends throughout the year focus on juice fasting, a sweat lodge ceremony, weight loss, smoking cessation, and yoga.

cooking, nutrition, and gardening to meditation and the healing arts. The after-dinner programming is the real wild card in the deck. One night it's handwriting analysis or hypnotherapy; the next could be drumming, storytelling, or acupuncture. The evening winds down with a 9pm movie in the lounge.

Activities & Recreation   Just being in the yoga studio, with its sky-bound, vaulted ceiling of beautiful Western redwood and heated floor, is motivation enough for taking a class here. A golden Buddha takes his place next to a stone fireplace up front that's often decked out with fresh flowers and candles. The indoor pool, Jacuzzi, and solarium all get plenty of light and big views. The fitness room, gym (with cardio and circuit machines), and yoga studio offer lots of space to move, with natural light and views of the 280 acres of forested land. One drawback is the coed sauna and steam rooms, with certain hours of gender-only restrictions.

WHERE TO STAY

In some lower-priced rooms, the older mattresses sorely need replacing. (A massage will feel twice as good after sleeping on them!) The linens and comforters are far from fancy, and the pine-wood paneling may not suit everyone's tastes. If you're picky about the look and feel of your room, ask plenty of questions about specifics when booking. Most have been designed with either a deck or a porch. And with the full schedule and other places to relax, you shouldn't be holed up in your room anyway. It's your own deal if you and a friend have sneaked in a bottle of wine and want to indulge, but don't even think about dragging on a cigarette—the penalty for de-fuming your room is $100. Smoking is prohibited everywhere at the New Age Health Spa.

WHERE TO EAT

The Dining Room   This is your one-stop (and one choice) for meals. A table tent on each table gives a nutritional breakdown of all items served that day. You will know exactly how many calories, carbs, and grams of protein your fish/chicken or vegetarian entree at dinner contains. A buffet holds fruits, dairy, and whole-grain cereals at breakfast, followed by a soup-and-salad bar and an entree at both lunch and dinner. The dinner bonus is a small portion of low-fat dessert. A list of side dishes may also be ordered to accompany these meals, ranging from seared tofu to a baked sweet potato. The one communal salt-shaker is kept up on the salad bar to discourage excess sodium use, though plenty of the soups and steamed veggies could use it. For the full New Age experience, opt to participate in a juice fast. With advance warning, the chef will substitute your portion at meals with fruit and vegetable juices, potassium broth, wheatgrass juice, and a special fasters' soup. On the day of your fast, you'll be seated at a table with fellow fasters, where you'll have plenty in common to talk about. ("I can't believe we missed the potage of broccoli at lunch!")

WHERE TO SHOP
The gift shop stocks workout clothing, aromatherapy everything, and essentials you may have forgotten.

Omega Institute

150 Lake Dr., Rhinebeck, NY 12572
⊘ **800/944-1001** • www.eomega.org

Getting there: Amtrak train from Penn Station to Rhinecliff, NY, then Omega shuttle from train station to center (runs once an hour and must be reserved in advance).
Subways: A, C, E to 42nd St./Port Authority or N, Q, R, S, W, 1, 2, 3, 7 to 42nd St./Times Sq.
Approximate travel time: 1 hr., 35 min., plus 20-min. shuttle ride.
Schedule: Trains leave Penn Station roughly once an hour. They leave Rhinecliff periodically throughout the day and evening. Times change, so check the schedule.
Transit cost: $58–$66 for the train round-trip, plus $5 each way for the shuttle.
Alternate Transit: From the end of May to the end of Sept, an **Omega charter bus** takes NYC guests from a pickup spot on the northeast corner of 31st St. and Eighth Ave. right to Omega's door for $60 round-trip. Timed to coordinate with both the weekend and 5-day workshops, the shuttle picks up participants in NYC at 4:15pm on Fri and Sun. Return trips leave Omega at 1:15pm on Sun and Fri. Travel time is approximately 3 hr. each way. Reservations must be made in advance and payment is required when the reservation is made.
Season: Apr–Oct.
Institute cost: Omega fees include housing, meals, and activities. A 2-night Rejuvenation Weekend, for example, costs around $365 per person with dorm housing. (Rates are less for camping, more for a double or single room.)

Head upstate and spend a few days immersed in learning something you always swore you'd get around to trying. Chances are this mega education center and retreat offers a weekend-long or 5-day workshop in just what you're looking for. Omega's dense, 125-page annual program catalog reads like a Learning Annex for the self-aware. Instructors are well-known gurus in their fields, which include arts, sports, languages, dance, astrology, spiritual practice, philosophy, empowerment, emotional healing, cooking, writing, and even workshops for refocusing a misguided career. There are classes just for educators and health-care professionals, and those just for women and just for kids. You can take classes in right-brain drawing, conscious horseback riding (as opposed to unconscious?), raw-juice purification, feng shui, belly dancing, flying trapeze, compassionate living, "shamanic journeywork," or meditative walking, among other things.

The 195 countryside acres—embroidered with gardens, woods, trails, and a secluded lake—feel like a small, self-sufficient town with a vision of oneness. Cars are left in the main parking lot, making strolling the preferred way to get around. Up to 450 upbeat guests find Omega each weekend, and the campus bustles with the energy of optimistic first-timers conversing with self-declared Omega addicts. By the end of the April-through-October season each year, the center will have hosted another 14,000 people from around the world.

Most guests enroll in one of the hundreds of weekend workshops (Fri evening to Sun at noon) or a 5-day workshop (Fri evenings to Wed at noon). But some stay for a month or more to participate in one of the intensive workshops or teacher trainings.

Glancing through the catalog or across the idyllic grounds, it's hard to believe that the nation's largest holistic education center is nonprofit. The name alone attracts global teachers and participants. One week Goldie Hawn is co-leading an evening session

Tip

Cellphones are frowned upon and may only be used in the main parking lot or one of the phone booths around campus. Not surprisingly, smoking is also discouraged. But there is one smoking-permitted location on campus—just ask, if you dare.

and panel discussion on Mindfulness Studies for Young People (part of her Bright Light Foundation work); the next, Robert Bly is heading up a class that combines poetry, storytelling, and group discussion. Deepak Chopra is a regular instructor of personal transformation classes. Other author/teachers include Dan Millman (*Way of the Peaceful Warrior*), Nick Bantock (*Griffin and Sabine* series), Pam Houston (*Cowboys Are My Weakness*), and Susan Orlean (*The Orchid Thief*).

But nonprofit it is. Generous donors have helped Omega build and maintain this peaceful—and environmentally sensitive—escape for the past 30 years. This is a place where recycling, water conservation, and energy efficiency are nonnegotiable.

An Omega weekend starts on a Friday evening. After check-in (4–7pm) there's a guest orientation and a dinner buffet before your chosen program gets underway with an evening workshop session. Workshops, meals, and bouts of free time fill your Saturday. Checkout time on Sunday is a bright and early 9am. You can take an optional class before breakfast, then have a hearty meal and finish your last workshop at noon.

In addition to the activities on your specific program's schedule, open classes are offered throughout the day in tai chi, meditation, yoga, and movement. In the evenings, programs might include lectures, dances, concerts, or films. Nighttime quiet hours are from 10pm to 7am, but the Wellness Center, library, and cafe stay open until 11pm.

Can't decide on a specific workshop? You don't have to. Omega's **Rejuvenation Weekends** are a design-your-own experience that lets you balance the yin of activity with the yang of restfulness. The price of the weekend includes optional programs and classes (like the open classes mentioned above as well as other classes with topics like organic gardening and art), trail walks and other recreation, a 1-hour massage, and use of the sauna. The weekends work well for coordinating your own minireunion with friends, accompanying someone who wants to enroll in a specific workshop, or simply to schedule a couple of days in which you don't have to answer to anyone but yourself.

GETTING AROUND
Instead of booking the Omega shuttle from the train or bus station, you can call for a local cab; try **Red Hook Taxi** at ✆ **845/758-1478.**

WHAT TO DO
Omega offers plenty of **recreational opportunities.** Volleyball, basketball, and tennis courts; several trails; a lake for swimming, canoeing, and kayaking; and hammocks for dozing all make for a nice break from your chosen themed program.

Events: Arts Week
The institute's grounds come alive in a festival of music, dance, painting, sculpture, theater, and writing. Faculty stage performances, participants' talents are showcased, and everyone can try a flying trapeze.

Wellness Center Improve your body, mind, and spirit with treatments that start at $45 for a half-hour of therapeutic or aromatherapy massage and go up to $80 per hour for acupuncture or astrological counseling; $115 per hour for nutritional counseling; and $250 for an hour with an M.D. who will help revamp your lifestyle with a holistic health consultation. Bring a towel and check out the coed sauna, where swimsuits are optional. There are a couple of slots with designated hours for women only and men only, too.

The Library Opened in 2002, the library contains books and audio materials largely devoted to spiritual studies—some the work of past and current Omega faculty. The square-on-square architecture of the building was inspired by the eight petals of the lotus blossom.

The Sanctuary Remove your shoes before entering this sacred space on a hill in the woods. Any and all are welcome to stop by to meditate, pray, or just sit and reflect. This is also where the daily group meditations take place.

WHERE TO STAY

Comfortable but not air-conditioned, the housing options here run the gamut of price and privacy. Book a private cabin, bunk it in the dorms, rough it in a tent cabin, or bring your own tent and get back to nature. The choice is yours.

WHERE TO EAT

Dining Hall Omega serves a primarily vegetarian menu that appeals to most nonvegetarians as well. Many of the fruits and vegetables served are organic and come from the Hudson Valley, including some from Omega's own gardens. Omega's kitchen staff turns out dishes like lemon-roasted mahimahi and tofu stir-fry with spicy peanut sauce.

Omega Café This air-conditioned cafe also features a deck overlooking the garden. Both are pleasant places to indulge in a pastry, fair-trade coffee, organic tea, or locally made ice cream. You'll also find heartier lunch items like an Asian-greens salad and a free-range-chicken sandwich. Pull out one of the board games or bring your laptop and take advantage of the free wireless Internet. It might be the best way to send and receive communications, as cellphones are somewhat taboo.

WHERE TO SHOP

Omega Bookstore Open from noon to 10:30pm (with a siesta break in the afternoon), this gift-friendly store has books, CDs, cards, meditation supplies, clothing, jewelry, accessories, fitness wear and gear, and even musical instruments from faraway lands. Toiletries and camping essentials are also available.

Sky Lake Lodge Shambhala

Mountain Rd., Rosendale, NY 12472
☎ **845/658-3251** • www.sky-lake.org

Getting there: Adirondack Trailways bus from Port Authority to Rosendale, NY, then a shuttle provided by the lodge.
Subways: A, C, E to 42nd St./Port Authority or N, Q, R, S, W, 1, 2, 3, 7 to 42nd St./Times Sq.
Approximate travel time: 1 hr., 45 min., plus a 5-min. shuttle ride.
Schedule: Buses leave Port Authority once or twice an hour and return from Rosendale on a similar schedule.
Season: Year-round.
Cost: $41 round-trip for the bus, $5 each way for the shuttle.
Lodge cost: $235–$500 for all-inclusive retreats.

Sky Lake Lodge is not a quick-fix factory for those who've hopped on the retreat circuit. Nor does it take a "diner menu" approach to weekend self-exploration, claiming to offer something for every appetite. It's evident by the mere 18 guest beds that Sky Lake isn't taking out glossy ads in self-help magazines to bring people in.

Sky Lake is a quiet place for meditation and study. It was built on a strong foundation of community involvement by active members who practice "mindfulness-awareness meditation" and seek to weave their contemplative practices into their daily lives. Many faces you'll see on one of the weekend retreats are the same faces that were probably also there during that week. Members and volunteers serve as weekend staff, help with administrative tasks, till the gardens, and meditate together on a regular basis.

A "Shambhala" (meaning, roughly, a mystical place of peace and serenity) is intended to be a quiet place of contemplation, reflection, and introspection. You needn't ascribe to a distinct set of beliefs to partake; Sky Lake welcomes anyone interested in meditation as a practice and anyone who strives to spread gentleness and nonaggression on their thoughtful path through life. The main principles of Buddhism form the slow and steady undercurrent at Sky Lake Lodge. While

Events: Buddhist Teachings

Also at this location, the Shambhala School of Buddhist Teachings offers a 2-year cycle of study in which students delve into the realm of Shambhala Buddhism and meditation. Students do not need to be or become a Buddhist to enroll in these courses, although that opportunity is provided.

some members do attend the retreats, nonmembers and first-timers make a good showing as well.

A weekend retreat at Sky Lake Lodge packs a full schedule. Because enrollment is limited and the lodge sleeps less than 20, each weekend has an intimate feel and a good deal of small-group interaction. In your free time, you can meander the grounds of the Mid-Hudson River Valley retreat center. There's a spring-fed pond with a rustic gazebo alongside and miles of secluded hiking trails. (If you were to keep going on some of them, the trails eventually intersect with those on the grounds of the lovely Mohonk Preserve, adjacent to Sky Lake.) The lodge's peaceful ambience is true to its claim to be "a genuine haven from the rigors of urban life." Some weekend programs are part of a larger, long-term cycle of Buddhist study classes and therefore have prerequisites. But every other month or so a program is offered that is open to all—often with a theme of yoga, art, or nature.

Sky Lake is at the northern crest of the Shawangunk Ridge, its 18 acres blanketed in cedar and white pine and ancient lichen-covered rocks and ponds. Among the

> **Tip**
>
> Sky Lake Lodge is a gay-friendly community.

wildlife that call it home are birds, deer, fox, and other Catskill creatures. The natural environment is considered to be an honorary member of the community here. A recent renovation used locally milled pine and cedar that had fallen on the property, so no trees were cut in the process.

Sky Lake Lodge is part of Shambhala International, a worldwide network of meditation centers founded by Chogyam Trungpa Rinpoche, a master of the Shambhala and Tibetan Buddhist traditions. The organization is now guided by his son Sakyong Mipham Rinpoche, who is also the founder of Sky Lake Lodge, a nonprofit organization.

GETTING AROUND

The Trailways stop is outside a hardware store in Rosendale, New York. No taxis are available in Rosendale, so you'll need to schedule a pickup through the lodge (from the Rosendale bus stop to the lodge and back) in advance. The cost is $5 each way.

The limited free time you have during a scheduled retreat weekend is well spent hiking the trails on the property and otherwise enjoying the great outdoors.

WHERE TO STAY

All rooms are double occupancy with two beds and one bathroom (the exception is one room that sleeps four, with a bathroom—if you

> ### Tip
>
> Sky Lake offers the option of making a bed-and-breakfast-style reservation instead, for a quiet and contemplative atmosphere without the retreat activities. The weekend rate is $120 per night for two people. Without a car, however, it's difficult to do anything but roam the grounds.

happen to be assigned to this room because of popular demand for lodging, you will receive a small discount). (Register early through the website if you plan to room with a friend.) There are no televisions or telephones in the rooms here. Laptops are taboo and some cellphones won't get reception. Each room is shaded by tall pine trees and uses a ceiling fan instead of air-conditioning. Rooms are heated in the fall and winter.

WHERE TO EAT

The number and type of meals served depends on the retreat. Sometimes three meals a day will be served in the dining room and included in the price. Other times the group may form a carpool and have dinner together at a local restaurant. Either way, a refrigerator is provided for guests who like to bring their own snacks.

Tai Chi Chuan Class at Wave Hill Gardens

Lower Lawn, West 249th St. and Independence Ave., Bronx, NY 10471
📞 **718/549-3200** • www.wavehill.org

Getting there: The A train to 207th St. or the 1 train to 231st St. Either way, connect to a Bronx bus (see "Transit Facts," below) from the subway to Wave Hill.

Subways: 1 train to 231st St. or A train to 207th St.

Approximate travel time: 1 hr., 15 min. from Times Sq./42nd St.

Schedule: Subways and buses run fairly regularly and do not require advance scheduling.

Alternate Transit: Take a Metro-North Hudson Line train from Grand Central to Riverdale. Wave Hill is a pleasant but steep and uphill 15-min. walk from the station. Head up 254th St., turn right onto Independence Ave. and continue 2 long blocks to the main gate at 249th St. On weekends (Apr–Oct) a free Wave Hill shuttle meets northbound trains at 10:45am, 11:45am, 12:45pm, 1:45pm, and 2:45pm. Return shuttles leave Wave Hill's main gate at 1:20, 2:20, 3:20, 4:20, and 5:20pm to meet Manhattan-bound trains. Check schedules for times, as they may change. Cost is $9.50 round-trip off-peak and the train ride takes 25 min.

Hours: Tai chi classes are held Sat mornings, with a 1-hr. beginners class at 10am and a 1-hr. intermediate class at 11am. Wave Hill is open Tues–Sun Apr 15–Oct 14 9am–5:30pm. The rest of the year it closes at 4:30pm.
Cost: $10 ($7 for members) for the class, which includes admission to Wave Hill for the day; $4 MetroCard.

If you can move through the slow, graceful motions of tai chi, you will be able to move the same way through life.

—Unknown

In its highest form, *tai chi chuan*, commonly known as **tai chi,** combines holistic health with ancient Chinese philosophy. Many of the repetitive motions that have been practiced for more than 700 years originally derived from the martial arts, and possibly from the instinctual activities of animals and birds. To observe someone who has devoted years of his life to studying tai chi can be a near spiritual experience. But even a newbie to this living art form can find that focusing on a deliberate series of smooth, graceful motions is an excellent way to combine exercise and balance with purposeful relaxation.

Tai chi aside, Wave Hill is, on its own, a pretty relaxing place to visit. The 28-acre public garden and cultural center overlooks the Hudson and, across the water, the Palisades. The land was developed for use as a country estate in 1843 and was later leased by Theodore Roosevelt and Mark Twain (among others) before being turned over to New York State in 1960. To this day, this pastoral escape retains a country element with its wild gardens, unusual plants, and second-growth woodlands—all laid out in what the gardeners like to call a "carefully cultivated serendipity." Also on the grounds are greenhouses, grasses, galleries, a huge Italianate pergola, and garden pools dotted with water lilies.

> **Tip**
> Wave Hill allows no pets, radios, bikes, kite flying, or outside blankets and chairs. Tripods and easels are allowed only in certain areas. Picnics are restricted to the Glyndor Gallery Picnic Area only. And, of course, don't pick the flowers, climb the trees, or take plant cuttings.

As long as the weather permits, the year-round Saturday tai chi classes are held outdoors on the Lower Lawn. In cold or inclement weather, class is moved to Armor Hall, where large windows frame sweeping views of the river and the trees.

Sifu Jack Chu, Wave Hill's Yang-style instructor, feels the gardens are a spectacular setting for his classes. "Tai chi chuan is based on the laws of nature and draws its energy from the earth. Wave Hill, with its surrounding trees, flowers, and open air make it an ideal location for relaxation and meditation through movement," he says. Many of the names of tai chi postures are even drawn directly from nature, like White Crane Spreads its Wings and Waving Hands in the Clouds.

Some participants like to think of their tai chi classes as movements linking meditation with yoga postures. Others swear it's all about controlled breathing, while still another group waxes poetic about the harmony the poses create between energy and mass as they circulate "chi" throughout the body. The truth is, ask 10 people what they believe tai chi to be, and you'll get 10,000 answers. If you're even slightly curious, join a class at Wave Hill and begin to formulate an answer that stems from you. If you're shy about showing up or have been known to fall over in yoga class doing Warrior III, you'll feel most at home in the beginners class. The intermediate class, with just 20 to 30 people, tends to be consistently smaller than the beginners class. In summer both class sizes swell as word gets out about this leafy classroom.

Jack, who began studying tai chi as a boy with his grandfather, loves to see beginners in class. "It's a slow, nonstressful mixture of movements that is suited for many ages and levels of skill. I try to make the movements as simple as possible—and always fun, too."

TRANSIT FACTS

To take the subway to Wave Hill, you can either: 1) Take the A train to 207th St. and connect to the Bx7 bus on Broadway, or 2) take the 1 train to 231st St. and connect to either the Bx7 bus or the Bx10 bus on 231st Street (northwest corner, by Chase Bank). Whichever you chose, exit the bus at 252nd Street. Then cross over the bridge, walk 2 blocks down 252nd Street, turn left onto Independence Avenue, and proceed 1 long block to the garden's main gate at 249th Street. When returning, catch the Bx7 or Bx10 bus on the southbound Henry Hudson service road at 249th Street.

Events: Wave Hill

Special events take place almost every day throughout the year at Wave Hill. These range from gardening demos and garden walks to family art projects, music performances, art exhibits, and workshops—even Caribbean-style barefoot dancing. If you want to make it a full day after tai chi class, plan to attend class on one of the many days when a garden walk or demonstration starts. In between, have lunch at the cafe, check out the galleries, and do some nature exploring. Garden and conservatory tours are given every Sunday at 2:15pm. Go to **www.wavehill.org** for details.

WHERE TO EAT

Wave Hill Café This polished-wood and stainless-steel cafe is a popular post-class stop for an Illy coffee or loose-leaf tea. It also serves soups, salads, and sandwiches. Tues-Sun 10am-4pm.

WHERE TO SHOP

Wave Hill Shop Gardening, naturally, is the theme here. In addition to tools and trinkets for the urban garden, Wave Hill stocks children's items, jewelry, home decor, botanical books, and its own branded line of spa products. The linen and room spray, candles, hand salve, and bath gel come in two scents: Cypress & Cassis and Fig. All proceeds from the shop are planted back into the gardens and programs of Wave Hill. (You can also shop online at www.wavehill.org.)

Historic Places

THE HISTORY OF THE NORTHEAST IS, IN ESSENCE, THE HISTORY OF the beginnings of this nation. In 1524 Giovanni da Verrazzano became the first European to reach New York Harbor. Dutch fur traders settled on Lower Manhattan in 1613 in a small settlement then known as New Amsterdam. The Pilgrims weren't far behind, arriving at Plymouth, in Massachusetts, in 1620. These historic settlements were among the earliest in American history (to say nothing of the thousands of years of habitation by indigenous tribes), and the careful preservation of the area's important artifacts, landmarks, and architecture has made this region one of the most history-saturated in the country.

On a simple day trip or weekend escape from New York, you can find yourself transported to centuries past—and appropriately enough, you won't need a car (or a time machine) to get there. Colonial taverns share old post roads with sturdy Federal public buildings; centuries-old battlefields are tucked in forested glens a whisper away from Gilded Age mansions. West Point, nearly lost due to Benedict Arnold's treachery, keeps alive a narrative timeline of America's defenders of freedom. Mystic, Connecticut, offers a firsthand look at how shipbuilding, sea commerce, and whaling were critical to New England's development. At Philipsburg Manor, visitors are shown a poignant look at slavery's role in the economic growth of the region. Throughout the region is splendid evidence of the Rockefeller family's farsighted preservationist zeal and commitment to architectural integrity.

Each of the historic sights and attractions in this chapter is a mere day trip—and an easy mass-transit ride—away from New York.

Sunnyside & Lyndhurst

Sunnyside: West Sunnyside Lane off Rte. 9, Tarrytown, NY 10591
⌀ **914/631-8200** • www.hudsonvalley.org
Lyndhurst: 635 S. Broadway/Rte. 9, Tarrytown, NY 10591
⌀ **914/631-4481** • www.lyndhurst.org

TRAVEL TIME FROM NEW YORK CITY

Tarrytown, NY	48 mins via Metro-North/taxi
Lenox, MA	3.5 hrs via Peter Pan or Bonanza Bus Lines
Mystic, CT	2.5 hrs via Amtrak
Katonah, NY	1 hr via Metro North
West Point, NY	2 hrs via Shortline Bus
Sleepy Hollow, NY	48 mins via Metro-North/taxi

Getting there: Metro-North Hudson line train from Grand Central to Tarrytown, plus a cab from the station.

Subways: 4, 5, 6, 7, S to Grand Central/42nd St.

Approximate travel time: 38 min. for express train, 50 min. for local, plus 10-min. cab ride.

Schedule: Trains leave Grand Central twice an hour on weekends and return from Tarrytown on a similar schedule.

Transit cost: $15 round-trip off-peak, plus $8 cab fare.

Alternate Transit: NY Waterway offers **weekend ferry service** from West 38th St. at the Hudson River in Manhattan to Tarrytown. Several tour packages are offered that include round-trip ferry transportation and bus transportation and admission passes to nearby historic landmarks. To tour Lyndhurst, purchase the **Lyndhurst Cruise package** ($42); add a visit to Washington Irving's Sunnyside for $7. Or purchase the **Sleepy Hollow Cruise package** ($46), which includes a visit to Sunnyside as well as nearby Philipsburg Manor. Both cruises depart at 10:30am and return to Manhattan at 6pm. For information and reservations, call ✆ **800/53-FERRY** or go to **www.nywaterway.com**.

Hours: Weekends mid-Apr through Oct 10am–5pm (call each property for weekday and off-season hours).

Admission cost: Admission to each site: $10 adults, children under 12 free (includes guided tour). If you plan to visit both sites, buy a 2-site ticket for $16 at either site.

Spend an afternoon just north of the city touring two historic homes separated only by a wooded walk along the Croton Aqueduct Trail. The homes—one the romantic but modest residence of author Washington Irving, the other a showy Gothic Revival castle—make an interesting juxtaposition when toured one after the other. Especially when you consider that Irving was personal friends with the William Paulding family, who built this dramatic castle just down the road from his workaday house. But more about that later. . . .

Your day visiting these Tarrytown homes might go something like this: Take a cab from the train station to Sunnyside for a tour, follow the aqueduct trail to Lyndhurst, have lunch at the museum cafe, then tour the castle before heading back to the station to catch the train back to the city.

WASHINGTON IRVING'S SUNNYSIDE

Docents in period clothing lead the tour through Washington Irving's vine-covered riverfront home. After many years living and writing abroad—he wrote the *Legend of Sleepy Hollow* and *Rip Van Winkle* while in England—Irving returned to his beloved valley in 1835 to build Sunnyside estate. What he created in the end is rather humble, but the Hudson River views are heavenly. The interior of the author's home looks just as it did when he died there in 1859, surrounded by family. The man who so eloquently fictionalized New York history through his tales—and grew famous in the process—never married or had children of his own. (His only fiancée died from tuberculosis at the age of 17.) Instead, he often had the company of his brother and his nieces, many of whom lived with him off and on. They adored their uncle and became as dear to him as if they were his own children.

Sunnyside began as two rooms on 10 acres, for which Irving paid $1,800 in 1835. A bargain indeed, all the more so considering the fact that the railroad paid him $3,500 in 1849 to get him to stop fighting with them. (The noise from the trains traveling by the house drove Irving to wage battle with the MTZ.) Inside, see his study, his shaving blade, his version of a La-Z-Boy chair. It's not a fancy house—it's even a little musty—but it's the house of a real man who turned down all sorts of jobs—including the chance to run for mayor of New York City—because he simply wanted to write. For this, Irving eventually became the first American to earn a living on writing alone. When he died around the eve of the Civil War—just after finishing a multivolume work on the life of his namesake, George Washington—the church bells tolled for an hour through the streets of New York City. Irving is buried in nearby **Sleepy Hollow Cemetery** (www.sleepy hollowcemetery.org).

To reach Lyndhurst from Sunnyside: Take the lane back up the way you came in the cab. You'll see a flat, wide dirt path off to the left before you reach the main road—this is the Croton Aqueduct Trail. It's is an easy, 10- to 15-minute walk that leads you through the woods, then along a long stone wall to your right, before opening up to the Lyndhurst property. Follow the signs to the visitor center down a path to your left.

LYNDHURST

Looking more like a cathedral than a family home, the Lyndhurst mansion and 67-acre park has earned a name for itself as one of the foremost examples of Gothic Revival architecture in the U.S.—where castles, in general, aren't that easy to come by.

The stately structure made of "Sing Sing marble"—that is, gray limestone quarried by prisoners a few towns up the Hudson River—served a series of owners, the first of which was William Paulding (1770–1854), a former mayor of New York City. Designed in 1838 and completed in 1842, the home is the handiwork of architect Alexander Jackson Davis, who also designed much of the home's Gothic furniture to match. While Paulding originally named his home "The Knoll," critics preferred to call it "Paulding's Folly"—the style was considered unusual, and even off-putting, for the postcolonial era. Local merchant Philip Hone wrote of the estate: "In the course of our drive, we went to see Mr. William Paulding's magnificent house, yet unfinished, on the bank below Tarrytown. It is an immense edifice of white or gray marble, resembling a baronial castle, or rather a Gothic monastery, with towers, turrets, and trellises; minarets, mosaics, and mouse-holes; archways, armories, and air-holes; peaked windows and pinnacled roofs, and many other fantastics too tedious to enumerate, the whole constituting an edifice of gigantic size, with no room in it; great cost and little comfort, which, if I mistake not, will one of these days be designated as 'Paulding's Folly.'"

Tip

A new riverfront trail between Sunnyside and Lyndhurst is in the works.

From its carved wooden coat rack sporting two hunting hounds and a wolf with a duck in his mouth to a Gothic dining room, stained-glass windows, a celestial bedroom ceiling, a secret bathroom, and a mini-museum picture gallery, the mansion is certainly a stark contrast to modest Sunnyside. During Paulding's residence, however, there was significant carriage and foot traffic between the two homes: The Paulding and Irving families were close friends until an engagement between Paulding's son, Phillip Paulding Rhinelander, and Irving's niece, Julia, was broken, after which the friendship cooled.

In 1961 Lyndhurst was given over to the National Trust for Historic Preservation by the relatives of railroad magnate and Wall Street tycoon Jay Gould. As the third major owner, Gould had used the house for 12 years as a summer home and country retreat.

GETTING AROUND

Taxis should be waiting at the station in Tarrytown; if not, call **Knapp McCarthy Taxi** (✆ **914/631-TAXI**). Give 10 to 15 minutes' advance notice for cabs to show up at the properties for pickup. Most rides cost $4 to $8. It's common for Tarrytown taxi drivers at the station to group passengers together, even if they are traveling to different destinations.

WHAT TO DO NEARBY

Also in the area (and in this book) are **Kykuit—The Rockefeller Estate, Philipsburg Manor, The Union Church at Pocantico Hills,** and **Stone Barns Center for Food & Agriculture**—a working farm and educational center with a fresh-from-the-fields, Zagat-rated restaurant (see chapter 5).

WHERE TO STAY

Castle on the Hudson   After visiting Lyndhurst, nothing less than a night spent wining, dining, and drifting off to sleep in a castle will do—and Tarrytown happens to have its very own. Service is top-notch, the restaurant trumps many Manhattan big names, and relaxation comes easy when you're safe inside these thick stone walls. (For more on the hotel, see chapter 4, "Romantic Weekends.") 400 Benedict Ave. ✆ **914/ 631-1980.** www.castleonthehudson.com. Doubles start at $320 per night.

Events: Legend Weekend Halloween Activities

A reading from Washington Irving's spooky *The Devil and Tom Walker,* guided woodland walks, and 19th-century magic shows, puppet shows, and ghost stories for kids are offered at Sunnyside during Halloween weekend. A Victorian Halloween Party is held at Lyndhurst the same weekend.

Events: Independence Day 1856 at Sunnyside

Sunnyside celebrates July 4th in true 19th-century style with rousing speeches, period music, and traditional country dancing. Play "Town Ball" (19th-c. baseball) against the costumed guides, take a house tour, or learn to make ice cream the old-fashioned way. Pack a picnic or get a snack from on-site vendors.

Tarrytown House Estate and Conference Center   Just a couple miles from Lyndhurst and Sunnyside, this hotel has loads of amenities: indoor and outdoor swimming pools, tennis and volleyball courts, a fitness center, billiards, and the Sleepy Hollow Pub for bowling and beer. The hotel offers a 1-night package that includes admission to these and other historic landmarks nearby. 49 E. Sunnyside Lane. ✆ **800/553-8118.** www.tarrytownhouseestate.com. Doubles start at $199 per night.

WHERE TO EAT

Winding stone steps lead up to a small picnic area that's shaded under a grove of pine trees at Sunnyside. But the only dining option on these two properties is the restored **Carriage House Cafe** at Lyndhurst. Open May through October, the cafe offers indoor and outdoor seating options, but you're also welcome to order a picnic lunch and take it out onto the grounds. Fare includes soups, salads, sandwiches, desserts, and even wine. (Open May–Oct Wed–Sun 11am–3pm in season.)

WHERE TO SHOP

Each of these historic homes has its own museum shop with gifts, jewelry, artwork, reproductions, and books on the Hudson Valley. Sunnyside also devotes a large section of its shop to the literary works of Washington Irving and books on Sleepy Hollow folklore.

Lenox, MA

Lenox, MA 01240
✆ **413/637-3646** • www.lenox.org

Getting there: Bonanza Bus Lines or Peter Pan Bus Lines from Port Authority to Lenox. Call the resort for a pickup when you arrive—it's just a few minutes down the road.
Subways: A, C, E to 42nd St./Port Authority or N, Q, R, S, W, 1, 2, 3, 7 to 42nd St./Times Sq.
Approximate travel time: $3\frac{1}{2}$–4 hr.
Schedule: Each company offers several buses each day. Call or check the websites for times.

Season: Year-round.

Cost: Bus fares are $77 round-trip on Peter Pan, $69 round-trip on Bonanza. The experiences are indistinguishable, so choose based on the schedule that works best for you.

In the Gilded Age of turn-of-the-20th-century America—when the nation's industrialization brought near incomprehensible wealth to an elite society—anyone who was anyone summered in the Berkshires. The fetching hill country of eastern Massachusetts drew a fashionable resort crowd from across the region—wealthy landowners who built some 75 extravagant "cottages" where they could vacation in the warmer months. Ventfort Hall, now a museum, was one of these cottages. Others scattered around this picturesque town have since been restored as inns, restaurants, offices, even private homes. Edith Wharton's estate is open for tours, as are her Italian-influenced gardens, still tended as they were when she lived there.

The Gilded Age moneyed class—the Vanderbilts, Astors, Morgans, Westinghouses, and Andrew Carnegie—all looked to Lenox as a favorite summer retreat. They were not alone: Writers like Wharton, Mark Twain, Herman Melville, Daniel Webster, Henry James, and Nathaniel Hawthorne were also drawn to the Berkshire hills. These days, the region's fresh air, mountain views, spas, culture, and great restaurants continue to draw waves of admirers each year spring through fall. In Lenox they also come for the palpable 19th-century ambience and the town's wealth of historic sights and attractions.

GETTING AROUND

The bus drops passengers off in town right outside the chamber of commerce (5 Walker St.), where you can pick up free maps and brochures of the area. It's within easy walking distance of downtown and many inns. The bus picks up passengers for the return to New York right across the street.

If you like to walk, you won't need anything but determination to power you around Lenox. Use the maps and brochures you picked up at the chamber of commerce to help you navigate your way around town. Some of the attractions outside the downtown village area are slightly spread out, but it's nothing a New Yorker can't handle. Bike rentals are available at **Mean Wheels Bike Shop** (57A Housatonic St.; ✆ 413/637-0644).

WHAT TO DO

The Mount: Edith Wharton's Estate and Formal Gardens Whether you cab it or take the easy half-hour walk from town, a visit to the Mount is worth the trip. The guided mansion tour offers a

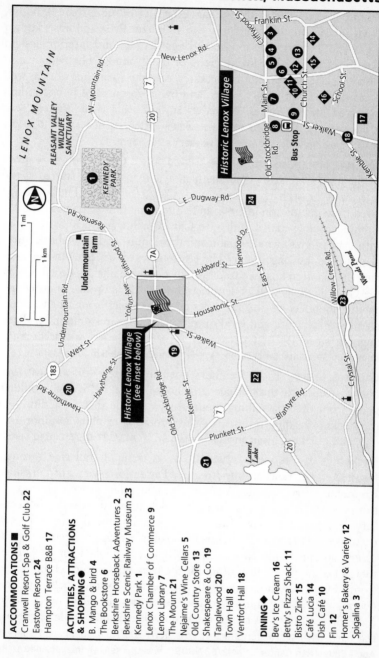

Lenox, Massachusetts

Historic Lenox Village

ACCOMMODATIONS ■
Cranwell Resort Spa & Golf Club **22**
Eastover Resort **24**
Hampton Terrace B&B **17**

ACTIVITIES, ATTRACTIONS & SHOPPING ●
B. Mango & bird **4**
The Bookstore **6**
Berkshire Horseback Adventures **2**
Berkshire Scenic Railway Museum **23**
Kennedy Park **1**
Lenox Chamber of Commerce **9**
Lenox Library **7**
The Mount **21**
Nejaime's Wine Cellars **5**
Old Country Store **13**
Shakespeare & Co. **19**
Tanglewood **20**
Town Hall **8**
Ventfort Hall **18**

DINING ◆
Bev's Ice Cream **16**
Betty's Pizza Shack **11**
Bistro Zinc **15**
Café Lucia **14**
Dish Café **10**
Fin **12**
Homer's Bakery & Variety **12**
Spigalina **3**

glimpse into the life of this celebrated writer of more than 40 books. Wharton was the first woman to win a Pulitzer Prize and was a known talent and authority in architecture, gardening, and interior design. The Terrace Café has lovely views of the grounds. The Mount also hosts special events, including lectures, readings (from her work as well as from others), a poetry series, and live recordings of public radio's "Selected Shorts" series. 2 Plunkett St. (just south of the Routes 7 and 20 intersection). ⊘ 413/637-1899. www.edithwharton.org. Admission $16 adults, free for children under 12. May–Oct weekends 9am–5pm.

Ventfort Hall: Museum of the Gilded Age Guided tours are given on the hour of this 1853 Elizabethan-style mansion that starred as the exterior of the orphanage in the movie *Cider House Rules.* The house was saved from demolition in 1996, and visitors can now step inside and see a dining room paneled with rare Cuban mahogany, a billiards room with stained-glass windows and spiral columns, and an alabaster fireplace in the drawing room. (The last tour leaves at 2pm.) In the summer, the mansion hosts a theater production with Shakespeare & Co. in the Great Hall, as well as demonstrations such as bronze pouring and an afternoon lecture-and-tea series covering topics from art and architecture to literature and local history. The house restoration has been ongoing since 1997. 104 Walker St. ⊘ 413/637-3206. www.gildedage.org. Admission $9 adults; $4 children. Mon–Fri 11am–2pm; Sat–Sun 10am–3pm.

Lenox Library If the weather's not cooperating—or you just love books—stop into this former courthouse, circa 1815. You wouldn't guess from the unassuming, Federal-style facade that, in addition to the stacks, a reading room, art gallery, rotating exhibits, outdoor garden, and gift shop await inside. 18 Main St. ⊘ 413/637-0197. Closed Sun.

Berkshire Horseback Adventures A tranquil trail ride through forested and somewhat hilly Kennedy Park affords views of Berkshire County at every clearing. A knowledgeable guide answers your questions about the region and the park, which at the turn of the 20th century was home to the grand, 400-room Aspinwall Hotel. It was destroyed by fire in 1931, but its foundation can still be seen in several places, Because only two to four people are booked for each ride, there's no stopping and waiting for the back horses to catch up to the front. One-hour rides are $50 per person; 2-hour, half-day, and overnight trips are tailored to your level of skill. Head north down Main Street/Route 7A out of the main village about a mile to the big red barn with white fencing on your left. 293 Main St., at the Aspinwall Adult Equestrian Center. ⊘ 413/637-9090. www.berkshirehorseback.net. Daily mid-May through Oct.

Events: Autumn Tub Parade and Colonial Tea at Ventfort Hall

The English tradition of parading opulently decorated horse-drawn carriages through the streets of town harkens back to the Berkshires golden age. Back then, the wealthy—before they left their "summer cottages" for the season—would pluck the finest blooms from their gardens, decorate their horse and "tub" (carriage), and try to one-up one another in an entertaining display of ridiculous opulence the whole town could enjoy. The tradition continues today at the close of each summer season with a decorated tub parade—one of only two modern-day tub parades still held in the U.S. Early to mid-Sept.

Berkshire Scenic Treks and Canoe Tours   If they're not too busy, the people who run this custom-tours company—Hilary and her son Alex—will pick you up at your inn and take you to the river or the mountain to begin your adventure. Tailor-made hikes are popular, but canoe treks are the bulk of the business. Hilary and Alex share an enthusiasm for the Housatonic River's abundant wildlife, plant life, and life in general. They'll point out tree swallows and muskrats, explain the dusk-time activities of beavers, and wax poetic on the plight of the Native Americans who once called this home. Gliding quietly down the marsh-lined waters, trekkers have glimpsed beavers building dams, moose along the bank, and the occasional black bear. ⌀ **413/442-2789.** Spring-fall by reservation only. 2-hour guided canoe trips start at $30 per person, with 2 people per canoe.

Kennedy Park   Hike the seven rambling trails—15 miles in total—throughout this 108-acre hardwood forest park on the edge of the Village. In the winter it's a popular place for cross-country skiing. Out along Route 7A past downtown; maps available at the Lenox Chamber of Commerce. 5 Walker St. ⌀ **413/637-3646.**

Berkshire Scenic Railway Rides and Museum   Journey in a 1920s coach car from Lenox to Stockbridge on a 2½-hour ride that's narrated by a conductor in full vintage uniform. The museum is housed in a vintage railway coach. Once in Stockbridge, a free trolley takes you to Main Street and the Norman Rockwell Museum. 10 Willow Creek Rd., at the east end of Housatonic St. ⌀ **413/637-2210.** www.berkshirescenicrailroad. org. Tickets $13 round-trip; admission to the museum is free. Trains leave Lenox at 10am and 1:30pm on weekends and major holidays Memorial Day weekend through October.

Shakespeare & Co.   Eight performances a year take to three stages for both indoor and outdoor shows day and night. The season runs June through October. 70 Kemble St. ✆ **413/637-3353. www.shakespeare. org. Tickets free–$75.**

Tanglewood   The summer home of the Boston Symphony Orchestra (and host to numerous top-notch concerts) is what turns this town upside down every July and August. Picnic on the lovely lawns if you can get tickets ($11–$96). ✆ **888/266-1200. www.bso.org.**

WHERE TO STAY

Lenox is home to one of rural New England's largest concentrations of private-mansions-turned-inns. These charming inns are best enjoyed from September to June when the town is quieter, the restaurants less insane, and the prices not so inflated. Unless you're coming specifically for the celebrated Tanglewood concerts (and reserve at least 6 months in advance if you are), you'd do best to avoid the concert-season months of July and August when inns often charge somewhere in the realm of $350 per night, with a 3-day (sometimes even 4-day) minimum stay required for weekends.

   Many of the inns in town are not suitable for children, so if you have your family in tow, check out the casual, all-inclusive **Eastover Resort** (430 East St.; ✆ **800/822-2386;** www.eastover.com). It's not in the town center, but it has both indoor and outdoor pools and plenty of planned activities. Rooms have neither air-conditioning nor TVs.

Cranwell   A member of the Historic Hotels of America, this hilltop Gilded Age mansion is now a rambling full-service resort. Frederic Law Olmstead (of Central Park landscaping fame) designed the 380 lush acres. Dine in the resort's romantic Wyndhurst and Music Room restaurants in the main mansion or tee off on the 18-hole championship golf course; weekend rates start at $79 for 18 holes. Cranwell is also home to an elegant state-of-the-art-spa, with whirlpool, sauna, fireplace lounge, 60-foot indoor pool, natural-light fitness center, and spa boutique. 55 Lee Rd. ✆ **413/637-1364. www.cranwell.com. Doubles start at $175 a night; a 2-night spa package starts at $390 a person.**

Hampton Terrace B&B   Just a couple blocks from the bus stop, this inn couldn't be better located or better appointed for a rejuvenating weekend away. Rooms in the main house are warm and inviting—with beds that make it hard to wake up and rooms that make it hard to leave the house. Out back, a new pool is open to guests, and behind that are the Carriage House rooms and three new amenity-laden suites. Many rooms have fireplaces, claw-foot tubs, and/or whirlpool baths, and all are of generous proportions. A full breakfast is served by candlelight and classical music. The Southern hospitality of the inn's gracious owners even extends to the family dog, who is always happy to greet a new guest. (If this B&B happens to be full, the owners have great relationships with nearby inns and can give you a good referral.) 91 Walker St. ∅ 800/203-0656. www.hamptonterrace.com. Off-season doubles start at $140 per night including breakfast.

WHERE TO EAT

Lenox has no shortage of restaurants. Most are very good, but few offer a bargain—you'll eat well during your stay here, but you'll pay for it. It's a good idea to make reservations for weekend dinner wherever you go.

Betty's Pizza Shack   This surfer-themed hangout is a little slice of Santa Cruz in the Berkshires, with Baja burritos ($6.50–$8.50), "long board" and "short board" pizzas, and beer by the bucket. 26 Housatonic St. ∅ 413/637-8171. Pizzas $9.75-$17.

Bistro Zinc   This is the kind of warm, ambient place—all yellow walls and tile floors—that has people peering in wistfully from the street and wishing they'd eaten here instead. The French bistro menu (with Asian undertones), desserts you'll dream about, a popular crowd scene, and a disarming staff of waiters make this the Lenox spot du jour. 56 Church St. ∅ 413/637-8800. Entrees $18-$28.

Café Lucia   This northern Italian restaurant has been a Lenox favorite for 25 years, where folks come for the *osso buco con risotto* or *bistecca alla fiorentina*. 80 Church St. ∅ 413/637-2640. Entrees $19-$32.

Dish Café   A delicious place to have a lunch or dinner of soup and salad, a burger, the flatbread special sandwich of the day, or the "über-mac" with fontina and prosciutto. 37 Church St. ∅ 413/637-1800. Entrees $16-$20.

Fin   This sushi-and-sake bar serves a traditional Japanese menu of sushi, sashimi, and rolls, with a few tricks thrown in for fun (read: a deep-fried California roll). The calamari salad over baby arugula with a sweet chili vinaigrette is tops. Sake is served hot or cold, the fresh fish is wild (not farmed), and the sushi-house decor is decidedly a departure for the Berkshires. 27 Housatonic St. ∅ 413/637-9171. Entrees $12-$23.

Homer's Bakery & Variety   Thoughts of Homer's old-fashioned cake donuts with a hot cup of coffee gets locals out of the bed in the morning. 27 Housatonic St. ∅ 413/637-3066.

Spigalina   Mediterranean cooking in a large, dining space with an intimate atmosphere. 80 Main St. ∅ 413/637-4455. Entrees $15-$30.

WHERE TO SHOP

B. Mango & bird   Modern housewares, furniture, glassware, bath products, candles—things to make your place look good, smell good, and feel good when you come home. **74 Main St.** ∅ **413/637-2011.**

The Bookstore   Take time to peruse the many stacks of books in this large store, as well as its music section and secondhand-books annex next door. **9 Housatonic St.** ∅ **413/637-3390.**

Nejamie's Wine Cellars   Your stop for wine, cheese, and specialty foods to take to a Tanglewood concert or back to your inn's front porch. Tastings every Saturday from 1 to 5pm. The gourmet picnics-to-go should be ordered in advance; $40 serves two. **60 Main St.** ∅ **800/946-3978.**

Old Country Store   Seasonal items, toys, gadgets, crafts, accessories, garden goods, and kitsch. **67 Church St.** ∅ **413/637-9702.**

Mystic, CT

Mystic, CT 06355

∅ **877/286-9784** · www.mycoast.com or www.mysticmore.com

Getting there: Amtrak train from Penn Station to Mystic, CT
Subways: 1, 2, 3 to 34th St./Penn Station or A, C, E to 34th St./Eighth Ave.
Approximate travel time: 2½-3 hr.
Schedule: Trains leave Penn Station several times a day and return from Mystic on a similar schedule.
Cost: $78-$102 round-trip.

First settled in 1684, this 19th-century shipbuilding town on the banks of the Mystic River was built by the hands of those in the maritime industries: shipbuilders, captains, sailmakers, merchants, carpenters. Venture along the residential side streets, where many of the clam-shell-white houses bear a small badge of honor: a plaque bearing the date when the house was built plus the name and occupation of the original master.

Though Mystic is not quite as walkable as some other small towns—the seaport is a 15-minute walk from downtown, the aquarium is a mile and a half out—it's a place that has taken pains to preserve its heritage and integrate that history into the day-to-day life of the town. Mystic is a skilled old storyteller, capable of making you feel the sea's influence everywhere you go. Tall ships dock in the seaport, and a river meanders through town; nautical prints line the walls of art galleries and

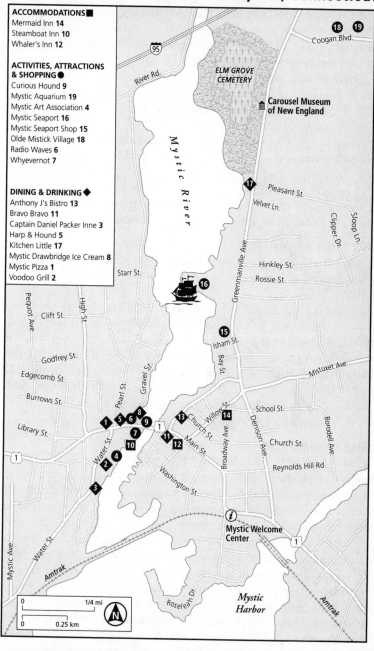

Mystic, Connecticut

ACCOMMODATIONS ■
Mermaid Inn **14**
Steamboat Inn **10**
Whaler's Inn **12**

**ACTIVITIES, ATTRACTIONS
& SHOPPING** ●
Curious Hound **9**
Mystic Aquarium **19**
Mystic Art Association **4**
Mystic Seaport **16**
Mystic Seaport Shop **15**
Olde Mistick Village **18**
Radio Waves **6**
Whyevernot **7**

DINING & DRINKING ◆
Anthony J's Bistro **13**
Bravo Bravo **11**
Captain Daniel Packer Inne **3**
Harp & Hound **5**
Kitchen Little **17**
Mystic Drawbridge Ice Cream **8**
Mystic Pizza **1**
Voodoo Grill **2**

Coogan Blvd.
River Rd.
ELM GROVE CEMETERY
Carousel Museum of New England
Mystic River
Pleasant St.
Velvet Ln.
Clipper Dr.
Sloop Ln.
Greenmanville Ave.
Hinkley St.
Rossie St.
Starr St.
Isham St.
Bay St.
Pequot Ave.
Clift St.
High St.
Godfrey St.
Edgecomb St.
Burrows St.
Pearl St.
Gravel St.
Mistuxet Ave.
Willow St.
School St.
Church St.
Denison Ave.
Church St.
Borodell Ave.
Library St.
Water St.
Main St.
Washington St.
Reynolds Hill Rd.
Broadway Ave.
Mystic Welcome Center
Mystic Ave.
Water St.
Amtrak
Roselea Dr.
Mystic Harbor
Amtrak

0   1/4 mi
0   0.25 km
N

seafood restaurants. The 1922 Bascule Drawbridge leads from the seaport side of town to the several-block downtown area of shops and restaurants. Every hour the old bridge still stands up to take a bow, letting all makes of sailboats pass safely beneath.

Mystic is magical for anyone with a passion for the sea, with all manner of sea creatures at the aquarium, whaling lore and artifacts on display at the seaport, and many opportunities to get out on the ocean in a vessel and see the town from the water.

Not too much happens around downtown Mystic at night, but the **Harp & Hound** traditional Irish pub (4 Pearl St.; ✆ **860/572-7778**) offers a warm atmosphere notches above your typical beer dive (probably helps that one of the owners is originally from Ireland). Order an Irish or Scotch malt or one of the ales on tap, and if you're there on the right night, enjoy a live session of Irish music.

GETTING AROUND

Amtrak is set just off the downtown and close to most accommodations. From the train station to Whaler's Inn, for example, it's a 5-block walk.

Mystic is fairly walkable in nice weather. That said, the downtown shops are just over half a mile from the seaport and about 1½ miles from the aquarium and Olde Mystick Village—all walkable if you have the time and inclination. In the summer you can also rent bikes from **Mystic River Bike & Moped Rental** (15 Holmes St.; ✆ **860/572-0123**). If you need a taxi, call **Yellow Cab** at ✆ **860/536-8888.** And if you want to cruise the countryside, an **Enterprise Rent-a-Car** is in town (✆ **800/536-6829;** www.enterprise.com).

WHAT TO DO

Mystic Seaport: The Museum of America and the Sea In the harbor are historic ships restored to their old-time greatness and other, newer ships that have been reconstructed with old-world techniques from exacting historic models/blueprints. The sounds of tall ships being restored by hand ring out in the old shipyards. Nearby, a re-created 19th-century coastal community is filled with busy "townspeople" minding the local businesses that would have kept the seafaring village afloat. Also here is the country's leading maritime museum. Few places have been as exacting at preserving a moment in time as the Mystic Seaport, where you can watch a ship smith forge iron implements, marvel at the mammoth scale model of the town and its river life, circa 1870, walk through the skeleton of an old schooner, get an up-close look at sailor's scrimshaw, and enter an almost ghostly gallery of restored wooden figureheads from ships that roamed the world. But the pride and joy of this educational center is the world's oldest wooden whaling ship, the *Charles W. Morgan*. Visitors are welcome to explore its depths and an adjacent exhibit on the hard life of a whaler.

I know that people have come to town and been dissuaded by the $17 admission fee. But no one should make a trip to Mystic without seeing the seaport. Mystic is the seaport and the seaport is Mystic—there is no better way to experience the town from a historical perspective. **75 Greenmanville Ave.** ✆ **860/572-5317. www.mysticseaport.org.**

Boating on the Mystic River   There are plenty of ways to take a boat ride in season here, depending on the type of trip you have in mind and the desired level of historical authenticity. At the seaport, take a 30- or 90-minute cruise downriver on the 1908 steamboat *Sabino* (the oldest coal-fired wooden steamboat still running) or a half-hour cruise on the catboat *Breakneck Marshall* with a skipper pointing out landmarks along the shore. A diesel-powered Herreshoff called *Resolute* also takes passengers out for a spin. (Rides are $4–$12/person.) You can even rent a **sailboat** or **rowboat** and take your own self-guided tour ($10–$20 per hour).

Three thousand square feet of sails grace the *Mystic Whaler*—and you may even get a chance to raise and lower them. The 83-foot windjammer offers day sails, lobster-dinner sails, and 2- to 5-day sails from May through August. On each sail, passengers can participate as honorary crew by taking a turn behind the wheel or learning a little

---

Events: Mystic Seaport

Mystic Seaport has a busy year-round schedule of nautical-themed events. Musicians rock the docks at Mystic Seaport in mid-June at the **Annual Sea Music Festival.** Restored powerboats and sailboats of the great nautical eras converge on Mystic for the **Antique and Classic Boat Rendezvous** in mid- to late June. The **Melville Marathon,** a 24-hour marathon *Moby-Dick* reading, is held on board the world's last wooden whaling ship at the end of July/beginning of August. Head to the open-air sheds on the riverbank for **Lobsterfest** on Memorial Day weekend. Warm up with a bowl of "chowda" in the cool sea air at **Chowderfest** on Columbus Day weekend. Enjoy an evening of spooky tales and ghoulish fun during **Nautical Nightmares: Maritime Ghost Stories at Mystic Seaport** in mid- to late October. During **Lantern Light Tours,** from early to mid-December, the town hosts horse-drawn sleigh rides, St. Nick, and evening performances evocative of Christmas Eve 1876.

coastal navigational skills. Day sails (5 hr. with lunch) and lobster dinners (3 hr.) are $80 per person. ✆ **860/536-4218**. www.mysticwhaler. com.

A replica of a 19th-century coastal trading schooner, *ARGIA* departs May through October for half-day sails, sunset cruises, and 40-minute tours of the harbor. ✆ **860/536-0416**. www.voyagermystic.com. Tickets $25-$38 per person.

Mystic Aquarium   Pet a baby gator, pose with tropical birds, and put your hand in a touch tank to pet the backs of steel-gray rays as they float by. Touch pools are a big thing here—and each is full of critters found off the Connecticut coast. Ever seen a blue lobster? One in every two to three million is born that way, and you can see one here up close. Sea-lion shows and penguin and beluga whale feedings provide some of the best entertainment the aquarium has to offer. Beyond sea creatures, the Return to the Titanic scale model, Hidden Amazon rainforest exhibit, and 3D-XD motion-ride theater appeal to kids. Validate your ticket and you can use it for 3 days.

For a memorable hands-on experience, empty your piggy bank and reserve a spot in Mystic Aquarium's **Penguin Contact** ($62 per person) or **Beluga Whale Contact** ($165 per person) programs. In less than an hour, you'll meet the animal's trainers and even have the uncommon opportunity to touch these creatures with your own hands. 55 Coogan Blvd. ✆ **860/572-5955**. www.mysticaquarium.org. Admission $18 adults, $13 children 3-17.

Mystic Art Association   View ongoing exhibits and juried shows of regional artists' work in a sprawling riverfront gallery. Events include fine-art sales, workshops, lectures, and classes. 9 Water St. ✆ **860/536-7601**. www.mystic-art.org.

Sailing Adventure

Lose yourself out at sea for a day, 2 days, or a long weekend aboard Mystic Seaport's 1932 classic schooner, *Brilliant*. You're both passenger and crew as you learn to sail, help with cooking and cleaning, and take an adventure that may include stops at Shelter Island, Block Island, and Newport. On board, your captain and mate head a crew of about a dozen people much like yourself. Teamwork, leadership, and living at sea are the theme—the water, the wind, the sun, and the stars are your guide. Sails are $170 to $720 per person. For more information, call ✆ **860/572-5323** or go to **www.mysticseaport.org/brilliant**.

WHERE TO STAY

Mermaid Inn of Mystic This Victorian B&B is just a short walk from downtown. A full breakfast is served daily. 2 Broadway Ave. ☎ 860/536-6223. www.mermaidinnofmystic.com. Doubles $150–$225 per night.

Steamboat Inn Ten guest rooms and suites with river views (and sometimes, noise from the steady river traffic). Some rooms have a fireplace, and all have DVD players and whirlpool tubs. 73 Steamboat Wharf. ☎ 860/536-8300. www.steamboatinnmystic.com. Weekend doubles $190–$300 per night.

The Whaler's Inn Check into this hotel for the floral-print charms of an inn, the privacy of a hotel, and modern comforts like cable TV, free Internet access, a continental breakfast, complimentary magazines, and an ideal downtown location. Rooms in the main building have a more traditional hotel look, while those in the 1865 house next door have four-poster beds and wingback chairs. 20 E. Main St. ☎ 860/536-1506. www.whalersinnmystic.com. Weekend doubles $115–$249 per night with a 2-night minimum most weekends and holidays.

WHERE TO EAT

Anthony J's Bistro Don't leave town without eating here at least once . . . a day. It's that good. The name is nondescript, but the restaurant is anything but. Fabulous service, outstanding specials, and a homey atmosphere with booths built for two. The slant is Italian, but the chef always has some surprises up his sleeve. 6 Holmes St. ☎ 860/536-0448. www.anthonyjsbistro.com. Entrees $16–$30.

Bravo Bravo Serving Italian classics and then some, this contemporary restaurant sits inside the Whaler's Inn but stands tall on its own merits. 20 E. Main St. ☎ 860/536-3228. www.whalersinnmystic.com/bravo. Entrees $17–$25.

The Captain Daniel Packer Inne It's a bit of a walk from downtown, but inside this historic inn you can dine in the downstairs pub or the more formal dining rooms upstairs with burnished wide-plank floors and wood-burning fireplaces. 32 Water St. ☎ 860/536-3555. www.danielpacker.com. Entrees $20–$29.

Kitchen Little With nearly more letters in its name than seats in the restaurant, this pancake-and-omelet house is a favorite spot among locals for breakfast—though few brave the weekend crowds of tourists. It's nothing spectacular, but every small town has their beloved place for bacon and eggs. Besides, it's fun to marvel at how such a large menu comes out of what is possibly the smallest commercial kitchen in several states. 135 Greenmanville Ave. ☎ 860/536-2122. Main dishes $3.45–$13.

Mystic Drawbridge Ice Cream   Homemade ice cream has been served to Mystic's pedestrian crowds in this downtown store since the 1800s. Today's homemade flavors include Mystic Mud, Vermont Maple Nut, Chocolate Chambord, and Ginger Spice. 2 W. Main St. ∅ **860/572-7978.**

Mystic Pizza   Yes, it's *the* original Mystic Pizza, with the "Slice of Heaven" T-shirts just like Julia Roberts wore in the movie, and plenty of booths. The Hollywood-movie inspired surge of business caused the family to expand the place to twice the size of its original 1973 incarnation. 56 W. Main St. ∅ **860/536-3700.** www.mysticpizza.com. Large pizzas $10-$16.

Voodoo Grill   Creole, Cajun, Southwestern, and barbecue come together on the spicy menu in a place that proclaims, "Mama never cooked like this!" And unless your mama made deep-fried alligator bites, crawfish and corn chowder, catfish fritters, or jambalaya sandwiches, they're right. Open-air patio, Saturday-night karaoke, and lots of hot sauce. 12 Water St. ∅ **860/572-4422.** www.thevoodoogrill.com. Entrees $6.95-$17.

WHERE TO SHOP

Curious Hound   Freshly baked and gourmet goodies for your furry friends, plus boutique accessories for pets—and their owners—who demand the best. 5 W. Main St. ∅ **860/536-1468.** www.curioushound.com.

Mystic Seaport Shop   Easy to enter whether you're visiting the seaport or not, this enormous two-story store is a one-stop nautical department store. Ships sail across glazed pottery, lobsters crawl across neckties, and many children's toys, puzzles, and games recall past times of eras gone by. The second floor has a collector's maritime art gallery with original artwork, prints, and model ships for sale. 75 Greenmanville Ave. ∅ **860/572-5315.**

Olde Mystick Village   The colonial architecture, country landscaping, gazebo, and duck pond are meant to resemble a New England village green circa 1720. But of the 60 stores specializing in art, antiques, clothing, crafts, gifts, home furnishings, New England goods, and jewelry, some feel more authentic and crafts-oriented than others. Depending on your taste, it's either cute and quaint or an old-fashioned theme mall. Coogan Blvd. ∅ **860/536-4941.** www.oldmysticvillage.com.

Radio Waves   Antique radios from the 1930s to 1950s, jazz CDs, plus knickknacks for the home that aren't music-related at all. 4 W. Main St. ∅ **860/572-4435.**

Whyevernot   Artistic housewares, clothing, jewelry, linens, paper goods. 17 W. Main St. ∅ **860/536-6209.**

Afternoon Tea at the Caramoor House Museum

149 Girdle Ridge Rd., Katonah, NY 18229
☎ **914/232-5035**, ext. 221 • www.caramoor.org

Getting there: Metro-North Harlem line train from Grand Central to Katonah, NY, then a 5-min. cab ride from the station to Caramoor.
Subways: 4, 5, 6, 7, S to Grand Central/42nd St.
Approximate travel time: 1 hr., 5 min.
Schedule: Trains leave Grand Central about once an hour. They leave Katonah on a similar schedule.
Transit cost: $18 round-trip, plus about $8 each way for the cab.
Alternate transit: If you're making the trip for a Sat or Sun musical performance during the summer, consider taking the **Caramoor Caravan.** The coach leaves from several points in Manhattan, arriving at Caramoor 2 hr. before the concert–leaving you just enough time to picnic on the grounds. Caravan is $21 per person round-trip (www.caramoor.org).
Hours: Teas are hosted May through mid-Oct Thurs-Fri 1:30-4pm. General house tours are Wed-Sun 1-4pm during the same season.
Tea and museum costs: Afternoon tea and house tour costs $29 per person. House tours alone are $9.

You can enjoy an afternoon tea at any number of classic old venues in the city—even if the Plaza is no longer one of them. But for something even more decadent, set a spring day aside to take your tea at the utterly fascinating Caramoor House Museum. This estate, best known for its musical performances, offers docent-led tours of a remarkable mansion followed by a formal tea service in the rustic Summer Dining Room overlooking the Spanish Courtyard. What a very civilized way to while away an afternoon!

Built between 1929 and 1939, this Mediterranean villa–style summer palazzo features an inner courtyard, eclectic furnishings, and complete rooms transported from across the continents. It was built by Walter Rosen and Lucie Bigelow Rosen, Caramoor's founders. The name may not ring a bell, but the Vanderbilts and the Rockefellers weren't the only society-era family who had money and knew how to spend it. An ambitious young man who graduated from Harvard in 3 years, Walter Rosen formed his own law firm and was later involved in investment banking. Lucie Bigelow Dodge had the good fortune to be born into a prominent New York family; her grandfather, John Bigelow, was minister to France under Abraham Lincoln and a founder of the New York Public Library. This house was their dream home—a place to hold the treasures from their travels, host friends they met along the way, and

Events: Music at Caramoor

Musical performances are Caramoor's main attraction, with an international summer music festival that lines up chamber music and string quartets as well as modern jazz, opera, and performances by cabaret singer-songwriters. Venues include the grand Venetian Theater and under the stars in the Spanish Courtyard. The **Caramoor Indoors** concerts in spring and fall are best appreciated when held in the house museum's intimate and lavish Music Room. One way to enjoy the music of Caramoor along with a tour of the house is the **Performer's Showcase,** Wednesday from 11am to 3pm. The package combines a music recital, house tour, BYO picnic lunch, and self-guided tour of the formal gardens ($16). Caramoor loves to throw in a musical surprise now and then as well. Last fall they hosted an old-time square dance under a tent, complete with a Southern string band, bales of hay, and a pulled-pork dinner with all the trimmings. Check the website's online calendar for listings and tickets.

raise their two children, Walter and Ann. (You have to wonder what the punishment was for running in the house or dropping a Ming vase, for example. Everything in sight is worth an absolute fortune.)

The home's yellow stucco exterior and terra-cotta roof tiles are unusual for Westchester, but it's what's inside that really stands out. More than 3 centuries of global art, antiques, and furnishings blend seamlessly in rooms where Renaissance, medieval, and Asian art commingle handsomely. Silk wallpaper from the Far East, a bed once owned by a pope, a 14-century tapestry from Florence, and a relief by Donatello are just a few of the treasures. Entire rooms, walls and all, were transferred from overseas to be faithfully reconstructed in the house.

The Rosens also had an affinity for the avant-garde: Guests dined on 14 red lacquer chairs with jade-green cushions, and in lieu of wallpaper, patterns are painted right onto the walls. Lucie's pure jade, eight-paneled screen from 19th-century China is believed to be one of only two in the world.

Today, 20 of the family's rooms are open to the public. And because of the way the house was laid out, you'll finish your tour right back where you started, in the Music Room—which the staff likes to call the "jewel of the house" and "the heart of Caramoor." The Rosens were known for the concerts they hosted in this room—Lucie herself was an accomplished musician who performed at Carnegie Hall, and Walter played piano. They invited musicians, celebrities, and international dignitaries to dine and enjoy chamber music—a tradition that continues today at the Caramoor Center for Music and the Arts, of which the house museum is a part. (The home was bequeathed as such following son Walter's death in 1968.)

After your tour, it's time for an alfresco tea in an alcove off the Spanish Courtyard. The china laid out on your table is the very same used by Walter and Lucie to entertain at their own tea parties. A proper affair, your choice of tea arrives with the classic tri-tiered tower of tidbits: English scones served with clotted cream and preserves, a selection of tea sandwiches, and tiny, work-of-art desserts—all garnished with fresh flowers. (If you loved the egg salad, fret not—your server will come around with a seconds tray.) You'll likely share your afternoon tea with ladies of a certain age from neighboring Hudson River towns. They remark on the weather as they tip the dainty china cups, *always* with the pinky extended.

Tickets for afternoon tea can be purchased online, and reservations do need to be made in advance. For reservations less than a week prior to a tea, call ✆ **914/232-5035,** ext. 221, or e-mail museum@caramoor.org.

GETTING AROUND

If you're only interested in a quick afternoon tea, catch the 11:48am train from Grand Central; it arrives in Katonah at 12:51pm. To get to Caramoor, take one of the cabs waiting at the station; if not, call **Katonah Taxi** (✆ **914/232-5772**) or **Sam's Taxi** at (✆ **914/666-6002**). Even after you catch the cab, you'll have a little time to browse the gift shop or walk the grounds. After tea, call a cab to make the 4:26pm train from Katonah back to NYC. (Schedules and times change often; check times when you plan your trip.)

West Point

United States Military Academy, West Point, NY 10996
✆ **845/938-2638** • www.usma.edu

Getting there: Shortline bus package from Port Authority to West Point.
Subways: A, C, E to 42nd St./Port Authority or N, Q, R, S, W, 1, 2, 3, 7 to 42nd St./Times Sq.
Approximate travel time: 2 hr.
Schedule: Buses leave Port Authority at 8:30, 8:45, and 11:15am. They leave West Point at 3:07pm daily, with a 2nd bus on Sat, Sun, and holidays leaving at 5:07pm. Times change, so check the schedule to be sure.
Season: Year-round.
Hours: West Point is open to the public 9am–4:45pm daily. Closed for Christmas, Thanksgiving, and New Year's.

Cost: $40 round-trip includes bus transportation, sightseeing tour, complimentary movie at the visitor center, and a 10% discount coupon for lunch at area restaurants.

Alternate Transit: If you want to visit West Point on your own instead of with Shortline's package, take a **Metro-North Hudson line train** from Grand Central to Croton-Harmon, about an hour from the city ($15 round-trip off-peak). From there, West Point is 15 miles by cab.

George Washington considered West Point one of the most important points in North America. From its position on the high ground above a narrow curve of the Hudson River, fortifications could control all north/south traffic on the Hudson River. Without it, the fledgling Continental Army could not have mounted a sustained defense of the Colonies in the face of British might.

Almost 220 years later, West Point maintains its critical importance to America, albeit in different ways. It is a symbol of our revolutionary roots, a place to learn about the history of the American military, and a place to honor those who fought and continue to fight for our country. Perhaps most important, it is the place where many of the future leaders of our armed forces are trained to serve and lead.

Today nearly three million people visit West Point each year, making it one of the top-three tourist attractions in New York State. Anyone interested in military history, arms and armor, or the history of the state of New York should plan a visit. And anyone interested in the sheer physical beauty of a historic school perched on the cliffs of the Hudson River should make a visit as well. Fortunately, Shortline Bus Lines offers a day trip that makes a visit to the Point easy and affordable.

When you arrive at the West Point visitor center, head inside to sign up for a guided tour (included in the cost of the day trip). While you're waiting, check out the life-size barracks room to get a peek into the life of a West Point cadet. Videos detailing cadet life and West Point history are shown here every 30 minutes.

The guided tour is inspiring; see the gorgeous Gothic **Cadet Chapel** (one of five chapels on campus) and **West Point Cemetery,** the final resting place of such legends as Generals George Custer and Winfield Scott. Take in the breathtaking view from **Trophy Point,** and visit the home of Army Football, **Michie Stadium.** (*Note:* Tours are not offered on days when Army football has a home game.) Along the way, view memorials to the living and dead from every American armed conflict and monuments to legendary military figures, and learn about West Point's role in American history, at home and abroad—from Benedict

---

Events: Army Football Games

The season runs from the beginning of September through the beginning of December, culminating with the season finale, the Army-Navy game. About a half-dozen games each year are home games. Tickets are $27 to $31, except for the Army-Navy game, which is $50 to $85 and sells out far in advance. Tickets are available at www.goarmysports.com. No tours, however, are offered on game days.

Arnold's betrayal during the Revolutionary War to the education of the Army's military leaders of the future.

After the tour and a quick lunch, pay a visit the **United States Military Museum,** the country's oldest and largest museum devoted to the military. Since 1854, it has been the repository for some of the rarest and most fascinating military artifacts from America's storied military past. Currently, the museum boasts 135 exhibits covering every American armed conflict, plus one of the finest collections of small arms in the world.

TRANSIT FACTS

You many want to spend half your day at the nearby Woodbury Common Outlets; if so, choose any of the New York City–bound Shortline buses that leave frequently from the outlets to return to Port Authority Bus Terminal (see Woodbury Common below).

GETTING AROUND

A guided tour of West Point is included in the price of your Shortline bus ticket package. Take advantage of the tour, and of your guide's wealth of information. West Point is enormous—local knowledge will help you orient yourself and fill in some of the fascinating history of the place.

If you decide to take the Metro-North train to West Point instead of the Shortline bus package, you will need to take a cab from the station to West Point. Taxis meet most trains at the station, or try **J & S Taxi** (✆ **914/271-3333**) or **Larry's Taxi** (✆ **914/271-3777**).

WHAT TO DO NEARBY

Woodbury Common   If you feel like combining a day learning about military history with shopping, you're in luck; the Shortline bus also offers a combo trip that stops at both West Point and the Woodbury Common Outlets. Arrive at West Point at 10:30am, then depart promptly at 1pm for premium shopping at Woodbury Common's 220 stores featuring Nike, Diesel, Polo, Gucci, and many more. Package price is $41. Contact Shortline for more information and to check times, as they are subject to change. 498 Red Apple Court, Central Valley, NY 10917. ℘ 845/928-4000. www.premiumoutlets.com/woodburycommon.

WHERE TO STAY

For the West Point gung-ho, Shortline offers an overnight package that includes a stay at the historic **Thayer Hotel** (674 Thayer Rd.; ℘ 800/247-5047; www.thethayerhotel.com), the elegant, recently renovated "Pride of the Hudson Highlands" that overlooks the Hudson River and sits at the south entrance of West Point. The Thayer also boasts a decadent Sunday brunch that is famous throughout the region. Package price is $125/person double occupancy. The packages can be booked directly through Shortline bus lines; for information call ℘ **201/529-3666** or go to www.shortlinebus.com.

Tip

Be realistic about the amount of time you want to budget for visiting West Point. If you plan on staying for lunch and spending a significant amount of time in the United States Military Museum, a half-day may not be enough time, and you may want to consider overnighting here.

WHERE TO EAT

Park Restaurant Since it opened in 1935, the Park Restaurant has been providing comfort food in a casual setting just 3 blocks from West Point. When you step through the double doors and spot the comfy leather booths or the serious bar with liquor bottles lined up like soldiers, the tone is set. In the summer, sip a delicious frozen cocktail like the Dirty Banana or a nonalcoholic mixed-fruit smoothie while snacking from a colossal menu featuring scores of salads, wraps, and sandwiches, in addition to seafood, grilled, and Italian entrees. 451 Main St. ℘ 845/446-8709. All entrees under $10.

Schade's Deli & Restaurant Schade's Restaurant, located across from the West Point visitor center, is another casual but excellent option for lunch at the Point. Service and food are both quite good, and the menu has an excellent selection of pizzas in addition to other Italian and American options. 54 Main St. ℘ 845/446-2626. All entrees under $10.

WHERE TO SHOP

West Point Gift Shop Plenty of stuff for the military aficionado. And, if you have a hankering for some Army athletics paraphernalia, this is the place. Inside the visitor center. ℘ 845/446-3085.

Kykuit–The Rockefeller Estate & Philipsburg Manor

Kykuit: Rte. 9, Sleepy Hollow, NY 10591
✆ **914/631-9491** · www.hudsonvalley.org
Philipsburg Manor: 150 White Plains Rd., Tarrytown, NY 10591
✆ **914/631-3992** · www.hudsonvalley.org

Getting there: Metro-North Hudson line train from Grand Central to Tarrytown, plus a cab from the station.

Subways: 4, 5, 6, 7, S to Grand Central/42nd St.

Approximate travel time: 38 min. for express train, 50 min. for local, plus 10-min. cab ride.

Schedule: Trains leave Grand Central twice an hour on weekends and return from Tarrytown on a similar schedule.

Transit cost: $15 round-trip off-peak, plus $8 cab fare.

Alternate Transit: NY Waterway offers weekend ferry service from West 38th St. at the Hudson River in Manhattan to Tarrytown. Several tour packages are offered that include round-trip ferry transportation, and bus transportation and admission passes to nearby historic landmarks. To tour Kykuit, purchase the **Kykuit Cruise package** ($64), which includes visits to both Kykuit and Philipsburg Manor. Or, purchase the **Sleepy Hollow Cruise package** ($46), which includes a visit to Philipsburg Manor as well as nearby Sunnyside. Both cruises depart at 10:30am and return to the city at 6pm. For information and reservations, call ✆ **800/53-FERRY** or go to **www.nywaterway.com**.

Season: Both houses are open from late Apr through early Nov. Philipsburg Manor has a longer season but is closed Jan, Feb, weekdays in Mar, and every Tues.

Hours: The Manor is open 10am–5pm (last tour at 4pm) in high season with shortened hours in the off season. Kykuit's timed tours are scattered throughout the day from 9am to 4pm.

Admission cost: Kykuit tours $19–$36; Philipsburg Manor admission $10.

Four generations of Rockefellers lived in one of these homes; nearly two dozen 18th-century African slaves lived and worked in the other. A day roaming these two properties will undoubtedly lend two radically different perspectives about how the past influences the present—and what it would have been like to live here, depending on whose home one happened to be born into.

Unless you're in a real hurry, it doesn't make sense to tour one of these and not the other. You can purchase tickets for both right at Philipsburg Manor—which acts as the visitor center for both the manor and Kykuit (pronounced *Ky*-kit). A **free shuttle** makes the 8-minute ride from Philipsburg Manor to Kykuit and back again. The shuttle is timed to arrive at Kykuit right when your tour begins. Along the short drive, an audio narration provides some background about the estate and what you're seeing outside as you enter the grounds. (One fact, for instance, is that John D. Rockefeller installed the golf course here even before he started work on the house or the gardens.)

For the Rockefeller Estate, it is highly recommended that you reserve tickets online in advance and pick them up at the Kykuit ticket desk at Philipsburg Manor. When you do, you'll receive a coupon for discounted admission to Philipsburg Manor—for which you do not need advance tickets and you can purchase them right there. Most people like to tour Kykuit first—it is much larger and more elaborate—and then come back to Philipsburg Manor and have lunch and a tour before heading back to the city. (If you don't buy tickets for Kykuit in advance, know that they may sell out by midday.)

When you pick up your tickets, you will also receive a voucher for free admission to the **Union Church of Pocantico Hills.** This church, just a few miles away, is famous for its dramatic stained-glass windows by Henri Matisse and Marc Chagall. A trip to the church requires an additional cab ride.

KYKUIT–THE ROCKEFELLER ESTATE

While waiting for the shuttle from Philipsburg Manor to Kykuit (Dutch for "high point" or "lookout"), catch the 10-minute ongoing film about the background of the Rockefeller family and their opulent estate. Then it's off to tour the Hudson Valley's most exceptional property, where you'll be guided through the first floor of the main house, formal gardens, an art gallery, and the carriage house; you'll also see an astonishing private collection of 20th-century sculpture. John D. Rockefeller, philanthropist and Standard Oil businessman, built and lived in this 40-room home with its 20 bedrooms and more than 70 pieces of sculpture; three more generations continued to live here, too. While the house is certainly elegant—with original artworks by Rodin, Alexander Calder, and Toulouse-Lautrec—it's also a family home that feels lived in and accessible: a family home that happens to have an enormous window that looks out on the Palisades and takes two people just to open it, a roomful of china from around the world, and the white buttons on the walls used to call the staff of servants. Downstairs in the gallery hangs a series of Picasso tapestries specially commissioned by the family. Your tour ends in the coach house, which displays a century's worth of carriages and cars, from a 1924 Ford Model T to a 1959 Chrysler Ghia limo.

The **House and Inner Garden Tour** ($22) is only one of five ways to tour the estate and is recommended for first-time visitors. The 3-hour **Grand Tour** ($36) adds a visit to the second-floor balcony, while the **Garden and Sculpture Tour** ($22) skips the house and carriage house to highlight the flora and works of art. A **Time-Saver Tour** ($19) cuts to the chase, for those on a tight schedule.

PHILIPSBURG MANOR

Possibly the most unusual of the area's historic homes is this simple stone manor house and grounds where much milling, farming, and trading took place. Through costumed guides, vignettes, and demonstrations, this "living-history museum" relates the experience of its 23 enslaved Africans who tended the farm and mill for a wealthy Anglo-Dutch family in the late 17th/early 18th century. (Tours are dated for 1750.) Much of what you'll see has been reconstructed and refurnished based on research and speculation, but the demonstrations, especially of open-fire cooking and the making of herbal medicines, and those at the reconstructed, water-powered gristmill and millpond, are interesting. You can even buy a muslin bag of stone-ground wheat flour or yellow corn meal ($3 a bag) to take home that were made by the mill's gigantic stone grinder. A slave garden has been re-created to the times, and historic breeds of cows, sheep, and chickens live here along with lamb and geese.

GETTING AROUND

Taxis are generally waiting at the station in Tarrytown. If not, call **Knapp McCarthy Taxi** (✆ 914/631-TAXI); give 10 to 15 minutes' advance notice for cabs to show up at the properties for pickup. Most rides cost $4 to $8. It's common for Tarrytown taxi drivers at the station

---

Events: Philipsburg Manor

Philipsburg Manor has a number of worthwhile annual events. On a Sunday in mid-May, **Pinkster Day Festival at Philipsburg Manor,** an African-American celebration of spring that dates back to the 17th century, means a festive day of music, food, drumming and traditional dance, African folktales, and demonstrations of traditional African instruments. On Labor Day weekend, the **Green Corn Festival** incorporates folk tales, song, and dance into a weekend celebration of Native American culture and traditions. On the last weekend of October, the **Fall Harvest Activities at Philipsburg Manor** features colonial chores and activities for children such as corn shelling, pumpkin carving, and the cooking of pumpkin recipes on an open hearth.

to group passengers together, even if they are traveling to different destinations.

WHAT TO DO NEARBY

Next to Philipsburg Manor, on the opposite side of Route 9, is **Sleepy Hollow Cemetery** (540 N. Broadway), where Andrew Carnegie, Walter Chrysler, Elizabeth Arden, and William Rockefeller have all found a final resting place. For more information, visit www.sleepyhollow cemetery.org or call ✆ **914/631-0081.**

When in Tarrytown, also consider a visit to **Sunnyside** (Washington Irving's home), **Lyndhurst** (a Gothic Revival castle), or **Stone Barns Center for Food & Agriculture**—all recommended in this book. The **Rockefeller Estate Life Tour** ($34)—a new option that isn't offered every day—combines a tour of Kykuit's house and inner gardens with a visit to Stone Barns. Call Kykuit for details.

WHERE TO STAY

See the entry on Sunnyside and Lyndhurst in this chapter for information on where to stay in Tarrytown. Or consider the **NY Waterway ferry cruise package,** which includes visits to Kykuit, Philipsburg Manor, Sunnyside, and Lyndhurst, with a night at the Tarrytown House Estate and breakfast in the morning. Packages starts at $195 per person based on double occupancy. Call ✆ **800/53-FERRY** or go to www.nywaterway.com.

WHERE TO EAT

There is no cafe at Kykuit—nor are you allowed to bring food or beverages along. The informal **Greenhouse Cafe** (9am–4:30pm) at Philipsburg Manor offers a small selection of salads, sandwiches, and baked goods. You can eat in the sunny atrium or at the tables outside—both of which have a view of the manor across the footbridge.

WHERE TO SHOP

Kykuit has no gift shop, but the large one at Philipsburg Manor carries Hudson Valley books, items for the gardener, jewelry, and gifts.

Antiquing Tours

I'S FRIDAY NIGHT AND YOU'RE AT A FRIEND OF A FRIEND'S ULTRA-smooth dinner party. It's a catered affair because, well, they don't like to dirty their 1948 O'Keefe & Merritt stove. The phone rings—a clunky yet commanding ring you recognize from your youth—and you look over to see a mint-green, rotary-dial number straight out of the 1950s. It must weigh 6 lbs. "Where did you *find* that?" three people screech at once. "Oh, we buy all our vintage stuff in this cute little town up the Hudson," beams your hostess.

For savvy New Yorkers like our dinner hosts, it's no secret that outstanding vintage and antiques shopping is just a train or a bus ride away from the city. Some can be found just up the Hudson River—in quaint New York State towns like Hudson and Cold Spring—or down-shore in the equally quaint New Jersey towns of Red Bank and Lambertville. Bargains are lurking if you look hard enough—and the selection can be truly eclectic. And if you can fit your purchases in the bus baggage compartment or on the train, you won't need a car to drag it back home.

Next time you hear someone talking about a set of classic china they found upstate, or dishing about the vintage weather vanes they discovered in a country antiques emporium, you'll know what all the fuss is about. But this time you'll have your own dinner-party success story to match it.

Hudson, NY

Warren St., Hudson, NY 12534
℘ **518/828-3375** · www.columbiacountyny.org

Getting there: Amtrak from Penn Station to Hudson, NY.
Subways: 1, 2, 3 to 34th St./Penn Station or A, C, E to 34th St./Eighth Ave.
Approximate travel time: 2 hr.

Schedule: Trains leave Penn Station nearly every hour on the weekends and return from Hudson on a similar schedule.
Cost: Train fare $74 round-trip.

Plenty of urban antiques hounds have heard of Hudson, New York, and its store-lined streets. But not having a car can prove a hindrance to getting there. Hudson lies off the Metro-North grid, which means that even on a warm, sunny Saturday, the town still feels fairly undiscovered. The cost is higher to get there—you'll need to take Amtrak—but the payoff comes in the uncrowded stores, the laid-back attitude, and an accessible Hudson Valley enclave brimming with good taste.

The funny thing about Hudson is . . . well . . . a couple of things. First, for a town known for its antiques, its storefronts sell nonantique wares in an impressive amount of varieties and styles. So much so that you have to wonder if Hudson should actually be known for shopping in general. Upscale modern housewares, garden items, and thrift-store bric-a-brac all have their niches along Warren Street—the retail thoroughfare—as well as down some of the surrounding blocks. Shopkeepers—many of whom are NYC transplants—have loads of personality and take pains to stock goods that go beyond the same old stuff you see in the city. It's not unusual to see a celebrity on a shopping spree, a family looking at the real-estate listings for their summer home, or a retiree in a flashy vintage sports car just tooling through town on an afternoon drive. The *New York Times* has recently caught wind of Hudson, too, reviewing its stores and restaurants with growing frequency. But the town is never mobbed with shoppers and visitors, making it the best kind of day trip there is.

The other funny—nay, unfortunate—thing about Hudson is that, once you're off the beaten path, you may find some areas are still rough around the edges. That could be the reason that many shoppers make it a day trip, despite the emergence of several cute places to spend the night (see "Where to Stay," below). Like many upstate towns that thrived in another century, Hudson has seen hard times, and economic recovery has been slow in coming. Still, signs of Hudson's gradual gentrification pop up in restaurant menu items (and prices), increasingly sophisticated window displays, and new condos overlooking a waterfront park. It won't be long before the rough edges are smoothed out entirely. That's probably when you'll need to start making reservations for lunch. Sigh. . . .

GETTING AROUND

Amtrak lets you off within walking distance of downtown shopping. Pick up a map and restaurant guide inside the train station before

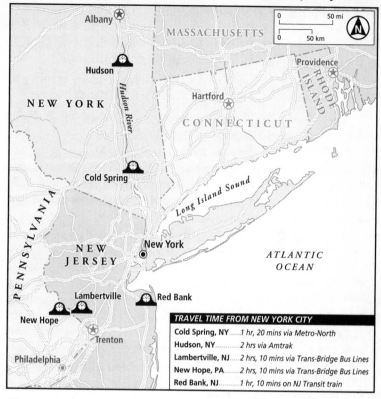

Albany

MASSACHUSETTS

Hudson

Providence

RHODE ISLAND

NEW YORK

Hudson River

Hartford

CONNECTICUT

Cold Spring

Long Island Sound

NEW JERSEY

New York

ATLANTIC OCEAN

PENNSYLVANIA

Lambertville   Red Bank

New Hope

Trenton

Philadelphia

TRAVEL TIME FROM NEW YORK CITY

Cold Spring, NY ......*1 hr, 20 mins via Metro-North*
Hudson, NY ....*2 hrs via Amtrak*
Lambertville, NJ .....*2 hrs, 10 mins via Trans-Bridge Bus Lines*
New Hope, PA ....*2 hrs, 10 mins via Trans-Bridge Bus Lines*
Red Bank, NJ ....*1 hr, 10 mins on NJ Transit train*

turning left out of the station, then making a right on Warren Street and walking a few blocks uphill to the main shopping strip. (You'll hit the lower address numbers first.) Spend the day moving up one side of Warren and down the other.

For a side trip to Olana, you'll need to call a cab. Taxis often wait outside the Amtrak station to meet trains, and it might be best to visit Olana first and reserve the rest of the day for downtown shopping. If you don't see any cabs, **Hudson City Taxi**'s headquarters are caddy-corner across the street (58 S. Front St.; ✆ **518/822-8880**). The ride takes less than 10 minutes and should cost about $12 each way. It adds up when you tack on the price of admission, but the house and the views are uniquely spectacular. Just make sure your taxi is not charged the $5 vehicle fee at the guardhouse to the property, since he or she is only dropping you off, not planning to park.

WHERE TO SHOP FOR ANTIQUES

You can print out a shopping map of the town at **www.hudson antiques.net**. Most of Hudson's 65 antiques shops are open Thursday to Monday from 11am to 5pm, but call ahead to make sure.

Boulay Antiques   Midcentury modern chairs, phonographs, and French Bull melamine tableware. 530 Warren St. ∅ **518/828-6979.**

Fern   Farmhouse-chic decor and housewares with decoupage globes, quirky clocks, vintage-inspired fabrics, and a back garden. 554 Warren St. ∅ **518/828-2886.**

Gottlieb Gallery   A stuffed warthog lives here among dramatic crystal chandeliers, gilt mirrors, bronze statues, French urns, and neoclassical marble busts. 524 Warren St. ∅ **518/822-1761.** www.gottliebgallery hudson.com.

Keystone   A sprawling store with room to showcase the biggest pieces in town, thus making it the most fun to walk through. Lanterns that once hung from vaulted church ceilings, stone urns and angels, and ironwork doors and gates just screaming to be transformed into headboards. 746 Warren St. ∅ **518/ 822-1019.**

Maren Dunn   Three floors of goods to explore when you climb the winding staircase. 422½ Warren St. ∅ **518/828-9996.**

> ### Tip
> For larger purchases, most stores will let you pay, leave your buys behind the counter, and pick them up at the end of the day. For *really* large purchases, inquire about delivery to the city.

Warren Street Antiques   A meandering hodgepodge of affordable retro goods. 322 Warren St. ∅ **518/671-6699.**

WHERE TO SHOP FOR ANYTHING ELSE

Hudson Home   Modern class in the form of fur pillows, cowhide rugs, linens, candles, and tailored fabric furnishings in a crisp, cream-and-black motif. 356 Warren St. ∅ **518/822-8120.**

John Doe's Records   A refreshingly grubby basement of thrift is an irreverent change of pace from so many other antiques stores. Paw through clothes, records, and other vintage castoffs priced to move. 18 Warren St. ∅ **518/828-4738.**

Knotty Woodpecker   Gnome T-shirts, velvet Buddhas, cowboy hats, and dazzling skirts. 323 Warren St. ∅ **518/828-2650.**

lili & loo   Handmade jewelry, plus African- and Asian-inspired home treasures made of wood, iron, linen, or leather. 259 Warren St. ∅ **518/ 822-9492.** www.liliandloo.com.

Olde Hudson Market   The queen bee of upscale importers, stocking edible treats up front and bath and body treats in the back. 434 Warren St. ⊘ 518/828-6923.

Shop Naked   Cowboy, the store's own Jack Russell, hangs out among impulse buys for those with a sense of humor. Photo lampshades, recycled material handbags, and a coffee bar in back. 10 Warren St. ⊘ 518/671-6336.

White Rice   Eclectic imports—from batik clothing to carved furnishings—from Bali, India, and Nepal. 531 Warren St. ⊘ 518/697-3500. www.white-rice.com.

WHAT TO DO NEARBY

Olana   You should definitely include a side trip to see this Moorish hilltop estate, which was owned, designed, and landscaped by the artist Frederic Church. Inspired by his extensive travels in the Middle East, the Hudson River School landscape painter began crafting his exotic Persian-style manor in 1870. He then continued to perfect its rich details—literally inch by inch of rich, complicated color palettes and stenciled patterns—for another 2 decades. Centered around an inner court, the house contains such ornate furnishings as Oriental rugs, hand-painted carved chairs, and a 3-foot-tall stuffed peacock, much of it built specifically for the house. Over the past century, the metallic shine of paints Church mixed by hand for the interior has faded, but the home's timeless splendor has not. The obsessive artist who controlled each facet of his estate left an unusual legacy of architectural beauty. If you can't bear to leave after a short film and a 40-minute, history-woven tour, you're free to traverse the 5 miles of carriage roads, some with 360-degree views. Plan ahead and bring a bag lunch: Visitors are welcome to picnic on the grounds. Because tickets can sell out for the whole day by early afternoon, make reservations for a tour in advance. 5720 Rte. 9G. ⊘ 518/828-0135. www.olana.org. Admission $7. Mid-Apr through Oct Tues–Sun 10am–5pm.

WHERE TO STAY

Once you step off Hudson's main drag, you may encounter parts of Hudson that are kind of a drag in and of themselves. That said, a good argument for spending a couple of days in the area is to have 1 day for shopping and another to tour the captivating Olana (see "What to Do Nearby," above). The following accommodations are drawing more and more people to spend the night in Hudson.

Country Squire B&B   Built in 1900 as a rectory, this 21-room downtown Queen Anne Victorian is all about making you comfortable. The guest rooms have the sweet flourishes you'd expect in a town known for its antiques: four-poster and sleigh beds, pedestal sinks, toile fabrics, and claw-foot tubs. A generous continental breakfast kicks off your day. 251 Allen St. ✆ 518/822-9229. www.countrysquireny.com. Doubles $125-$195.

Hudson City B&B The antiques continue inside this towering charmer. Adorable from the outside but a bit jumbled and frilly inside. 326 Allen St. ✆ 518/822-8044. www.hudsoncitybnb.com. Doubles $100-$175.

Union Street Guest Houses Modern with vintage touches, each of these sweet little suites has hardwood floors, Aveda bath products, and its own private entrance. The location is a plus: just 5 blocks from the train station and 1 block from downtown. The home is 1830s Greek Revival, but each room contains a minifridge and coffeemaker. (No breakfast is served.) 349 Union St. ✆ 518/828-0958. www.unionstreetguesthouse.com. Doubles $100-$400.

WHERE TO EAT

Bolgen & Moi Serving French cuisine with a Norwegian twist, this quirky bistro is known for its unusual chef's-choice tapas and fish and shellfish soup. 136 Warren St. ✆ 518/671-6380. Entrees $12-$29.

Ca' Mea Fine northern Italian fare with the option to dine outdoors. 333 Warren St. ✆ 518/822-0005. www.camearestaurant.com. Pastas $14-$15; entrees $16-$22.

Nola Bakery & Café If you time it right, the old-fashioned donuts will be hot from the oven at this sandwich-and-snack shop with indoor/outdoor seating. Or cool off with an iced coffee, smoothie, or Jane's ice cream (made in nearby Kingston). 454 Warren St. ✆ 518/828-4905.

Swoon Kitchenbar Both lunch and dinner are absolutely delicious at this bistro with a silver tin ceiling, mix-and-match cafe-style seating, and a jungle of plants throughout. In the afternoon enjoy the skirt-steak salad or a panini, followed by double chocolate chip cookies. At night order king salmon with white-bean puree or iron-pot lamb shank (served in a mini cast-iron pot). While you're waiting, sip on a passion margarita or huckleberry martini. The bar offers an extensive wine list. 340 Warren St. ✆ 518/822-8938. www.swoonkitchenbar.com. Entrees $16-$18; less for lunch.

Red Bank, NJ

Antiques District, Red Bank, NJ 07701
✆ **732/741-9211** · www.redbank.com

Getting there: NJ Transit's North Jersey Coast line train from NY's Penn Station to Red Bank, NJ.
Subways: 1, 2, 3 to 34th St./Penn Station or A, C, E to 34th St./Eighth Ave.
Approximate travel time: 1 hr., 10 min.
Schedule: Trains leave Penn Station once an hour on weekends and return from Red Bank on a similar schedule.
Cost: $22 round-trip.

What's not to like about a town that welcomes train passengers with a pink, gingerbread-style rail station? Built in 1875, this historic depot doubles as the town's visitor center. It's full of maps and brochures, with a friendly face behind the desk to answer any visitor's questions.

Home to the oldest antiques co-op in the country, Red Bank is a pleasant walker's town with an antiques district that runs parallel to the banks of the Navesink River. Antiquing is serious business here, and unless you're a discriminating collector willing to shell out big bucks, you may go home empty-handed. But there's nothing wrong with a day spent browsing the shops, stopping for a casual lunch, and tooling through this energetic small town whose main street leads to a lovely park overlooking the river.

If you need a break from the old, there's plenty of new here as well. High-end housewares and women's boutiques are interspersed with a big Restoration Hardware, a few teen-friendly specialty stores, coffeehouses, and chocolate shops.

A bustling river town back in the 1800s, Red Bank took its name from the clay banks of the river it borders. While it has long been known as a haven for antiques, the town is working hard to update its image with a lively year-round events calendar that includes a summer concert series in the park, street fairs, an annual sidewalk sale at the end of July, a huge Halloween parade, lots of holiday activities, and the state's largest fireworks display for Independence Day. Check the online calendar of events for details.

GETTING AROUND

Stop in at the visitor center upon arrival and pick up one of their free walking maps. Broad Street, a few blocks up, is the main artery of town, but most of the antiques stores are on Front Street.

WHERE TO SHOP

West Front Street, where most of the town's antiques stores are clustered, is considered the town's Antiques District, but a few more shops are dotted about town on Broad Street, Monmouth Street, and Shrewsbury Avenue.

Antiques Center of Red Bank   Housed in two adjoined buildings with a third one across the street, the Antiques Center should be your first shopping stop. Booths are set up for each vendor on two different floors. Some of the stuff is a bit stuffy—with chandeliers, china, silver, furniture (lots of walnut and mahogany), toys, and artwork comprising the bulk of the offerings—but it's fun to see several centuries of valuables all crammed together in one place. There's even a jewelry repair counter that can repair your precious jewels while you wait. The staff is happy to hold your purchases until the end of the day so you can pick them up on your way back to the train. **Antiques Center I & II: 195 W. Front St.** ∅ **732/741-5331. Antiques Center III: 226 W. Front St.** ∅ **732/842-4336.**

> **Tip**
>
> Most of the antiques and housewares stores in town can arrange delivery back to the city for a fee.

Funk & Standard Variety Store   A small-town Urban Outfitters–type place with trendy tops, posters, incense, jewelry, and various Paul Frank items. 40 Broad St. ∅ **732/219-5885.**

Gigi's House of Antiques   Two levels of European furniture, all gilt and fringe and crystal sparkle. The quarters are tight but the owners know their eras. 182 W. Front St. ∅ **732/747-3900.**

Jack's Music Shoppe   This shop has it all: In addition to aisles of CDs and DVDs, it also specializes in guitars, keyboards, and many other instruments, plus the sheet music to go with them. 30 Broad St. ∅ **732/842-0731. www.jacksmusicshoppe.com.**

Jay & Silent Bob's Secret Stash   A comics store owned by filmmaker Kevin Smith—of *Clerks* fame—who grew up nearby and shot part of his films *Chasing Amy* and *Dogma* right in town. The store, named after characters in many of his films (Smith himself plays Silent Bob), is jam-packed with related comics, *Mallrats* action figures, bumper stickers, posters, and frightening minibusts of both Jason and Freddy. 35 Broad St. ∅ **732/758-0508. www.viewaskew.com.**

Monmouth Antique Shoppe   Among the finds here are stained-glass windowpanes, an Asian antiques section, vintage prints and

---

Events: Red Bank Jazz & Blues Festival

Three days of entertainment contribute to New Jersey's largest jazz and blues fest with food, crafts, and fun stuff for the kids. It takes place in Marine Park in early June.

---

books, and vintage farm wares like salvaged barn windows. 217 W. Front St. ✆ **732/842-7377.**

River Bank Antiques   The antiques here are so immaculate, they look as if they were never used. Rattan and wicker furniture, carved dining chairs with upholstered seats, ornate chaise longues, a French desk set—and mod lamps and fancy hatpins thrown in for fun. 169 W. Front St. ✆ **732/842-5400.**

WHAT TO DO

Count Basie Theater   An endless stream of big-name musicians, actors, and comedians breeze through town to stop at this 1926 theater, named for the count, who was born right in Red Bank. In October the theater hosts a weekend-long International Film Festival. 99 Monmouth St. ✆ **732/842-9000.** www.countbasietheatre.org.

WHERE TO STAY

You can browse the town in a day, but for serious shoppers or those with tickets to a show at the Count Basie, Red Bank offers two convenient options for an overnight stay.

The Molly Pitcher Inn   Built in 1928, this grand hotel offers river views, inn-style furnishings, a bar, a fitness room, wireless Internet, and a small outdoor pool. 88 Riverside Ave. ✆ **732/747-2500.** www.molly pitcher-oysterpoint.com. Doubles $130 and up.

The Oyster Point Hotel   A more contemporary setting with the same river views. Amenities include a bar, a restaurant, and a fitness room. 146 Bodman Place. ✆ **732/530-8200.** www.mollypitcheroysterpoint. com. Doubles $120 and up.

WHERE TO EAT

Juanito's Mexican Restaurant and Bakery   Across from the train station. The scent will lure you in for very good, authentic fare that many locals swear by. 186 Monmouth St. ✆ **732/747-9994.** Entrees $11 and under.

The Melting Pot   Okay, it's a chain restaurant, but it's still fondue! The large menu includes four kinds of cheese fondue ($16 serves one or two people) and nine kinds of melted, chocolatey concoctions ($15–$18).

1st floor of The Galleria shopping center, 2 Bridge Ave. ∅ **732/219-0090**. www. meltingpot.com.

You're My Hero   If it's a beautiful day, pick up a sub sandwich and picnic on the waterfront. 17 W. Front St. ∅ **732/842-1855**.

Zebu Forno Bakery & Café   Refuel in style at the town's swankiest coffee shop. Besides espresso and bagels, the cafe does strong business with sandwiches, salads, wraps, gelato, four soups in a bread bowl, and custom pizzas. 20 Broad St. ∅ **732/936-9330**.

Lambertville, NJ & New Hope, PA

Bridge St.–both towns
∅ **609/397-0055** • www.lambertville.org
∅ **215/862-5030** • www.newhopepa.com
www.newhopepennsylvania.com

Getting there: Trans-Bridge Bus Lines from Port Authority to Lambertville, NJ.
Subways: A, C, E to Port Authority or N, Q, R, S, W, 1, 2, 3, 7 to Times Sq./42nd St.
Approximate travel time: 2 hr., 10 min.
Schedule: Buses leave Port Authority three times a day Sat-Sun (more often on weekdays) and return from Lambertville on a similar schedule.
Cost: $36 round-trip.

These two equally quaint and interesting towns are the fraternal twins of the antiquing scene with a slew of galleries to boot. Aside from the obvious difference between them—the towns sit on opposite banks of the Delaware River, and a bridge crossing the New Jersey–Pennsylvania border both connects and divides them—each has its own, distinct personality. You can visit these two intriguing towns in the same weekend and never get bored.

Let's start with Lambertville—the more mature, more focused sibling. Lambertville has several good wine shops and a mix of antiques and imported-goods stores. She dresses smartly at all times and goes to bed at a reasonable hour. Her crowd tends to be a bit older, she is prone to retail moments of over-the-top froufrou decor, and she's home to the local bus stop. She's spirited yet well behaved, and her quiet side streets of Victorian and Federal-style residences are a great joy to come home to after a day spent shopping and sightseeing.

New Hope is the history nerd with a wild-child side, a picturesque place with historic inns, a mansion, an old railroad, a theater, boat rides, and a curving European-style street called Mechanic. The wild-child

Lambertville & New Hope

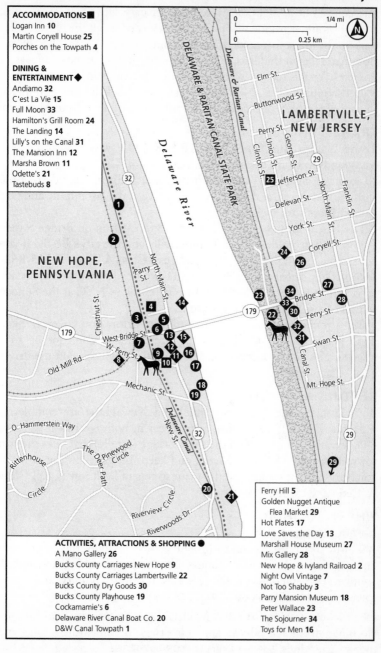

DELAWARE & RARITAN CANAL STATE PARK

Delaware River

Delaware & Raritan Canal

Elm St.

Buttonwood St.

LAMBERTVILLE, NEW JERSEY

Perry St.
Union St.
Clinton St.
George St.
Jefferson St.
North Main St.
Franklin St.

Delevan St.

York St.

Coryell St.

NEW HOPE, PENNSYLVANIA

Parry St.
North Main St.
Chestnut St.
West Bridge St.
W. Ferry St.
Old Mill Rd.
Mechanic St.

Bridge St.
Ferry St.
Swan St.
Canal St.
Mt. Hope St.

Delaware Canal

New St.

O. Hammerstein Way

Rittenhouse Circle
The Deer Path
Pinewood Circle
Riverview Circle
Riverwoods Dr.

0   1/4 mi
0   0.25 km

side comes out at night, at lively open-air bars, late-night restaurants, and a postdinner parade that promenades up and down the narrow sidewalks. The most haunted town in Pennsylvania also peddles hippie clothing, Tibetan Buddhas, $60 face powder, and sequined handbags. A French bakery is tucked in an alley along the river, and a brewery chain is in a shopping plaza. New Hope even has a hookah lounge to match all those boutiques of accessories from Indonesia, Tibet, and Morocco.

TRANSIT FACTS

Trans-Bridge Bus Lines (☎ **610/868-6001;** www.transbridgebus.com) tends to board early and leave on the dot. Get to the gate at least 20 minutes ahead of your departure time, confirm your destination with the bus driver, and board. Do *not* arrive at the last minute and take your chances with making it.

The bus drops passengers off at the Exxon station on Bridge Street, a short walk from downtown Lambertville and the city's B&Bs. If you have luggage and prefer to take a cab, call **Class A Taxi** (☎ **215/862-2660**). They can also take you around town or to any out-of-town side trips. The bus picks up for the return trip back to NYC at the Sunoco station across the street from Exxon.

Buy a round-trip ticket at Port Authority before you go, even if you don't know when you'll be coming back; they're good for up to 6 months. You can buy tickets on board on the way back, but the driver needs exact change.

GETTING AROUND

Both Lambertville (just 1 sq. mile) and New Hope are completely walkable. Bridge Street is the main street in both towns—it starts in one, traverses a footpath on the short bridge (⅕ mile) that links the two towns (over the Delaware River), and keeps on going in the other. If you want to venture beyond the main streets of both towns, call **Class A Taxi** (☎ **215/862-2660**).

WHERE TO SHOP
Lambertville

A Mano Gallery   As fun to browse as it is to shop, this large store housed in the old Five & Dime Building specializes in handcrafted, whimsical art, pillows, wine accessories, furniture, pottery, and accessories. 42 N. Union St. ☎ **609/397-0063.** www.amanogalleries.com.

Bucks County Dry Goods   Modern housewares, jeans, and trendy clothing—from silk pillows and retro rugs to embellished tanks and men's surfer duds. 5 Klines Court. ☎ **609/397-1288.**

Golden Nugget Antique Flea Market   The die-hards arrive at 6am sharp to snatch up the best of the day's antiques and collectibles. While the market advertises that it's open until 4pm, some vendors—cleaned out from frantic shoppers—start packing up as early as noon. Another reason to get there early: It can be a very hot shopping trip. The market has 60 indoor shops, 250 outdoor vendors, and two restaurants. Open Wednesday, Saturday, and Sunday from 6am to 4pm year-round. 1850 River Rd., Lambertville (1½ miles south of town). ✆ 609/397-0811. www. gnmarket.com.

Mix Gallery and Mix at Home   Two stylish stores, the first with findings from 1800 to 1960, the next full of midcentury mod and retro vintage for the home. Antiques at 17 S. Main St. (at Ferry St.), vintage at 65 Ferry St. ✆ 609/773-0777. www.mixgallery.com.

Peter Wallace   Don't miss this riverside gem. The deck has bubbling garden fountains, statuary, and iron tables and chairs. Inside, chandeliers hang overhead on three floors of decorative antiques. 3 Lambert Lane. ✆ 609/397-4914.

The Sojourner   A world market of imported sandals and clothing, loose beads, clunky jewelry, and lots of lanterns. 26 Bridge St. ✆ 609/ 397-8849.

New Hope

Cockamamie's   Art Deco barware and smoking accessories meet 1950s furniture and other treasures. 6 W. Bridge St. ✆ 215/862-5454.

Ferry Hill   Teapots and trunks, porcelain, Staffordshire, enamel jewelry, and bedside lamps make for a fancy-schmancy shop with a British touch. 15 N. Main St. ✆ 215/862-5335.

Hot Plates   A 1950s-diner theme is behind some of the china, glassware, and kitchen gadgets here. 40 S. Main St. ✆ 215/862-3220.

Love Saves the Day   An outpost of their Manhattan store, with the same vintage icons of pop culture, from leopard-print coats and 1980s prom gowns to Muppets drinking glasses and *Star Wars* anything. 1 S. Main St. ✆ 215/862-1399.

Night Owl Vintage   Dress yourself in vintage threads at this downtown store with good music and low prices. 10 Stockton Ave. ✆ 215/862-9685.

Not Too Shabby   A little bit country, a little bit frilly: collectibles, consignments, and housewares and gifts (candles, baskets, soaps) made by local artists and craftspeople. 29 N. Main St. ✆ 215/862-7093. www.nottoo shabbypa.com.

Toys for Men   In the Four Seasons Mall (a strange hodgepodge of shops to begin with) is this bizarrely named store of gadgets, board games, toys (for both kids and youngsters of the executive type), and gifts for the guys. 32 S. Main St. ✆ 215/862-5111.

WHAT TO DO

A great way to experience the two towns is by **bike.** The main streets see a lot of traffic, but the side streets and canal towpath are very bike-friendly. Bike rentals are $8 per hour, $22 for a half-day, or $32 for a full day (Body Tech Fitness, 2 Mt. Hope St., Lambertville; ✆ **609/397-6900**).

Delaware River Canal Boat Company   The most novel—and relaxing—attraction within walking distance sends passengers gliding down the canal on a barge pulled by two mules that walk on ahead along the canal towpath, which was built to tug barges hauling coal. Between 1832 and 1932, the mules were hauling 100 tons of the stuff each week—until they were edged out of the business by the railroad. Bordellos, brothels, and boat-supply shops sprang up along the canal banks. The canal was originally 60 miles long, and was dug hand-and-shovel by Scottish and Irish immigrants who were paid 75¢ a day plus a whiskey bonus (a better deal than the children mule-tenders who walked barefoot for 30 miles a day along that path and were paid a pittance). After your guide gives a local-history lesson (and some fun facts about mules), sit back and listen to a folk singer warble adaptations of songs sung along the Erie Canal in the old days. It's open April through November, with four 1-hour boat tours a day; admission is $10. 149 S. Main St. ✆ 215/862-0758. www.onthecanal.net.

Ghost Tours of New Hope   When the sun sets, the ghosts come out in New Hope—or at least the ghost stories do. These guided Saturday-night tours have been led by lantern light for more than 20 years through a town whose ghosts include a Revolutionary War soldier, a child along the canal path, and a distraught daughter whose father did not approve of her. After the tour, have a drink at the reputedly haunted Logan Inn and tell your own tales. Tours run from June through November plus Friday nights in October; admission $9. Meet at the cannon on the corner of Main and Ferry streets in New Hope at 8pm sharp. ✆ 215/343-5564.

Bucks County Carriages   Sit back in a fringe-top surrey or a canopied vis-à-vis carriage with two button-tufted seats for a slow and calmingly clompity 20-minute ride through either town. Lambertville carriages usually wait for walk-up customers outside Lambertville Station (11 Bridge St.); in New Hope carriages are found across from the Bucks County Playhouse. Make a reservation in advance or just hop on an empty one; $15 per person. ✆ 215/862-3582.

Events: Lambertville-New Hope Winter Festival

In early February, come for concerts, family activities, a parade, a chili cook-off, and ice-carving demos (www.winterfestival.net).

New Hope & Ivyland Railroad   Not a must-do (the narration is hard to hear, there isn't much to see, and flakes of black soot fly in through the train's open windows), but if you love trains, the steam or diesel locomotive toting restored 1920s passenger cars has its charms. The drinks on board are expensive, but first-class passengers ride in air-conditioned cars and get a soda and soft pretzel. The ride down to Lahaska and back is less than an hour; it's all very family-friendly. Tickets are $11 coach, $17 first-class, $7.75 for children. ⌀ **215/862-2332.** www.newhoperailroad.com.

D&W Canal Towpath   A favorite early morning walk for locals and tourists alike, this 30-mile scenic trail of compacted quarry grit has been used since the canal's coal-hauling years.

The Marshall House/Lambertville Historical Society   This historic home-turned-museum-of-local-history also offers information about the area and guided walking tours of town on the first Sunday of each month April through October. 62 Bridge St. ⌀ **609/397-0770.** www.lambertvillehistoricalsociety.org. Apr-Oct weekends 1-4pm.

Parry Mansion Museum   The tours of this restored 1784 house tend to be rather long-winded—especially on a hot summer's day without air-conditioning (which, at least, makes for an authentic experience). History buffs shouldn't miss it, however—the eight rooms reflect 125 years of decorative changes by the Parry family. Tours ($5) are given on Saturday and Sunday from 1 to 5pm, from late April through early December. 45 S. Main St. ⌀ **215/862-5652.** www.parrymansion.org.

Bucks County Playhouse   This former gristmill produces a lineup of classic musicals nearly all year long—with actors you might just recognize. Last season, *Gypsy, Hello, Dolly!* and *Dracula* hit the main stage. On weekends in October, catch a midnight showing of *The Rocky Horror Picture Show*—bring your own toast. 70 S. Main St. ⌀ **215/862-2041.** www.buckscountyplayhouse.com. Tickets $22-$27.

WHAT TO DO NEARBY

Odette's   After a dinner with views of both the Delaware Canal and the Delaware River, stay for Broadway songs and popular standards in the old-tavern Bar Room. At some point a singalong breaks out around the piano. Or buy tickets in advance for the East Coast's longest-running cabaret room. (*Tip:* If you're doing dinner and cabaret, make your reservations separately or risk eating your dinner in the actual theater, not nearly as nice as the restaurant's river-view dining rooms.) 274 S. River Rd., New Hope. ⊘ 215/862-2432. www.odettes.com. Tickets $8–$35 with $10 food or drink minimum. Closed Tues.

Bucks County River Country Get out on the Delaware River in a tube, canoe, raft, or kayak. About $20 per person for the day. 2 Walters Lane (8 miles away in Point Pleasant, PA). ⊘ 215/297-5000. www.river country.net.

WHERE TO STAY
Lambertville

Martin Coryell House Between shopping and dinner, guests can take a break on the prim Italianate front porch or in the Victorian parlor or formal library of this polished B&B. The welcoming Federal-style home (from 1864) has the nicest innkeepers to go along with the professionally decorated interior, pampering amenities, and three-course breakfasts served in a gorgeous blue-and-white dining room with a hand-painted ceiling mural. The murals are a theme throughout the house and continue along hallways leading up to rooms, which feature fireplaces, feather beds, and Jacuzzi tubs with double shower heads. The Emma Lily room has the sweetest pink claw-foot bathtub and roses on the walls. Myra's Suite has two rooms (one a TV lounge), five windows, and a view. In the morning, let Mary and Rich help you find the best places to shop or make dinner reservations for a special evening in town. (Check the website for packages to indulge in a massage, carriage ride, or chilled champagne during your stay.) 111 N. Union St. ⊘ 609/397-8981. www.martincoryellhouse.com. Weekend doubles $195–$295.

New Hope

Logan Inn At this large historic inn in the heart of downtown, request "the haunted room" (it's no. 6) only if you dare. The spirits in this particular room are not at all shy! 10 W. Ferry St. ⊘ 215/862-2300. www.loganinn.com. Weekend doubles start at $140. Mid-Feb through Oct.

Porches on the Towpath Close to the action yet set off the beaten path, this boxy Federal-style building lined with two stories of porches was built in 1830 as a granary. Rooms are filled with choice antiques, and some have views of the canal or a balcony. The ultracozy attic suite has a unique black-and-white antique claw-foot tub. A full breakfast is served out on the porch. 20 Fisher's Alley. ⊘ 215/862-3277. www.porches newhope.com. Weekend doubles $140–$250.

WHERE TO EAT
Lambertville

Many restaurants in Lambertville and (some in New Hope) are BYOB. A great bottle for your table can be selected from the thousands at **Welsh's Wines** (8 S. Union St.; ∅ **609/397-8243**). For an after-dinner cigar to go with your port, head to **Walker's Wine & Spirits** (86 Bridge St.; ∅ **609/397-0625**).

Note that many restaurants in both towns—for better or worse—still allow smoking. And reservations are highly recommended for dinner at all restaurants.

Andiamo A Culinary Institute of America (CIA) grad cooks up American, French, and Italian specialties, adding his own flair. Escargots in puff pastry have a garlic-butter-white-wine sauce, and the steak and chicken specials are worth deliberation. BYOB softens the tab. 13 Klines Court. ∅ **609/397-6767**. www.andiamonj.com. Entrees $18-$26. BYOB.

Full Moon Stop by until 3pm for omelets, French toast, salads, and sandwiches in a cafe with old-fashioned chairs and vaulted ceilings. Dinner is served on the night of the full moon—make reservations well in advance. 23 Bridge St. ∅ **609/397-1096**. www.nolegsneeded.com/fullmoon. Entrees under $10.

Hamilton's Grill Room Ask a waiter at any restaurant down the canal where he goes for a special dinner and you'll hear "Hamilton's." This contemporary Mediterranean restaurant features fresh seafood and meats fired on an open grill and elegant courtyard dining. 8 Coryell St. ∅ **609/397-4343**. www.hamiltonsgrillroom.com. Entrees $23-$32. BYOB.

Lilly's on the Canal A relative newcomer, Lilly's is popular for lunch and a casual dinner; its long sandwich list includes paninis and a Cubano with slow-roasted pork. 2 Canal St. ∅ **609/397-6242**. Entrees $10-$23.

New Hope

C'est La Vie French Bakery & Café If it's baked with butter and sugar, you can probably find it in the cases here. Chocolate-filled croissants, brioche, a dozen pastries, and assorted mousse desserts mix with more pedestrian treats like brownies, macaroons, and crumb cake. The cafe itself is nondescript, but a terrace is open for summer snacking. 20 S. Main St. (down the alley). ∅ **215/862-1956**. Individual baked goods $1-$3.50.

The Landing If you want to dine by the river, this is your spot. A huge terrace with umbrella-shaded tables can handle the crowds. The food is good, but the prices reflect the waterside views. 22 N. Main St. ∅ **215/862-5711**. www.landingrestaurant.com. Entrees $23-$33.

Events: Annual New Hope Outdoor Arts & Crafts Festival

A juried arts event that has run for more than 20 years in New Hope is held in early October (www.newhopechamberofcommerce.org/artsand crafts.htm).

The Mansion Inn   Torchieres light the golden-walled dining room of this lovely gingerbread mansion, all decked out in high ceilings, crystal water glasses, candlelit tables for two—and a four-diamond rating. The gracious waitstaff takes its job with a European seriousness and pride in the restaurant. The no-expense-spared menu incorporates elements like a champagne vinaigrette on the goat cheese salad, bourbon cream sauce on a center-cut and roasted filet mignon, and venison wrapped in smoked apple-wood bacon. Even amid all the upscale finery, the restaurant refuses to affect a stiff or uppity demeanor—rattan chairs and daisies in vases cut through any pretensions. The crowd here orders their wine by the bottle, and there's a reason the seasonal bread pudding has a reputation as the best dessert in Bucks County. 9 S. Main St. ∅ 215/862-1231. www.themansioninn.com. Entrees $16–$32.

Marsha Brown   Always packed because of its unusual venue—a 125-year-old converted stone church—this restaurant serves a delicious array of "refined Creole" cuisine. Very decadent, but the service can be spotty. 15 S. Main St. ∅ 215/862-7044. Entrees $21–$37.

Tastebuds   Despite the goofy name, this is one of the most cosmopolitan—and downplayed—restaurants in town. Most tourists never stumble upon it, but those who do are delighted. Walk in to what looks like someone's modern living and dining room and order from the small, seasonally inspired global fusion menu. Ultraromantic. 49 W. Ferry St. ∅ 215/862-9722. Entrees $12–$25. BYOB.

NIGHTLIFE

Lambertville is much quieter at night than bustling New Hope, and establishments tend to close earlier. In Lambertville the denlike fireplace lounge at **Left Bank Libations** (32 Bridge St.; ∅ 609/397-4745) is a cute place for a classic cocktail. Across the street the former 1867 railway station, **Lambertville Station,** sets up live jazz and blues on Friday and Saturday nights in the downstairs pub (11 Bridge St.; ∅ 609/397-8300; www.lambertvillestation.com).

In New Hope there's nightlife for all ages. A youthful set fills the outdoor deck at **Havana** (105 S. Main St.; ∅ 215/862-9897), where live music complements the mixed drinks and burgers. At **90 Main** (90 Main St.; ∅ 215/862-3030), a too-cool South Beach vibe almost feels out of place—but don't turn down the fab desserts. A walk down Main Street yields pizza joints and general hanging out. For those past 20-something, the large, ambling restaurant at **Logan Inn** has a bar with outdoor seating that's popular with locals and tourists alike for people-watching. **Marsha Brown** (see "Where to Eat," above) has a saucy scene for well-dressed couples. For dinner, **Zoubi** (5-7 Mechanic St.; no street numbers are posted, but go past the tall iron gate; ✆ **215/862-5851**; www.zoubinewhope.com) serves French, Asian, and Latin American cuisine—but go for a drink and you'll be instantly in the know. The patio is divine if you can get a table, and the exotic decor inside will appease if not.

Cold Spring, NY

Main St., Cold Spring, NY 10516
✆ **845/265-3200** • www.hvgateway.com/CS00.htm

Getting there: Metro-North Hudson line train from Grand Central to Cold Spring, NY. The town is just a short walk up the hill from the train station.
Subways: 4, 5, 6, 7, S to Grand Central.
Approximate travel time: 1 hr., 20 min.
Schedule: Trains leave Grand Central once an hour on weekends and return from Cold Spring on a similar schedule.
Cost: Train fare is $20 round-trip off-peak.

This little town tucked up off the Hudson River is one of the places people tend to head on their first mass-transit weekend getaway from NYC. And why not? Just a short jaunt from the train station, an adorable Main Street beams with antiques stores and all-American pride. Flags wave gaily from freshly painted front porches, shop owners call out a greeting, and the retail staples include vintage collectibles and ice-cream cones. In addition to nearby hiking and kayaking, you can eat lunch on the water, mosey among the independently owned shops, or have a sit along the renovated waterfront. Or stay the night. Cold Spring's B&Bs are part of the small, walkable downtown area—all of 8 blocks long. Plus, you'll get a true feel for the good old days: Some 225 of the town's buildings are listed on the National Register of Historic Places.

A naturally flowing stream in the front yard of the Cold Spring Depot (a restaurant and former train station) is said to be the source of Cold Spring's name. Whether George Washington really camped here, drank from the spring, and so named the town can never be proven, but the folk story lives on.

Events: Hudson Valley Shakespeare Festival

Hosted a few miles outside of town at the Boscobel Restoration from mid-June through Labor Day weekend, the three evening productions each season have drawn more than 25,000 people to come enjoy theatrical classics under the stars. Order locally catered gourmet picnics ($14–$22) and wine ($20 a bottle) at least 2 days in advance from the box office. Tickets go on sale in May and cost $25 to $38, depending on the day. There's even a $5 round-trip shuttle (the Bard Bus) from the Cold Spring train station—reserve a space when you order your tickets (Bear Mountain Bridge on Rte. 9D in Garrison, NY; ✆ **845/265-9575**; www.hvshakespeare.org).

Today's Cold Spring has decked itself out in a mix of contemporary boutiques (especially those with accessories to perk up your home), antiques stores, and cafes—something the *New York Times* likes to call the "SoHo-on-Hudson feel." It's no wonder the town is a weekend favorite with New Yorkers, which means it can be packed on Saturday and Sunday. Not every store is open every day, but most are open Wednesday through Sunday, making weekday trips toward the end of the week an option for those who wish to shop in peace.

GETTING AROUND
Call **West Side Taxi** (✆ **845/831-2400**) or **Highland Taxi** (✆ **845/265-8294**) if you need a lift.

WHERE TO SHOP
More than 30 antiques and vintage vendors under one roof can be found in several venues in Cold Spring: **Downtown Galleries** at 40 Main St. (✆ **845/265-2334**); **Bijou Galleries** at 50 Main St. (✆ **845/265-4337**; www.bijougalleries.com); and **Cold Spring Antiques Center,** 77 Main St. (✆ **845/265-5050**).

Decades White pottery, milk glass, black glass, and Fiestaware brighten the shelves of this shop—and your kitchen table. 131 Main St. ✆ **845/265-5082.**

Knittingsmith Enough yarn for a million and three sweaters plus a nice collection of knitting books and buttons. 35 Chestnut St. (Rte. 9D). ✆ **845/265-6566.**

Provincial Home A fine, old-world collection of European ceramics, linens, and glassware, as well as gourmet goodies and a pretty garden out back. 80 Main St. ✆ **845/265-5360.** www.provincialhome.com.

WHAT TO DO NEARBY

Boscobel Restoration   It's a quick cab ride to this 19th-century Federal-style estate and decorative-arts museum. Take a guided tour (free with the $10 admission), then wander through the gardens and orange orchard. Rte. 9D in Garrison, NY. ∅ **845/265-3638. www.boscobel. org.** Apr-Dec Wed-Mon 9:30am-5pm, including Thanksgiving and Christmas.

The Appalachian Trail & Breakneck Ridge   Both trails are nearby, just a short walk out of town. Stop in at Hudson Valley Outfitters to pick up maps and get pointed in the right direction.

Foundry School Museum   In 1818 an Act of Congress made it possible for Cold Spring to establish a local foundry, where much of the iron and casting technologies known today were first developed. The museum's building was built by the West Point Foundry in 1830 as a school for foundry apprentices and village children and served as such until 1889. There's much to learn about the area's industrial past here, such as this fact: In 1863, sleeping beds for local foundry workers were so scarce that they were used in 8-hour blocks and rotated through three shifts a day. 63 Chestnut St. ∅ **845/265-4010.** Tues-Wed 10am-4pm; Thurs 1-4pm; Sat-Sun 2-5pm.

Hudson Valley Outfitters Kayak   One block from the train station, this retail shop offers single and tandem rentals, instruction, and scenic tours of the Hudson. Rentals start at $45 for 4 hours; tours start at $75 and most include a waterproof lunch. Register for your tour at least 2 weeks in advance. Tours run April through October. 63 Main St. ∅ **845/265-0221. www.hudsonvalleyoutfitters.com.**

WHERE TO STAY

Hudson House Inn   It's not nearly as cute or put together as the Pig Hill Inn, but the full breakfast served on Saturday and Sunday gets a big thumbs up. (It also offers waterside dining for lunch and dinner.) Some rooms have river views and a small balcony. 2 Main St. ∅ **845/ 265-9355. www.hudsonhouseinn.com.** Weekend doubles start at $165.

Pig Hill Inn Bed & Breakfast   Most of the nine rooms have a fireplace; some even have four-poster canopy beds, Jacuzzi tubs, and handmade quilts or down comforters. A full breakfast is served in the glass-enclosed solarium, out in the terraced garden, or can be brought right to your room for a decadent breakfast in bed. The antiques scattered throughout are for sale, as are those in the inn's own gift shop. 73 Main St. ∅ **845/265-9247. www.pighillinn.com.** Weekend doubles start at $150 per night with a 2-night minimum.

WHERE TO EAT

Braserrie le Bouchon   A French sophisticate with bordello-red walls and ceilings, clandestine banquettes, and lots of mirrors. The upscale menu includes mussels, pâté, and steak frites. 76 Main St. ✆ **845/265-7676. Entrees $ 13-$24.**

Cathryn's Tuscan Grill   With a warm, wood-heavy interior, this is everyone's favorite spot for northern Italian and an interesting wine list. On Sunday a champagne brunch is served from noon to 3pm ($20). 91 Main St. ✆ **845/265-5582. Entrees $12-$26.**

Cold Spring Depot   Open more than 20 years now, this 1893 former train station at the foot of Main Street is the most popular outdoor dining spot in town. It also has a tavern and a casual main dining room serving dishes like Guinness potpie, meatloaf, and fish and chips—plus a lighter lunch menu and an ice-cream parlor next door. Weekend nights you might even catch some live jazz or Dixieland. Rumor has it that the railroad tracks are still haunted by a woman who was murdered there by her husband in 1898 as she tried to flee his hot-tempered ways on a train to Poughkeepsie. 1 Depot Sq. ✆ **845/353-8361. Entrees $13-$27; lunch less.**

Art Towns

NEW YORK CITY IS AN EMBARRASSMENT OF RICHES FOR ART LOVERS, but a growing number of enclaves outside the city are home to museums and art spaces developing thrilling collections of art and sculpture. The following towns have snagged big-time museums, but their many other charms make the trip that much more worthwhile.

Dia: Beacon

3 Beekman St., Beacon, NY 12508
✆ **845/440-0100** · www.diabeacon.org

Getting there: Metro-North's Hudson Line from Grand Central to Beacon, NY, then a walk or trolley ride to the museum.
Subways: 4, 5, 6, 7, S to Grand Central.
Approximate travel time: 1½ hr.
Schedule: Trains leave Grand Central hourly on weekends and return from Beacon on a similar schedule.
Hours: Mid-Apr to mid-Oct Thurs–Mon 11am–6pm; late Oct to early Apr Fri–Mon 11am–4pm.
Cost: Train fare $23 round-trip off-peak.
Museum Admission: $10, $7 for students and seniors.

Built in 1929, this nearly 300,000-square-foot building was originally a printing plant for the National Biscuit Company. While the Oreos and Ginger Snaps and Nilla Wafers were being baked inside the factory behemoth that is now Chelsea Market in Manhattan, their spiffy Nabisco packaging was being printed here in Beacon.

The art form has changed a bit inside these massive walls, where works of unusual proportion center on earth-inspired themes and media rather than disposable cracker boxes and bags. With its broad spans stretching between supporting columns and original shiny wood floors, the building provides an ideal showplace for Dia's outsized works. And the building's natural lighting is hard to beat: More than

34,000 square feet of skylights, all original to the building, bathe the pieces in northern light.

Dia was founded in 1974 as a nonprofit institution dedicated to supporting individual artists and offering a long-term, in-depth presentation of their work. The galleries have been designed to accommodate pieces from the 1960s to the present, many of which, because of their unusual size or makeup, could not be accommodated by more conventional exhibition spaces.

There are many possible paths to take through this sprawling museum—visitors have lots of room to spread out and roam. Much of the art has an organic feel, starting with the choice of materials—a mound of broken-glass shards, lines of stretched yarn, dirt, sand, and unfinished wood—all of it meant to invite the viewer into the piece. Some do that literally, such as Richard Serra's set of three structures composed of fluid ribbons and curls of 2-inch-thick steel standing 20 feet tall. Manufactured by a shipbuilding company outside Baltimore, each structure forms a room of tilting angles.

The artists fortunate enough to show their work at Dia: Beacon are also deeply involved with how the work is exhibited. Michael Heizer's massive *North, East, South, West* was designed in the late 1960s but never exhibited—no exhibition space was willing or able to take it on. Though not the desert landscape Heizer originally envisioned as a setting, Dia: Beacon agreed to make room for the four 20-foot-deep geometrical holes cut right into the floor of one gallery. Because of the danger factor involved, visitors must view the pieces from behind a glass barricade 10 feet back. Catch the 10:30am daily tour and venture behind the glass to peer down into the dark depths of the space. Vertigo sufferers, beware.

Not all of the art is so, well, earthy, but much of it revels in deceptive simplicity. One room is covered with tall, black words on the walls, another is aglow in eerie video projections, and one exhibit is done up entirely in tubes of fluorescent light. Andy Warhol's *Shadows* blankets a room's walls with 102 canvases of the same image spun out in different color palettes.

Tip

Keep in mind that in the colder months, some of the museum's cavernous rooms can be chilly.

Since it opened in 2003, Dia has not only provided a proper exhibition space for many artists, but it has done wonders for the town of Beacon. Named after Mount Beacon, where Revolutionary War troops lit fires to warn of British troops, the town was virtually reawakened by the presence of Dia. New

TRAVEL TIME FROM NEW YORK CITY	
Beacon, NY	1.5 hrs via Metro-North
North Adams, MA	4.5 hrs via Bonanza Bus Lines
Long Island City, NY	30 mins via NYC subway
Mountainville, NY	1 hr, 25 mins via Shortline Bus

businesses, restaurants, stores, and galleries flung open their doors for an emerging arts community, both local and weekenders. With a town trolley making everything that much more accessible, the village is truly on a roll. For more information on the town of Beacon, go to **www.cityofbeacon.org** or **www.beacon.mainstreetbiz.biz**.

GETTING AROUND

On Saturday and Sunday an old-fashioned trolley with wooden benches and gold poles makes a loop from the train station to Dia down Main Street and back to the train station ($2 for unlimited rides all day; you'll need exact change). The burgundy trolley may be waiting at the train station when you arrive to whisk you off to Beacon. In case it's not, it's an easy walk to Dia: Beacon. Just follow the silver guardrail in front of the station up the ramp that curves around to the right. Turn right off the guardrail, and stay on the sidewalk along the road running parallel to the tracks. After a few minutes' walk, you'll see the sign for Dia off to the right. Alternatively, exit the rear of the platform on the

---

Events: Gallery Talks

Held on the last Saturday of each month at 1pm, these talks feature writers, professors, art historians, and curators lecturing on a specific artist. Talks are free with admission, but reservations are required; call ⌀ **845/440-0100,** ext. 44. In addition, a guided tour through Michael Heizer's *North, East, South, West* is given at 10:30am on days of operation. To reserve, call ⌀ **845/440-0100,** ext. 42.

---

river (west) side. Turn left on Red Flynn Drive and follow it over the railroad tracks to Beekman Street and turn right. Continue on Beekman to Dia: Beacon, the next driveway on the right.

At Dia, the trolley picks riders up at a side door off the cafe and bookshop (you can't reenter the museum after exiting through this door). The schedule is a loose one, so allow time for walking from point A to point B in case the trolley doesn't appear on cue. When you do board, the spirited driver will give you pointers on where to stop in town so you can explore the full length of Main Street (instead of starting in the middle); he'll also let you know when he will be back around your way again. Stops are marked by signs in town, but just wave the driver down if you see him coming. It's a 5-minute ride from the main drag back to the train station.

WHERE TO STAY

Beacon has no overnight lodging to speak of—although a tourism rep for Ulster County wagers that the first person to open a hotel or inn will find it worth their while. Right now the closest accommodations are in Fishkill, about 5 miles east, or across the river in Newburgh, about the same distance (www.dutchesstourism.com/lodging.asp). Cold Spring, the stop before Beacon on the Hudson line, has a number of quaint B&Bs (www.coldspring.com). A comprehensive listing of accommodations is found at www.escapemaker.com/ny. Otherwise, Dia makes a fine day trip.

WHERE TO EAT

Café at Dia: Beacon   How many museum cafes offer egg creams? Chic salads (like mixed field greens with crumbled feta and marinated tofu), sandwiches (a vegan egg salad and a meatball sub with grated asiago), soups, and baked goods are all prepared on the premises using locally grown, organic ingredients whenever possible. Everything under $10.

Piggy Bank   Better than much of the Southern barbecue being peddled in Manhattan, the smoked pulled pork and Texas kettle beef here won't disappoint. Sit down to a basket of warm cornbread before you even order. Housed in a tin-ceilinged former bank from 1880, the restaurant takes pride in spice-rubbing their ribs and marinating them overnight before slow-cooking them over aged hickory wood and finishing them on a hot grill. Eat on the outdoor patio when the weather is nice. 448 Main St. ∅ **845/838-0028.** Entrees $7.75–$21.

The Upper Crust & Bakery at The Little Pie Shop   Browse the pies, pastries, breads, and baked goods to eat in the cafe or on the train ride home. 472 Main St. ∅ **845/838-2890.**

Yankee Clipper Diner   The real artifact from 1946, but renovated to a T. This diner is one of the first eateries you'll see when riding the trolley from Dia into town. 397 Main St. ∅ **845/440-0021.** www.beacon yankeeclipper.com. Lunch specials from $6.95.

WHERE TO SHOP

Bookstores   There are two on Main Street: **Beacon Books** (500 Main St.; ∅ **845/831-4920**) specializes in nicely priced used books. **World's End Books & Music** (532 Main St.; ∅ **845/831-1760**) mixes its used collection with records, CDs, hiking maps, local history guides, and Hudson River prints and postcards.

> **Tip**
>
> Dia has a gallery in Chelsea (548 W. 22nd St.; ∅ **212/989-5566**) with a rotating collection as well as public programming.

Dia Bookshop   A vast collection of books and DVDs on the artists featured in the museum as well as other artists, works, and art forms from the 1960s to the present day.

Hudson Beach Glass   An old firehouse is the appropriate home for this gallery, retail store, and glassblowing studio where you can watch live demos of glassblowing come to life before your eyes. Bowls, soap dishes, candle stands, and perfume bottles are among the delicate beauties for sale. 162 Main St. ∅ **845/440-0068.** www.hudsonbeachglass.com.

Events: Second Saturdays

On the second Saturday of each month, Beacon-area businesses host in-store events along the lines of art openings, poetry readings, live music, and art discussions. Ask for a Second Saturday brochure at Dia: Beacon for a schedule of events and a gallery guide to the town. Sponsored by the Beacon Arts Community Association (BACA), with more information at **www.beaconarts.org**.

Iron Fish Trading Co.   Antiques and locally made steel furniture and lighting. 504 Main St. ✆ **845/838-5486.**

Relic   Vintage fabulousness for the home. 484 Main St. ✆ **845/440-0248.**

20th Century Fox Antiques   An Art Deco, old Hollywood feel pervades this store, which is full of unusual and nostalgic temptations. 466 Main St. ✆ **845/831-6059.**

MASS MoCA/The Porches Inn

231 River St., North Adams, MA 01247
✆ **413/664-0400** • www.porches.com

Getting there: Bonanza bus line from Port Authority to Williamstown, MA, then a cab to the hotel.

Subways: A, C, E to Port Authority or N, Q, R, S, W, 1, 2, 3, 7 to 42nd St./Times Sq.

Approximate travel time: 4½ hr.

Schedule: Bus leaves NY at 10am and 5pm daily and returns at 10am and 4pm daily. Times change, so check schedule.

Cost: Bus fare is $76 round-trip.

Room rates: Double and suite rates $125-$435 per night. AE, MC, V.

One of the Berkshires' lesser-known destinations, North Adams, Massachusetts, is a postindustrial 1890s mill town that's just now starting to show the telltale signs of tourist potential that other towns nearby have enjoyed for years. It may not boast the high-end spas and boutiques of nearby Lenox, but North Adams is alive and well—and quietly swelling with an undercurrent of creative energy. A historical gem whose gritty roughness is well preserved, North Adams may be a town on the brink of becoming a lively artists' and culinary colony, but even if it never quite achieves the tourist potential of its sister communities, it offers two highly recommended reasons to visit.

The impetus behind North Adams's potential resurgence? In a word, art. Spend a day inside the massive **Massachusetts Museum of Contemporary Art (MASS MoCA),** an adrenaline-pumping museum of beyond-modern art that is cleverly housed in the town's former textile mill (see "What to Do," below).

The other compelling attraction in the **Porches Inn at MASS MoCA,** a romantic hotel set inside a strand of clapboard Victorian row houses, lovingly restored Martha Stewart–style. A hundred years ago, from the front porches of these same homes, working-class New Englanders watched the family breadwinners cross the street to report for work at the North Adams textile mill, one of many that helped power the region's once-mighty textile industry.

Today this comfortable hotel combines vintage elements, modern luxury, and the intimate hospitality of a small-town inn. Its many thoughtful touches and state-of-the-art amenities make it a favorite weekend hideout for New Yorkers who want to balance doing something with doing nothing at all.

The past is easy to conjure up as you walk the halls of the former row houses. The inn's wood floors and front doors are original, and photos of the painstaking restoration at different stages appear throughout the hotel.

On the walls of the rooms—each one is unique—ceramic plates from the 1940s and 1950s hang neatly, as does a cross-stitch that reads: LET ME LIVE IN THE HOUSE BY THE SIDE OF THE ROAD AND BE A FRIEND TO MAN. A wall safe hides behind a paint-by-numbers painting found on eBay, just like the mod pair of bedside lamps. But kitschy, granny-chic details don't detract from the decidedly modern feel. Sitting rooms with desks are a nice place to read or use the Wi-Fi if you brought along your laptop. Huge bathrooms with black slate floors have claw-foot tubs or showers with a rainwater showerhead and an oversize tub with massaging bubble jets. (The bathrooms are so pretty they make primping for

> **Pet-Friendly Rooms**
>
> A few select rooms are pooch-friendly (even if the bus is not). Porches keeps crates, bowls, and treats on hand for their special guests. Ginger even gets a letter welcoming her at check-in.

dinner a pleasure.) And when you come back from eating in town, the turndown-service elves have put mints on your pillows and left a newsletter of the next day's local activities and forecast.

But with comfy mattresses and creamy Frette linens, who wants to leave? Each room has a DVD player, so borrow from the inn's complimentary library at check-in—it's stocked with classics and new releases. The same vintage wardrobe that houses your TV also holds a wet bar and snack drawer. (Visit the tiny cash bar at the front desk for something fancier; you can take your drinks back to the room or to the adjacent lounge with leather club chairs and fireplace.) Two rooms have their own fireplaces; six have porches of their own. Suites for extended stays have kitchenettes. One two-floor suite has a spiral staircase and two bedrooms, one of them in a loft upstairs. The five separate gabled row-house buildings are smartly joined by indoor catwalks and courtyards.

Relax on 240 feet of front porches lined with rocking chairs. Out back, the blue-shale outdoor pool retains heat so well that the hotel can keep it at a balmy 84°F (29°C) year-round. Both the pool and hot tub are open 24 hours and are warm enough to enjoy even in the snow, when you can sneak over swaddled in the plushy robe from your room. The pool house also contains a sunny fitness room and a sauna.

In the morning a continental breakfast is served in the breakfast room as a small buffet or can be delivered to your room in a vintage-style aluminum lunchbox, complete with a thermos of steaming coffee and a copy of the *New York Times*.

Price categories for rooms are divided into high and low seasons; low season runs from early November through mid-May.

Note: If you love visiting the Berkshires, check out the entry on **Lenox, Massachusetts,** in chapter 7, and the entry on **Cranwell Resort** (p. 162).

GETTING AROUND

The Bonanza bus drops passengers off at the Williams Inn (✆ 413/458-2665) on the green on Main Street in Williamstown, about 5 miles from Porches. They can call a cab for you at the front desk. You can also try **American Cab Co.** (✆ 413/662-2000), **Berkshire Livery Service** (✆ 413/662-2609), or **Veteran's Taxi** (✆ 413/663-8300).

Though North Adams may not be loaded with things to do, it is easily navigated **on foot.** Careful planning before you head out is wise since the few stops you may want to make in town may be relatively spread out. If you need a **cab,** the Porches staff can call one for you.

The Berkshires have a lot to offer—if you have the time and means to explore further. This is one of those instances where renting a car once you're here is the smart, economical, and expedient way to get around and see the sights. **Enterprise-Rent-A-Car** is right in town and will pick you up from the hotel or even from the bus stop in Williamstown. Their 50%-off weekend rates for Friday-through-Monday rentals (closed Sun) start at less than $20 a day (303 State St.; ✆ 413/664-7620; www.enterprise.com).

WHAT TO DO

MASS MoCA   More than a century before housing large-scale works of art, the 27 buildings that currently make up the complex were built for Arnold Print Works, a textile printer, around 1872. In its heyday, Arnold was the largest finisher of cotton cloth in North America and the largest employer in North Adams, its workers living across the street, where Porches now stands. When the company was forced to

Events: MASS MoCA Saturday Nights

Saturday nights often host professional musicians, modern dancers, or singers or a weekend-long film festival. Check MoCa's special-events schedule online (www.massmoca.org).

close its doors in 1942, the building was taken over by Sprague Electric Company. When that company left town in 1985, North Adams's economy—and industrious spirit—took a nosedive. A year later a group of curators from nearby Williams College Museum of Art was introduced to the space by the mayor, who had heard they were looking for a space to exhibit works too unwieldy for traditional galleries. MASS MoCA opened its doors in 1999 (with Porches to follow in 2001), marking the beginning of the city's renaissance.

The museum presents its mission this way: "If conventional museums are boxes, MASS MoCA is an open platform—a welcoming place that encourages dynamic interchange between making and presenting art, between the visual and performing arts, and between our extraordinary historic factory campus and the patrons, workers and tenants who again inhabit it." Here the only thing polished is the floors, and interactive experience trumps order and arrangement. The statement-making art (which sometimes comes with a parental-advisory warning or two) surrounds you: suspended from the ceiling, projected on the wall, or built for you to walk inside it. The hulking old mill is just large enough to hold it. Exhibits, which range from pop art and found objects to collage, graffiti, and multimedia, are playful and often political. Some visitors may be frustrated by the strong countercultural slant, but everyone will find something to talk about later. 87 Marshall St. ⊘ 413/662-2111. www.massmoca.org. Admission $10 adults, $8 students, $4 children 6-16, free for children 5 and under. Sept 7-June 30 daily 10am-6pm; July 1-Sept 6 daily 11am-5pm.

What to Do Nearby

Appalachian Trail   A trailhead for this scenic Georgia-to-Maine hiking trail is just 1 mile away. Ask the Porches staff to point you in the right direction.

Beaver Mill Studios   This old converted cotton mill 1½ miles down the road from Porches is now brimming with arts and culture. It's located at 189 Beaver St. at the north end of North Adams. Inside the 130,000-square-foot, brick-and-stone structure you'll find:

Contemporary Artists Center (CAC) is a nonprofit artists center with five galleries. Check the calendar for 3-day workshops on print-making, painting, video arts, and more (∅ **413/664-8686;** www.the cac.org; May–Nov Thurs–Sun; hours vary).

At the **Dark Ride Project,** viewers take a seat and travel through "creative space" on a space-age vehicle called the Sensory Integrator (∅ **413/664-9550;** summer and fall Wed–Sun 11am–5pm; $10 integrator and galleries, $6 galleries only).

Drop in for a class at **Frog Lotus Yoga,** a large, airy studio with oak floors and high ceilings. Two yoga classes are offered Saturday and Sunday mornings, with more classes during the week ($12). Massage and Thai yoga bodywork are available by appointment (Studio 207; ∅ **413/664-8686;** www.froglotusyoga.com).

Natural Bridge State Park   Adjacent to the CAC, this abandoned quarry has North America's only marble dam. The "natural bridge"— created centuries ago with the melting of the glaciers—now arcs over a steep gorge and a rushing stream. Rte. 8. ∅ **413/663-6392.**

Williamstown, MA   On your way in or out of North Adams, make a stop at this quintessential college town to visit the **Williams College Museum of Art,** one of the most well-regarded college art museums in the U.S. (15 Lawrence Hall Dr., Suite 2; ∅ **413/597-2429;** www.wcma.org; Tues–Sat 10am–5pm, Sun 1–5pm; free admission). Also in town, the **Clark Art Institute** is a remarkable place in a remarkable setting. The museum, research center, and cafe sit on 140 beautiful acres, with the galleries looking out on Berkshires woods, lawns, and open fields. 225 South St. ∅ **413/458-2303.** www.clark art.edu. Admission $10, free Nov–May. Tues–Sun 10am–5pm.

Transit note: Both museums are within walking distance of the Williams Inn, the bus drop-off location.

Events: Williamstown Theatre Festival

For more than 50 years, fans of the stage have come from across the region for the vivacious main-stage productions, children's performances, and more held July and August (∅ **413/597-3400;** www.wtfestival.org).

WHERE TO EAT

Brewhaha   If you can't start your day without a full breakfast (two eggs, one meat, and a pile of potatoes)—or you just want some joe for your stroll about town—this is the spot. 20 Marshall St. ✆ **413/664-2020.** Everything on the menu under $10.

Dining at MoCA   In the early part of the day, MoCa's Lickety Split cafe serves breakfast, lunch, coffee, and ice cream. The museum's full-service restaurant, Café Latino, with its festive teal walls, serves Latin cuisine with a twist for both lunch and dinner; the backlit bar is popular for predinner drinks. Both establishments are new, created in response to museum-goers' requests. 1111 Mass MoCA Way, Building 11. ✆ **413/662-2004.** Entrees $9–$29.

Gideon's   Mediterranean cuisine from a star chef in a setting of exposed brick walls, candlelight, and a lovely bar. 34 Holden St. ✆ **413/664-9449.** www.gideonsrestaurant.com. Entrees $11–$28.

Gramercy Bistro   This chef-owned charmer offers a modern American menu based on local and organic ingredients. A list of more than 100 wines (by the glass, half bottle, or bottle) complements starters like Maryland crab cakes with wasabi vinaigrette and entrees such as the smoky paella with jumbo shrimp in a spicy red Thai curry sauce. 23 Marshall St. ✆ **413/663-5300.** Entrees $14–$21.

Milan @ 55 Main   Northern Italian considered by many to be the best in the Berkshires. Crisp white tablecloths, a checkered floor, and great pasta. 55 Main St. ✆ **413/664-9955.** www.milan55main.com. Entrees $17–$23.

WHERE TO SHOP

Hardware Shop   MASS MoCA's mega–gift shop of books, clothing, jewelry, toys for kids and pets, throws, housewares, cards, and office knickknacks. MASS MoCA. ✆ **413/664 4481,** ext. 8140.

Papyri Books   Used and out-of-print books for browsers, collectors, and anyone who likes a cup of tea and a comfy chair. First Friday art and music events on the first Friday of every month and wine and cheese readings on Saturday evenings. 49 Main St. ✆ **413/622-2099.** www.papyribooks.com.

Porches To-Go   In a tiny alcove across from the check-in desk, peruse the assortment of Porches signature items, travel candles, bath goodies, and artistic boutique-chic pick-me-ups. The Porches Inn.

Skidoo Vintage Modern   Midcentury clothing and accessories. 38 Eagle St. ✆ **413/664-8007.**

The Noguchi Museum

32-37 Vernon Blvd., Long Island City, NY 11106
☎ 718/204-7088 · www.noguchi.org

Getting there: N or W subway line to Broadway stop in Astoria, Queens, followed by a rather unscenic walk down 10 long Astoria blocks.

Alternate transit: A **Noguchi Weekend Shuttle Bus** ($10 round-trip, does not include admission) picks up passengers in front of Asia Society (Park Ave. and 70th St.) in NYC and runs a loop to the museum and back. Pickups at Asia Society are on the half-hour from 12:30 to 3:30pm, and leave Noguchi to come back to the city on the hour from 1 to 5pm. The 25-person bus loads on a first-come basis.

Subways: N, W to Broadway—4 stops into Queens.

Approximate travel time: 30 min. from midtown Manhattan.

Schedule: Subways run frequently throughout the day.

Hours: Wed-Fri 10am-5pm; Sat and Sun 11am-6pm.

Cost: $5 for adults, $2.50 for students and seniors.

Perched on a small triangle of land like a pelican on a pier post, the Noguchi Museum stands out. Never mind that its minuscule square footage nearly gets lost amid Long Island City's industrial landscape. But you'll find instant peace among masterful sculptural works in a building that seamlessly blends two indoor floors with a sculpture garden out back.

Isamu Noguchi (1904–88) was destined to live a life of contrasts. The child of an American mother and Japanese father, he was born in L.A., grew up in Japan, and then moved to Indiana with his family as a teen. (Talk about culture shock.) The varied textures and materials Noguchi later chose during his decades as a world-renowned sculptor reflect these disparate early influences. A tall piece, chiseled and raw, stands vulnerable, while another is smooth as bathwater. A gleaming, striped marble serpent shares the room with rough, pocked granite, weathered bronze, and silky orbs of clay. Some pieces rise up from the wooden floors; one seems to creep and crawl across it. Still others sprout from primitive blocks of tawny wood. In a piece titled

Tip

Although the museum is open year-round, the pieces in the outdoor sculpture garden are sometimes covered for protection when the weather turns crummy.

Remembrance, interlocking pieces of mahogany balance in the air. Downstairs, a lone stone is pierced with an aluminum bar.

A piece called *Walking Void #2*—shaped from black Swedish granite— tests the urge to touch to the max: What would it feel like under your fingers—dull or slick, soft or unforgiving? In winter you'll imagine it warm—with radiant heat from some hot inner core. On a blazing summer day, though, you can only imagine that it's a cool stone just plucked from a wandering river. These are the peaceful reflections that come from a few hours spent among this artist's nonliteral art.

Also known for his furniture and lighting designs, Noguchi's public works grace playgrounds, plazas, fountains, and parks throughout the globe. A quiet, second-floor room placed off to one side holds a memorial to those who died in Hiroshima.

GETTING AROUND
To get to the museum: From the N and W Broadway stop in Queens, walk 9 blocks west along Broadway toward the East River. Make a left on Vernon Boulevard and another left on 33rd Road to find the museum's entrance.

WHAT TO DO NEARBY
Socrates Sculpture Park   Just down the road and right on the water, this former landfill is now landscaped parkland filled with large-scale works by emerging artists. It's open 10am to sunset. On Wednesday evenings in July and August, the park shows films at sunset. 32-01 Vernon Blvd., at Broadway. ∅ 718/956-1819. www.socratessculpturepark.org. Free admission.

Museum of the Moving Image   If you don't mind the trek back up Broadway, 5 blocks past the N/W subway station is this homage to the big screen. Make sure you're interested in the current exhibits—the core content on the nuts and bolts of TV and moviemaking is a bit lackluster. From Friday through Sunday catch a film screening, included in the $10 admission. *FYI:* The museum is just a block from the G, R, and V trains. 35 Ave. at 36th St. ∅ 718/784-0077. www.moving image.us.

Events: Art for Families & Art for Tots
Hands-on workshops for families with children ages 2 to 11 take place on select Saturday mornings. For more information, go to **www.noguchi.org**.

WHERE TO EAT

Pick up the makings for a picnic on your way to the museum as you stroll down Astoria's Broadway. Rainey Park is across the street and a block south of the museum. You can dine on the grass with a skyline view of the city. It's not the fanciest patch of park in the city, but on a nice day, it does the trick.

Bel Aire Diner   A hulking, 24-hour beacon of Greek and American comfort foods, this sprawling diner is the obvious choice for juicy gyros or a BLT with fries. Consistently crowned the "Best Diner in Queens" by the New York *Daily News*. 31-91 21st St., at Broadway. ⓒ 718/ 721-3160. Entrees $8.95–$17; sandwiches are less.

The Museum Café   Just a small bar along one wall of the bookstore; choose from muffins, brownies, biscotti, juice, coffee, and a few assorted sandwiches.

WHERE TO SHOP

Costco   Shopping here may be the polar opposite of a visit to the minimalist Noguchi museum, yet, ironically enough, it's right up the street. *Note:* You'll need a membership card to get inside. 32-50 Vernon Blvd. ⓒ 718/267-3680.

The Museum Shop   Carries books and paper goods, Nelson clocks, a few pieces of signature furniture like the Noguchi Rocking Stool ($595–$650), and a selection of the artist's wasabi paper Akuri light sculptures (if $725 strikes you as steep for a floor lamp, IKEA does knockoffs). The shop closes 30 minutes before the museum does.

Storm King Art Center

Old Pleasant Hill Rd., Mountainville, NY 10953
ⓒ **845/534-3115** • www.stormking.org

Getting there: Shortline Bus package from Port Authority to Storm King includes round-trip bus fare and admission to the museum. Drops off and picks up at entrance to grounds.
Subways: A, C, E to 42nd St./Port Authority or N, Q, R, S, W, 1, 2, 3, 7 to 42nd St./Times Sq.
Approximate travel time: 1 hr., 25 min.
Schedule: The bus to Storm King leaves Port Authority at 10am. The return bus leaves Storm King at 4:47pm. Times change, so check schedule to be sure.
Hours: Apr 1–Oct 29 Wed–Sun 11am–5:30pm; Oct 30–Nov 13 Wed–Sun 11am–5pm.
Cost: Package cost is $36 for bus transportation and admission.

True fans of sculpture—especially gigantic, free-form sculpture unencumbered by museum walls—will enjoy the more than 100 works strategically situated throughout the 500 acres of former farmland now known as Storm King Art Center. Founded in 1960 by two private owners, the carefully landscaped lawns, hills, fields, and woodlands were originally intended to house a museum of works by Hudson Valley painters. But the owners' growing interest in sculpture led to a 1966 shopping spree in which they acquired 13 massive sculptures from upstate New York artist David Smith. The pieces were hauled back to Storm King and placed where they would best play off and interact with the stunning landscape.

By 1972, Storm King was commissioning site-specific works that would form permanent and meaningful relationships to their immediate natural surroundings and the distant mountain views. So as the land changes through the seasons, so does the art—the way it shines in the rain, glints in the sun, or stretches skyward from a mound of snow on an icy-gray November day.

When you first arrive at this unusual sculpture park, walk through the main gate and redeem your Shortline pass for a ticket and a map of the grounds. (The booth workers are used to ushering cars through, not pedestrians, so ignore any quizzical looks.) Your first instinct may be to head to the building up on the hill; it can be disorienting to look around and see only fields and sculpture without some major signage screaming at you about what is where and which is the right way to go. But at Storm King, there is no right way or wrong way—and there's very little signage to detract from the art. And all that's in the building on the hill is the museum bookstore and a small exhibit of photographs and sculptures. The building has no restrooms—they're outside in back—and no air-conditioning for those 93°F (34°C) days. So, forget the house on the hill. Just have a seat in the grass and plot your course.

A tram begins its 25-minute loop through Storm King at noon—a half-hour after your arrival—and stops for a quick look at most of the major structures. At several points you can hop off—Andy Goldworthy's 2,278-foot-long serpentine stone wall is a popular stop—and hop on again when the trolley comes back around. The only narration on the tram tour is a

> **Tip**
>
> If you're visiting in the summer, you may want to bring along bug repellent, sunblock, and sunglasses, and wear good walking shoes. A visit to Storm King can make for a long, hot day–or, in the off season, a long, *cold* day.

Events: "Highlights of the Collection" Walking Tours

Tours leave from the museum building at 2 and 4pm daily and are free with admission. These docent-guided tours last 45 minutes to 1 hour.

---

deep-voiced announcement of the sculpture's artist, material, and year of creation. To me, it's the only narration you need. The works, if you have an ear for them, tend to speak for themselves. Of course, to enhance your ride, you can also rent an **acoustiguide**—an audio tour with commentary from the museum's chairman and president, director and chief curator, the curator, and the artists themselves—in the Museum Shop for $5.

You can also tour the grounds on foot, strolling the trails and cutting across the plushy lawn. The grass is soft and the grounds are immaculately maintained, which makes it a great place to kick off your shoes and walk barefoot.

One note of frustration: The art center seems to have a larger rulebook than The Met. It *is* a museum after all, but the freeness of the open land and the playfully colossal art make the long list of rules feel somewhat stifling. No pets, no radios, no Frisbees, no ball playing, no "recreational items" of any kind. No eating anywhere but the one picnic area (in 500 acres!). And absolutely no touching the art or climbing on any of the sculptures. Yes, I understand that the many guidelines are in place to protect the art, the center, and the guests. All the same, this is an inspired marriage of art and nature, and the combination can result in the kind of playful spontaneity you won't see at The Met. (The rules would hit less harshly, too, were the staff a bit more friendly.)

Still, for sculpture buffs who love the idea of a museum with grass floors and a sky ceiling, there is no better place to roam. That core group of 13 David Smith sculptures began a collection that now includes modern works by revered sculptors Alexander Calder, Henry Moore, and Louise Nevelson. Other contemporary artists whose work is featured are Magdalena Abakanowicz, Alice Aycock, Mark di Suvero, Robert Grosvenor, Isamu Noguchi, Nam June Paik, and Ursula von Rydingsvard.

Some might complain that the pieces are repetitive and seldom go beyond the red, brown, silver, and black color scheme. Storm-King-o-philes will gush, however, about the harmony among the pieces, the brilliance of each placement, and the appreciation for a space where art is free to fulfill an artist's true desires—no matter how grand and far-reaching.

GETTING AROUND

The tram will take you in a loop around the grounds; feel free to explore the rest on foot.

WHERE TO EAT

Cold drinks and snacks (chips, candy bars, ice cream) are available from vending machines in the North Parking Area. No other food is sold on the grounds, so pack a picnic lunch and plenty of water. Unfortunately, you'll be confined to the picnic benches in the same parking area; no food (and, god forbid, no cooking!) is allowed on the grounds.

WHERE TO SHOP

The small shop in the museum building sells mostly books, along with some postcards and gifts.

Kid-Friendly Escapes

Y OU DON'T HAVE TO GO FAR FROM MANHATTAN TO FIND PLENTY OF transit-friendly, kid-friendly destinations. Even if you do have a car, nuisances like tolls, gas prices, parking, car seats, and weekend traffic can put a damper on a trip before it even gets underway.

Not having to drive frees you to focus on the tykes. The bus or train ride makes it easy to read together, play games, or work on a simple craft project. Or you can start a new book while your child checks out the latest handheld videogame sensation. Compose an easy-to-carry grab bag (or backpack) filled with activities and snacks for each child. And lay down the laws of good bus behavior before you get on board. Kids are often better behaved while riding among strangers than they are in their own vehicles.

The destinations in this chapter—museums, amusement parks, open places to run and play—make excellent getaways for kids who normally live and breathe a multiborough existence. Especially once you've made the liberating decision to leave that hassle-heavy beast of the highway at home.

Rye Playland

Playland Pkwy., Rye, NY 10580
✆ **914/813-7000** • www.ryeplayland.org

Getting there: Metro-North from Grand Central to Rye then the Rte. no. 75 bus from Rye station to the park.
Subways: 4, 5, 6, 7, S to Grand Central/42nd St.
Approximate travel time: 44 min., plus 12-min. bus ride.
Schedule: Trains leave Grand Central twice an hour on weekends and return from Rye on a similar schedule.
Season/Hours: May–Sept; weekends-only in the off-months. Hours change by the day but run noon–midnight in high season. Check website or call for hours on specific days; closed Mon except holidays.

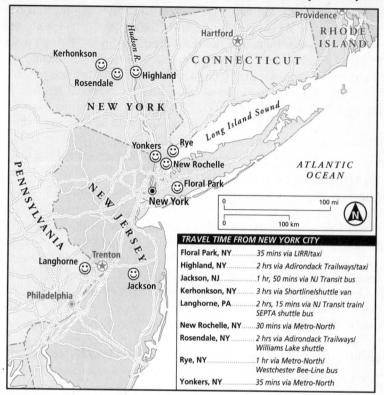

TRAVEL TIME FROM NEW YORK CITY

Floral Park, NY	35 mins via LIRR/taxi
Highland, NY	2 hrs via Adirondack Trailways/taxi
Jackson, NJ	1 hr, 50 mins via NJ Transit bus
Kerhonkson, NY	3 hrs via Shortline/shuttle van
Langhorne, PA	2 hrs, 15 mins via NJ Transit train/ SEPTA shuttle bus
New Rochelle, NY	30 mins via Metro-North
Rosendale, NY	2 hrs via Adirondack Trailways/ Williams Lake shuttle
Rye, NY	1 hr via Metro-North/ Westchester Bee-Line bus
Yonkers, NY	35 mins via Metro-North

Cost: Train fare is $14 round-trip off-peak for adults, $6.50 for children ages 5-11; bus fare is $1.75 cash each way. Playland admission is free; rides and activities have separate fees (see below).

Rye Playland's amusement park, beach, and boardwalk will entertain the kids, but for adults, it's a wonderful living museum of Art Deco design. Created by Westchester County in 1927, Playland's manicured lawns, boating lake, and some of the rides are pushing 8 decades old. Maybe your grandma smooched with her boyfriend in the dark tunnel of an old ride—back when they called the place Rye Beach.

Most of the rides are more country fair than if-you-dare, but that's part of the charm. Bring bathing suits for the beach, pack a picnic, take a pedal boat across the lake, and plan to stroll the boardwalk, with views of Long Island Sound. Clean, friendly, and adorably scenic, Playland has the strange distinction of being the only government-owned-and-operated amusement park in America.

Some scoff at the old-fashioned ways of Rye Playland—the pint-size rides, the single big coaster. And it's true: Today's sky-high expectations for slick rides that loop, dip, and reach speeds of up to 120 mph make Playland look like a set for a 1930s movie. (Or 1980s: Tom Hanks got hexed here in *Big*.) Of the 50 or so rides, more than half are for little kids. Also, Rye Playland—proudly listed on the National Register of Historic Places—has no intention of becoming the next Six Flags (or even 4½ Flags). Westchester remains content with its little park where families sunbathe and have fun along the wide wooden boardwalk with benches and lampposts that makes an embracing arc around the sea.

TRANSIT FACTS & GETTING AROUND

Mid-May through September, Metro-North's Playland package from Grand Central (or 125th St./Harlem) includes discount round-trip rail fare, a Fun Card, which is good toward admission to the park's rides, $1 pool/beach discount coupon, and shuttle bus to and from Playland. The cost is $30 for adults, $19 for children 5 to 11, and $14 for children under 5 (available at Grand Central).

One of Westchester's Bee-Line buses shuttles from the Metro-North station in Rye to Playland. The bus stops at the station 6 minutes after the train drops you off and picks up at Playland 18 minutes before the train leaves for New York City. For more information, go to beelinebus.westchestergov.com or call ✆ **914/813-7777.**

WHAT TO DO

Seven of the **rides** at Playland date from before 1930. The beautiful, 66-horse carousel (plus three chariots) is one; another is the Dragon Coaster. The latter is the park's most popular ride: a wooden coaster that shoots cars down right into the fuming mouth of the dragon—and comes out the creature's other end.

Teens gravitate toward the Zombie Castle, a nice long ride through the dark, and the goriest of the three new dark rides. And the almost unbraked Crazy Mouse never fails to jolt even the savviest coaster fanatic.

Some rides are pure ambience and very little motion; others are jerky scramblers. There is plenty for children of all shapes, sizes, and levels of courage. Kiddyland is filled with miniversions of the adult rides (a coaster, a carousel, bumper cars, and swings) and other challenges for a total of 26 rides and activities. Some have height requirements; others simply require that Timmy can sit up on his own. You have two options for paying at Playland: a **Fun Band wristband** or a **Fun Card.** The wristband is good for 6 hours of unlimited rides and costs $35 per person. Otherwise, you can buy a plastic Fun Card that uses points per

Events: July 4th Weekend

The park stays open late for evening fireworks celebrations. A special train and bus schedule accommodates the crowd.

ride instead of cash. Major rides cost between 2 and 4 points; Kiddyland rides, 2 points. The Fun Card, which also allows you to check your point balance, comes preloaded with 20 points ($24) or 36 points ($28), or you can spend a dollar a point for 1 to 19 points. See website for point specials.

Hunker down on the sandy, spacious **beach** that fronts the Long Island Sound. Music, a bit of honky-tonk, and restaurants complete the picture. It's open 10am to 6:30pm (weekends-only at the end of May through June; daily from then through Labor Day). Beach umbrellas and chairs can be rented for $3 a pop plus a $10 deposit. The beach is $3 for adults, $2 for kids. The Olympic-size pool nearby is an alternative: $4 for adults, $3 for kids. Lockers are available for 75¢.

Make time for the 19-hole **miniature golf** course in the shadow of the Playland tower ($4 per person). Or, if you're tired, take it easy in a two-person **pedal boat** ($8 per hour plus a $5 deposit) or a pedal boat built for four ($10 per hour plus a $5 deposit). The **Lake Cruise** might float your boat if pedaling seems a chore. It's a mere 10- to 15-minute ride on a retro pontoon boat, and there's usually a decent breeze ($3).

Check out one of the **free music** revues—from big band and blues to an Elvis tribute, depending on the day—daily throughout the summer and the

Midweek Escape

Weekends and holidays get very crowded here, but few people come during the week, even in midsummer. Try a Wednesday-night escape—tame crowds yet just festive enough with the boost in attendance for the 9:15pm fireworks.

free concert series on Thursday evenings in August. Bring a blanket to sit on the lawn. Captain Hook's on the Boardwalk by the Pier offers evening shows at 7:30pm. Younger kids can sing along at the free daily **puppet shows** at Kiddyland's Tiny Tot Theater.

With older kids, you can stay to see the **fireworks** that shimmer and fall over the water every Wednesday and Friday at 9:15pm in July and August. Get the best views from the boardwalk by the Log Flume and Playland Plunge.

Playland's **Ice Casino** draws folks in from the cold. From fall to spring, the ice-skating pavilion offers open skating times, lessons, and hockey games. Friday evening is Party Night and Saturday evening is Family Skate.

WHERE TO EAT

Throughout the park, you'll find pizza, cotton candy, and other amusement-park staples. **Burger King, Nathan's, Ranch 1,** and **Caliente Mexpress** also have their own Playland outposts. Or you can use the charcoal grills in Playland's picnic area overlooking Playland Lake to make your own meals.

Captain Hook's Fry-'em-up seafood on the boardwalk. Clams, cod, and a view of the Long Island Sound. Sandwiches $3-$5.50.

Hudson River Museum

511 Warburton Ave., Yonkers, NY 10701
✆ **914/963-4550** · www.hrm.org

Getting there: Metro-North Hudson local line train to Glenwood Station.
Subways: 4, 5, 6, 7, S to 42nd St/Grand Central.
Approximate travel time: 35 min., plus 10-min. walk.
Schedule: Trains leave once an hour throughout the day.
Hours: The museum is open Wed-Sun noon–5pm and in summer only, Fri 5–8pm. Planetarium shows are 12:30, 1:30, 2:30, and 3:30pm Sat-Sun; Fri summer shows, 7pm.
Cost: $12 round-trip off-peak train fare. Museum admission is $5 for adults and $3 for children and seniors. Planetarium admission is $2 for adults and $1 for children and seniors. The museum, including the 7pm planetarium show, is free Fri 5-8pm in summer.

Lots of museums claim to have something for everyone, but this one truly does. Kids, parents, and grandparents will have plenty to see and do at this community museum, which is part historic mansion, part art gallery, and part science exhibition space and planetarium.

When it opened in 1924, the Victorian-style Glenview Mansion housed the museum, a creation of John Trevor, a Renaissance man who loved both art and astronomy. The planetarium used to be in the dining room. Now, six rooms of the mansion have been meticulously restored with period furnishings on permanent loan from the Metropolitan Museum of Art. Paintings from the Hudson River School decorate the walls. Delicately painted tiles on a faux fireplace depict fairy tales—entertainment for children a century ago. And in the billiard

Events: Astronomy Day

Every spring the planetarium's day to shine includes telescope viewing and workshops. The schedule is set early in the year; for details, call ✆ **914/963-4550** or go to www.hrm.org.

room, kids today can play with 19th-century versions of dominoes and pickup sticks.

Head into the main museum building, which dates from the late 1960s, to check out the rotating displays of contemporary art. Neon lighting, interpretive videos, and Tiffany lamps have at some point all found a home in this space. Regional artists are often featured.

But the true highlight here is science, not art. The dynamic, interactive Hudson Riverama offers an intimate portrait of New York City's favorite river. Screens display video panoramas of various sites along the 315-mile-long body of water that stretches from the Big Apple up to Albany and beyond, into the Adirondacks. Put on headphones to listen to songs about the Hudson. Pick up binoculars and look out the window at the river itself. Peer into aquariums to see what swims beneath the surface. (Who knew that seahorses lived in the Hudson?) Kids will appreciate the simplified descriptions of the river and its creatures that appear at their eye level, beneath the usual text placards. They can also get worksheets to fill with rubber stamps of animals as they walk through the exhibit (adults can do it, too).

The biggest star of this museum is the 128-seat **Andrus Planetarium.** In addition to general audience shows about celestial events, the Hudson River's formation, and Native American legends, the planetarium puts on age-specific shows for preschoolers and young readers. The free Friday-night presentations in the summer are popular with teens looking for a dark, cozy, and cheap date. There are also regular Spanish-language shows. Most programs last about 45 minutes. Call ✆ **914/963-2139** or check the website for a current schedule of stargazer shows.

Don't forget to admire the views outside the museum, too. The museum's tranquil setting on a hill overlooking its namesake makes it seem a lot farther than 45 minutes away from the city. It's small enough to see in a few hours, but the planetarium alone might have the kids asking to return soon.

TRANSIT FACTS & GETTING AROUND

Sit on the left side of the train (facing forward) on the ride from NYC for fabulous views of the Hudson. From Glenwood Station, exit on

Glenwood Avenue and make a left onto Ravine Avenue, which leads to Trevor Park. Walk up through the park to the museum.

You can also take Metro-North's Hudson train line to the Yonkers station. Trains run often (every half-hour), but you'll need to take a taxi to the museum. The ride will only set you back about $5, but taxis aren't readily available from the station and can be tough to spot since they're often unmarked. This might be a good time to call a car service if you don't feel like walking and want more train time options. Try **Family Car Service** (✆ 914/963-2222) or **Yonkers Limousine Car Service** (✆ 914/476-8080).

WHERE TO EAT

Museum Cafe   Stop for a bite to eat and to watch the boats sailing by on the Hudson. A variety of low-priced options (about $5.50) are available, from hummus to grilled cheese to chicken parmesan. Wed-Thurs noon-3pm; Fri-Sun noon-4pm.

WHERE TO SHOP

Hudson River Museum Gift Shop   For many years, the gift shop was in the colorfully zany mock-up of a bookstore created by the artist Red Grooms. Now the shop's amazing selection of merchandise takes center stage and you can see Grooms's art inside the museum. Leave some time to browse among the many and varied gifts, including astronomy books, educational toys, decorative mirrors, embroidered pillows, and cool greeting cards.

Williams Lake

Binnewater Rd., Rosendale, NY 12472
✆ 845/658-3101 • www.willylake.com

Getting there: Adirondack Trailways bus line from Port Authority to Rosendale, NY, then call for a free pickup.
Subways: A, C, E to Port Authority or N, Q, R, S, W, 1, 2, 3, 7 to 42nd St./ Times Sq.
Approximate travel time: 1 hr., 45 min. bus ride, plus 10-min. ride to resort.

Schedule: Buses leave Port Authority once or twice an hour and return from Rosendale on a similar schedule.

Cost: Bus fare is $41 round-trip; rates start at $149 per night per person for the weekend.

Whatever happened to that cute little place where your parents (or grandparents) used to spend a week every summer by the lake? It's still there, the same as ever. Which, depending on your taste, can be either a very good thing or too fuddy-duddy for words.

A little bit *Dirty Dancing*, a little bit summer camp, Williams Lake will make you feel as if you're erasing decades from your life. It happens as soon as you're shown to your room at this 1950s-fabulous throwback to a simpler place and time.

Some call Williams Lake "The Poconos of Upstate, NY." It's one of those rare holdouts, a mountain resort that can take you back to the good old days—or it can take you there for the very first time. Imagine a little dance hall and corner bar in the basement lounge. A dining room that serves four-course dinners (all included in the price), with a lake view. The kind of place where canoes and rowboats wait by the shore, ready for you to push them off whenever the whim should strike. There are woods for exploring, fish for catching, a video-game room for rainy days, and lots of the house dessert—Scandinavian pudding—because diets don't matter around these parts. You'll even find a new golf academy, with 3-hour sessions to improve your game ($45). In the morning, wake up to a sunrise over the lake and 600 acres of peace and quiet, only to do it all over again.

It's brought to you by a dedicated group that believes that family fun doesn't have to mean flashing lights, moving parts, and high-speed Internet-meets-Disneyland. And they've been proving it every year since 1929. There's an undeniable reverence here for the way people used to pass the time—and it's terribly contagious. The lake remains a popular and economical getaway for families and family reunions, with a gracious staff that wants only for guests of all ages to have a great day, every day.

Events: Williams Lake

Check their online calendar for **theme weekends** devoted to big-band music, a murder mystery, and the like. Come to the lake for **holiday weekends** like Thanksgiving dinner with all the trimmings or a retro-style New Year's Eve party.

GETTING AROUND

The express bus stops just once in New Paltz before pulling into the hardware store in Rosendale. Call when you arrive and a staff member will come pick you up.

Bring your bike and hit the trails (see chapter 2 for more on taking your bike on Metro-North) or ask about renting one from **Table Rock Tours** (✆ 845/658-7832), down the street in Rosendale.

WHAT TO DO

That depends on the season. In the summer the trout-stocked lake offers nonstop **fishing, swimming,** and **boating.** Scheduled **nature walks** and **water volleyball** are open to all. **Tennis courts, basketball, shuffleboard,** or **lessons at the golf academy** suit the sporty types. In winter bundle up and go **cross-country skiing** through the woods, **ice-skating** on the lake, **snowshoeing** along the side of the lake, or search for that perfect fireside seat in the lounge. Any time of year, the **Finnish sauna** is there for your pleasure, as are the **miles of trails** leading up to Catskills' mountain views. In the **game room,** parents can vie with kids for use of the Ping-Pong, billiards, board games, and video games.

Fishing

You'll need a fishing license before you can catch anything, so get one at **Paragon Sports** (867 Broadway; ✆ **212/989-8686**) in the city before your trip.

After dinner, relax together at the **family show**—magic, comedy, or a wildlife presentation, perhaps—complete with free popcorn. Sometimes the whole family gets caught up in square dancing or country line dancing. Then the kids go off to bed and the dance floor fills with dressed-to-two-step couples who are still crazy after all these years. General manager, Ernie Bruno, is the man behind the smooth vocal stylings of swingin' standards, disco, golden oldies, and rock of the ages. He even takes requests. This is a man who loves what he does and wants to meet and greet every guest at Williams Lake—some of whom have been coming for the past 20 years.

WHERE TO STAY

Three motel-style buildings are just steps from the main lodge. None are fancy, and all have that time-warp quality to them. But they're family-friendly, and most are nonsmoking. The Chalet building is the newest, with two huge rooms on the second floor that have balconies looking out on the lake. Rooms on the second floor with lake views and balconies are the most desirable in general.

Rates include three meals a day and use of all facilities. Gratuities are not included; there is also an extra charge for sodas and bar drinks, video games, horseback riding, ski rentals, and a few other activities.

WHERE TO EAT

Your family will have a table reserved in the main dining room, where you'll enjoy three meals a day (and not one request to help with the dishes). Four-course dinners include soup; salad; entrees like prime rib, flounder stuffed with crabmeat, or fettuccine carbonara; and a choice of old-fashioned desserts.

On hot summer days, kids can stay in their swimsuits and eat lunch on the patio. Once a week when it's nice out, everyone grabs burgers, beer, and thick slices of watermelon at a lakeside barbecue and cook-out.

New Roc City

19-33 Le Count Place, New Rochelle, NY 10801
℘ **914/637-7575** • www.newroccity.com

Getting there: Metro-North New Haven line from Grand Central to New Rochelle, NY.
Subways: 4, 5, 6, 7, S to Grand Central.
Approximate travel time: 30 min.
Schedule: Trains leave Grand Central about twice an hour and return from New Rochelle on a similar schedule.
Hours: Daily 11am–11pm (some places open as late as 2am on weekends).
Cost: Train fare is $12 round-trip off-peak for adults, $6 for children ages 5-11; activity prices vary.

This just may be the perfect rainy-day destination for restless city kids. Every day of the year, New Roc City is filled with kids celebrating birthdays, sports wins and losses, mini–family reunions, and just celebrating being a kid.

A short walk from the train station, this 1.2-million-square-foot complex can keep toddlers to teens amused for the full 12 hours it's open each day (though you and your wallet will certainly grow tired long before that threshold).

Make sure to ask about New Roc's **package deals. Wacky Wednesdays** cost $20 per person and are in effect for any 4 hours between 4 and 10pm. A wristband allows access to all rides including laser tag, bumper cars, and the Space Shot, and the Turbo Card is good for all nonredemption video games. A complimentary pizza-and-soda buffet is included from 6:30 to 8pm. **Monday Madness,** also $20 per person, runs between 4 and 10pm, but it's good for 2 hours of unlimited go-carting plus pizza and soda from the Pit Stop Café.

GETTING AROUND

New Roc City is within walking distance—about 1½ blocks—of the New Rochelle station. Follow signs or ask the station agent for directions upon arrival.

WHAT TO DO

The Fun House   A supersized arcade with hundreds of video and prize games. Kids love the MaxFlight virtual-reality roller-coaster simulator, state-of-the-art laser-tag arena, and bumper cars. Favorites? They got 'em: Dance Dance Revolution, Daytona USA, Hyper-Bowl, Pacman, air hockey, and video bowling for starters. A kiddy center has an old-fashioned carousel and a helicopter ride.

> ### Pace Yourself
> Don't try to do the whole place in 1 day—it's huge and can be pretty exhausting for anyone over 18.

Tower Space Shot Ride   On the New Roc City rooftop, this thrill ride sends kids up an 185-foot tower before they sail back down with a few bounces along the way. If they keep their eyes open, they can see Manhattan, Long Island Sound, and lots of Westchester County. Open spring and summer, weather permitting.

New Roc-n-Bowl   Glow-in-the-dark bowling with special-effect lights, sounds, and rock 'n' roll. Air-hockey tables, a concession stand, and weekend DJs, too.

New Roc Speedway   Westchester's only indoor go-cart track lets kids beat their personal best with computerized timing and scoring.

Events: Birthday Parties

New Roc Fun House will host **birthday parties** for your birthday boy or girl and a whole mess of their friends. The party starts with an interactive show and continues with eating, singing, dancing, games, and prizes. Packages include pizza, soda, a Carvel ice-cream cake, and more. Call ✆ **914/637-7575,** ext. 223, for more information. The Putting Edge also offers pizza and golf parties; call ✆ **914/632-3346** for details.

Putting Edge Mini Golf More glow-in-the-dark fun. Each hole is set up as a different adventure, from underwater sea scenes to spooky forests and medieval times. The music is loud; the competition fierce. Call ahead to reserve a tee time.

Regal Cinemas and IMAX Theater Eighteen movie theaters with stadium seating. Plus, Westchester's first and only IMAX with a six-story screen and 2-D and 3-D technology kids love.

Ice Skating Center An NHL-size skating rink with 50-foot ceilings for open skating and special events.

Rack & Cue Bigger kids test their skills on one of 25 tournament-size pool tables. There's a snack stand and a beer-and-wine bar for those old enough.

WHERE TO EAT

New Roc City has several dining options. **Galaxy Grill** is inside the Fun House. **Pit Stop Café** is inside the New Roc Speedway. **Zanaro's** offers gourmet pizzas and imported Italian pastas served in individual or family-style portions. The chain **Applebee's Neighborhood Bar and Grill** has a substantial kids' menu.

WHERE TO SHOP

There is a Modell's and a Stop & Shop as part of the complex, but if they can't redeem the game tickets they won in the arcade to buy something, the kids probably won't be interested.

Sesame Place

100 Sesame Rd., Langhorne, PA 18229
✆ **215/752-7070** · www.sesameplace.com

Getting there: NJ Transit Northeast Corridor line from Penn Station to Trenton, NJ, then the SEPTA shuttle bus from Trenton train station to Sesame Place.
Subways: 1, 2, 3 to 34th St./Penn Station or A, C, E to 34th St./Eighth Ave.
Approximate travel time: 1 hr., 24 min. train ride, plus 50-min. bus shuttle.
Schedule: Trains leave Penn Station for Trenton at least once an hour on weekends. Buses leave Trenton for Sesame Place at 25 min. after every hour. Times change, so check schedule to be sure.
Season: Early May through late Oct (weekends-only Sept-Oct).
Hours: 10am-8pm in high season (closes earlier in low season).

Cost: Train fare: $20 round-trip for adults off-peak, $9.75 round-trip for children off-peak; SEPTA shuttle bus requires exact change: $6 round-trip for adults, $1 for children.
Park admission: $40; free for children under 2.

This is *the* place to eat breakfast with Big Bird, do the chicken dance with Elmo, or get a big blue hug from Grover. Sesame Place is the nation's only theme park based on the award-winning, 25-year-old show *Sesame Street*. To meet these "friends" in person and spend a day in their world can be an experience on par with a trip to Disney—yet it's less than 2 hours from home.

The park is perfect for kids ages 4 through 7 who feel comfortable in the water. Littler ones can splash in many of the play areas, but there's a lot that will be out of reach for them. Every corner of the 14-acre park has something going on though, from live shows and parades to thrill rides, water rides, face painting, and photo ops with the lovable roaming characters—including the newest one, Baby Bear.

TRANSIT FACTS & GETTING AROUND

From the Trenton train station, you can also take a cab to Langhorne instead of hopping the 50-minute SEPTA bus. Fare to Sesame Place or the Sheraton is about $25 and takes about 15 minutes.

New Jersey Transit offers a package that includes a round-trip ticket from any point on the Northeast Corridor Line and a $4 savings coupon off theme park admission. SEPTA shuttle service runs between Trenton Train Station and Sesame Place for $6 each way for adults and $1 for children. Purchase the package at Newark Penn Station, New York Penn Station, Hoboken Terminal, and from ticket agents and ticket vending machines along the Northeast Corridor Line. Contact NJ Transit at ✆ **800/626-RIDE** or SEPTA at ✆ **215/580-7800.**

At the park, stroller and wheelchair rentals are available.

WHAT TO DO

More than a dozen **water rides, slides, fountains,** and **pools** give the whole family a chance to cool off. Bump leisurely along in an inner tube on Big Bird's Rambling River or pile into a large raft to brave the six-story-high Sky Splash ride, where you'll glide under an 8-foot rubber duckie before taking a plunge to the bottom. Of the high-and-dry **rides and attractions,** the Vapor Trail steel roller coaster is the park's biggest thrill. (It's one of only several nonwater rides; children must be at least 7 years old to ride alone.) Another popular stop is Big Bird's Balloon Race, where everyone can appreciate the breezy views from hot-air-balloon-shaped cars that lift you up and away. And if the tykes have tired of the teacups at Grover's World Twirl, scale Cookie Mountain, join in Ernie's Bed Bounce, or count the 60,000 plastic balls in the Count's Ballroom. A full-size, outdoor re-creation of Sesame Neighborhood as it appears on TV includes a play firehouse with coats and boots for dressing up.

Among the live shows, the **"Rock Around the Block" parade** marches to a dancing beat, starring every character in the park. Don't miss the chance to wave to Prairie Dawn, Telly Monster, and Zoe Ballerina.

Why rush home? Purchase Elmo's Two-Day Ticket and receive 2 days' admission for the price of one.

A few rules: Large ($7) and small ($5) lockers can be rented for the day to store essentials. Major credit cards are accepted at most vendors (no personal checks, however), and ATMs are available in the park.

Swim diapers are mandatory for diaper-wearers and appropriate swim attire is required on all water attractions. Bring water shoes, too; if you don't have them, you can buy them at the park.

No pets, picnic lunches, coolers, radios, or alcoholic beverages are permitted through the park gates. Smoking is limited to designated areas only.

What to Do Nearby

If your kids like Sesame Place, they may also like the **Crayola Factory** ($\oslash$ **610/515-8000;** www.crayola.com) in Easton, about 1½ hours away. You'll enter a colorful, creative space where the daily activities might include T-shirt making, storytelling, spin art, and demonstrations about how crayons and markers are made. Also on-site, the **National Canal Museum** has a neat model-train exhibit. Nearby **Hugh Moore Park** draws families to its mule-drawn canal boat ride and the Easton Museum of PEZ dispensers. Several restaurants are in town, and a

> ### Rainy Days
>
> If the skies open up on the day you visit, Sesame Place offers a "Sunny Day Guarantee": If it rains continuously for an hour or more, Sesame Place will give you a free ticket to come back to the park another day during the season.

local cab service can zip you to nearby hotels such as the Holiday Inn Express. Public transportation is available on Trans-Bridge Bus Lines from Port Authority to the bus station in Easton, Pennsylvania, half a block from the Crayola Factory.

WHERE TO STAY

Sheraton Bucks Count   The closest hotel to Sesame Place, it's just across the street from the park. The hotel provides a free shuttle, so you don't have to cross the highway on foot. The shuttle guarantees pickup every half-hour, but usually runs more frequently. The hotel's indoor pool and health club are a welcome respite after the park. Kids under 10 eat free at the restaurant. From the hotel, you can walk to a slew of suburban stores and restaurants; a Burger King, Boston Market, Taco Bell, a pizzeria, and Krispy Kreme are all within a block or so of the hotel. Lodging packages, available through Sesame Place, include accommodations and 2-day park passes. 400 Oxford Valley Rd. ✆ 215/547-4100. www.sheraton.com.

WHERE TO EAT

Throughout the park, eateries and ice-cream places serve summer favorites for all ages. An additional ticket is required for **Dining with Big Bird and Friends,** a special, buffet-style breakfast or dinner hosted by costumed characters. If the kids can't get enough of those larger-than-life friends they've seen on TV, this is an easy way to get some extra one-on-one time. The **Sesame Café** is an air-conditioned dining room with an expanded menu, serving club sandwiches, grilled-chicken Caesar salads, and chicken parm with penne pasta. **Food Factory** has outdoor seating with pizzas, chicken fajitas, and more.

WHERE TO SHOP

With so many adorable things to buy, you won't leave the park empty-handed. Clothing, plush toys, character-shaped balloons, and family caricatures are just a few things that might fill up your shopping bag. If the kids forgot their swim shoes or sunblock—even their swim trunks—**Trader Bert's Treasures** will suit them right up.

Queens County Farm Museum

73-50 Little Neck Pkwy., Floral Park, NY 11004
✆ **718/347-3276** • www.queensfarm.org

Getting there: LIRR from Penn Station to Little Neck and a taxi 2½ miles to museum.
Subways: 1, 2, 3 to 34th St./Penn Station or A, C, E to 34th St./Eighth Ave.
Approximate travel time: 30 min., plus a few minutes' cab ride.
Schedule: Trains leave about twice an hour during the day.
Hours: Mon-Fri 9am-5pm; Sat and Sun 10am-5pm.

Cost: $6 round-trip off-peak, plus cab fare ($5-$6 plus tip). Admission to the museum is free, though some special events have an admission charge, as do special activities (hayrides are $2, and so forth).

Although the Queens County Farm Museum is open year-round, it's at its best during special events. Every weekend in October, the museum sets up a corn maze and a seasonal vegetable stand, which adds to the agrarian atmosphere. Dating back to 1697, the 47-acre working farm holds several claims to fame. It's New York City's largest remaining tract of undisturbed farmland, it's the only working historical farm in the city, and it's the longest continuously farmed site in the state.

Its grassy fields and contented farm animals may not offer the same thrills-and-chills to children as, say, an amusement park or even a zoo. But it sounds like a barnyard and smells like the country, and many families are happy to pack a picnic and take in some fresh air. Smaller children enjoy chasing each other barefoot on the lawn, feeding the goats, *bahhh*-ing back at the sheep, and riding on a truck piled high with sweet-scented hay.

Colonial artifacts fill the farmhouse museum. Tour the house on weekends—it's cool in the summer and a fire is going in the winter. You'll sit on a bench in the kitchen and learn about traditional cooking, clothing, chores, games, and survival skills of those times. A tour of the main floor holds children's interest just long enough, as engaging tour guides try to involve them the best they can.

Also on the property are a greenhouse (the plants inside are for sale), farm vehicles, an orchard, and an herb garden. The small Museum Store sells fresh eggs and honey, and hayrides ($2) bump around the farm on weekends and during special-event days.

WHAT TO DO: EVENTS

The museum has a long list of events each year, but some offer more to do than others. While the Berry Festival, for example, fell short of berry-related fun with loose berries for sale and little else, the following events are some of the best all year. All are held rain or shine.

Children's Carnival   Just like it sounds: rides, games, hayrides, petting zoo, and kid-friendly entertainment, held in mid-April. The $8-per-person admission includes all rides.

Annual Thunderbird American Indian Mid-Summer Pow Wow   A 3-day celebration of culture at the end of July represents more than 40 Indian Nations. The area's oldest and largest powwow features intertribal Native American dance competitions, plus arts, crafts, and things to eat. Admission is $9 for adults, $4 for children.

Annual Queens County Fair with Amazing Maize Maze During this late-September fair, contests award blue ribbons for livestock, produce, and crafts. Visitors can also join in pie-eating and corn-husking contests, pig racing, hayrides, a petting zoo, carnival rides and games, and a make-your-own scarecrow station. Stop by the Bavarian Garden where Irish and German bands entertain. The 2½-acre corn maze challenges kids to find clues and solve puzzles to find their way out. Admission is $6 for adults, $3 for children.

Children's Fall Festival Come in costume for Halloween. The autumnal activities include sack races, trinkets in the haystack, pony rides, a petting zoo, and the annual haunted house. Country-western music and dancing accompany craft and food vendors. Admission is $4 per person (all ages); it's $3 extra for the haunted house (ages 4–12).

WHERE TO EAT

There is no cafe at the museum, but all events invite food vendors, who sell a mix of seasonal goodies and street-fare standards, such as funnel cake, kettle corn, ice cream, sausage, corn dogs, curly fries, and soda.

Two Hudson Valley Family Ranches

Pinegrove Dude Ranch
30 Cherrytown Rd., Kerhonkson, NY 12446
℘ **845/626-7345** · www.pinegroveranch.com

Getting there: Shortline bus from Port Authority to Kerhonkson, NY, then a free shuttle to the ranch.
Subways: A, C, E to Port Authority or N, Q, R, S, W, 1, 2, 3, 7 to 42nd St./Times Sq.
Approximate travel time: 2½–3 hr. on the bus, plus a 10-min. shuttle ride.
Schedule: Buses leave Port Authority 4 times a day and return from Kerhonkson 3 times daily.
Season: Year-round.
Cost: Bus fare is $38 round-trip.
Ranch rates: Rates start at $229 per adult and $115 per child for a 3-day, 2-night weekend package. Children 3 and under stay free.

Rocking Horse Ranch Resort
600 Rte. 44-55, Highland, NY 12528
℘ **845/691-2927** · www.rhranch.com

Getting there: Adirondack Trailways bus from Port Authority to New Paltz, NY, then a cab to the ranch.
Subways: A, C, E to Port Authority or N, Q, R, S, W, 1, 2, 3, 7 to 42nd St./Times Sq.

Approximate travel time: 1 hr., 45 min., plus 10-min. cab ride.

Schedule: Buses leave Port Authority about once an hour and return from New Paltz on a similar schedule.

Transit cost: Bus fare $38 round-trip.

Alternate Transit: You can also take the Metro-North Hudson line or Amtrak train to Poughkeepsie to get to Rocking Horse. It's also about 10 min. from the train station. On Metro-North the ride takes 1 hr., 50 min. and costs $26 round-trip off-peak for adults, $13 for children. On Amtrak the train also goes to Poughkeepsie; it's a little shorter and about the same price ($33–$44 for 1 adult and 1 child, round-trip).

Season: Year-round.

Resort rates: Rates start at $199 per adult for a 3-day, 2-night weekend package, and $75 per child. Children 3 and under stay free.

Ever send the kids off to summer camp and wish you could go along, too? Horseback rides on a sun-dappled trail, afternoon swims in the lake, and an endless daily schedule of sports, games, lessons, contests, crafts, parties, dances, and singalongs from which to choose sure sounds better than another day at the office. After dinner, snakes of smoke from a crackling bonfire fill the night air, but so do the sounds of karaoke, a high-energy magic show, a movie, or a children's comedian floating up from the downstairs lounge. Adults can join in activities just for them.

These ranches may not offer the rugged terrain and workday rigor of those in Montana or Wyoming, but here in the Shawangunk Mountains, just a couple hours from New York City, they have a beauty of their own. And they work hard to embody the Western spirit. Pinegrove, in particular, feels like a dude ranch, and—for experienced riders—offers the only cattle drive in the East. Rocking Horse keeps many gentle horses as well, but the place plays up the theme a bit slicker and feels a little less ranchy and a little more resorty.

Suit up the family in a few good pairs of Levis and head for the hills. Both ranches are all-inclusive—meals, activities, entertainment, and most equipment are covered. And both family-owned ranches have created a casual, comfortable, safe, and affordable place for families to spend time together—and apart. If the kids want to go off and play "Let's Make a Deal" at 3pm by the pool, you know where they'll be. And hey . . . the beer volleyball tournament for the adults starts right around the same time just a few steps down the hill. Getaways to the ranch are designed to be free of the hassles and worry involved in planning and financing a traditional vacation, so it's a good option for a family reunion, too.

Ranch life at both resorts overlaps a great deal. Both have an indoor pool and an outdoor pool with water slides. Both offer a load of sports, including volleyball, basketball, tennis courts, archery, riflery, a rock-climbing wall, shuffleboard, an arcade, horseback riding, fishing, and paddle boating on the lake. In the winter both get out the cross-country skis, ice skates, and snow tubes. The daily activity list for each ranch is nearly overwhelming. Pinegrove has a better hayride, but Rocking Horse has a fancier minigolf course. Pinegrove has Paintball and Lazer Tag, while Rocking Horse has a teepee village, water-skiing, a horse-drawn sleigh, and a deluxe playground. Both have a fitness center and the option of child care.

THE PINEGROVE DUDE RANCH EXPERIENCE

A small line in the Pinegrove brochure reads "Down-home friendliness is our first concern." You feel it all over this 600-acre nature preserve. One of Pinegrove's biggest strengths is the people who work there. They're not afraid to put on a big foam cowboy hat and lead some country line dancing. Even if you're just here for the weekend, the staff might already greet your kids by name because they are genuinely involved in making sure you're all having a good time. Pinegrove runs with the ranch theme, complete with Wild West decor, from the farm-animal petting zoo to an adults-only Silver Dollar Saloon that has swinging doors and a guitar wrangler in the evening. To keep current, the ranch has added a new fitness room. You can even book a Swedish massage while the kids are upstairs playing "Name That Tune" or gorging themselves in the pudding-eating contest. Overall, Pinegrove is less flashy, more personal, and very friendly and engaging.

THE ROCKING HORSE RANCH RESORT EXPERIENCE

Rocking Horse Ranch has manicured lawns. While it does the cowboy thing to some extent, Rocking Horse doesn't want its lodge to look like a hundred ranch hands have been traipsing through it all day. The lakeside minigolf course is within sight of the Big Banana Boat Rides (summer only). The indoor pool has a cool, interactive beach-ball-basketball-fountain thing in the middle, akin to what you'd find at a water park. Everything here is slightly more tidy and new and upscale. Rocking Horse Ranch is very organized and separates some of the activities for parents and kids more than Pinegrove does. The Jacuzzi is adults only, and an adult-humor comedian performs after the children's one finishes up and the kids go off to make sundaes. Overall, the people behind Rocking Horse have put a great deal into making their resort a comfortable, exciting, and pretty place to relax.

GETTING AROUND

Pinegrove offers free pickup service from the bus station in a cow-print van. Just give the ranch a call when you're getting close. For Rocking Horse, take a cab from the New Paltz bus station to the ranch ($15), which is about 10 minutes away. It's a one-cab-company town, and Glenn Stage Coach (aka **New Paltz Taxi**) is based at the bus station. Call ahead, though, to make sure one's available (℘ **845/255-1550**).

Everything you need is right on the ranch (at both ranches), so you don't need to plan any side trips. I guarantee you'll be too busy to take them anyway!

WHERE TO STAY

Each ranch offers a handful of room configurations to fit your family's size and preferences. All rooms have private bathrooms, TV, air-conditioning, and daily maid service. Some also come with sitting areas, sofa beds, minifridges, and coffeemakers.

Holiday weekends often require a 3-night minimum. There are plenty of kids who come up with just one parent; everyone fits in and everyone is welcome. Pinegrove even offers special rates for single parents and active-duty military personnel—just ask.

Note: Rocking Horse Ranch does not suggest tipping your maid or the restaurant waitstaff, whereas Pinegrove does. But you should always, of course, tip for good service.

WHERE TO EAT

You'll eat heartily at either ranch. All three meals are included in the price of your accommodations. The ranch assigns your family a table, which is yours for your stay. Menus range from steak and seafood to grilled cheese and chicken fingers—and special diet needs are easily met. Expect both buffet- and table-service-style meals, with an emphasis on the latter. Both places also host special events that feature food—pool parties with appetizers, watermelon-eating contests, marshmallow roasts, and cocktail parties.

Pinegrove's **Chuck Wagon Snack Bar,** open 10am to midnight, doesn't charge for the small burgers, baskets of fries, fruit, or ice cream should anyone get hungry between meals. Kids can order anything they want, when they want it. (They're going to get used to this. . . .) At Rocking Horse the **Cactus Grill** snack bar has a similar setup, but you will have to pay for each item. (Pinegrove's fitness center also sells Starbucks coffee for a dollar.)

WHERE TO SHOP

The gift shops stock souvenirs for the kids and any essentials you may have forgotten to bring along. Per the theme, Pinegrove's store has a more Western slant to it: No one leaves without trying on a cowboy hat, ya hear?

Six Flags Great Adventure & Hurricane Harbor

Rte. 537, Jackson, NJ 08527
Ø **732/928-1821** • www.sixflags.com/greatadventure

Getting there: NJ Transit bus no. 308 from Port Authority Gate 324 to Six Flags.

Subways: A, C, E to Port Authority or N, Q, R, S, W, 1, 2, 3, 7 to 42nd St./Times Sq.

Approximate travel time: 1 hr., 50 min.

Schedule: Buses leave Port Authority at 9:30am and 2:30pm and leave from Six Flags at 8:30 and 10pm. Times change, so be sure to check the schedule.

Season/Hours: End of Mar through the end of Oct. Park hours vary during the season. Sat in high season 10am–11pm.

Cost: $50 for transportation and theme park admission (which includes the Wild Safari); or $48 for transportation and water park admission. Children's package prices are $37 and $35, respectively. Bus transit alone is $25 per adult round-trip and $12 per child round-trip.

As soon as the snow melts, this huge New Jersey theme park entices people to leave the comfort of their homes to stand in line for hours at a time. In the last few years, Six Flags has pumped up the volume in the park. It has added new shows starring exotic animals and superheroes (though not together), a new jungle-themed **Golden Kingdom** section of the park, and the world's tallest, fastest roller coaster—**Kingda Ka.**

For New Yorkers, Six Flags is the best big-ride amusement park in the region—and it's easy to access via mass transit. It's not officially summer until you've bought four pairs of Old Navy flip-flops, panned the Hamptons, eaten a chocolate-dipped cone from the Mister Softee truck, and put Six Flags on your calendar.

TRANSIT FACTS

Ticket packages are available from NJ Transit ticket agents at Port Authority. The bus stops in front of Six Flags, and it's an easy walk to Hurricane Harbor.

GETTING AROUND

Six Flags and Hurricane Harbor are within walking distance of one another. The guided shuttle from Six Flags to Wild Safari leaves from next to the Northern Star Arena.

WHAT TO DO

Like all amusement parks, weekends on the season's fringes and week-days throughout the season are your best bets. That said, this Warner Brothers–themed park is notorious for closing certain rides when they're not running the place at full capacity—or for any other reason. On any given day, Batman & Robin: The Chiller ride may be out of commission. (Very un-superhero-y of them.) Worse, when Kingda Ka—a hydraulic-launch rocket coaster—opened in May 2005, chaos ensued. The term "opened" was used loosely—just weeks after the ride premiered, it promptly closed down for 2 months of repair work. People came in droves expecting to board the 128-mph thrillster that towers 456 feet high and is over in less than a minute. The situation improved—after plenty of media footage of disgruntled visitors. Kingda Ka is 151 feet higher than the Statue of Liberty and it absolutely dwarfs London's Big Ben—it's the tallest, fastest ride on the planet.

> **Tip**
>
> Buy your season pass at the tail end of the summer, and you can get a visit in before using it the whole next season.

The 12-acre **Golden Kingdom** caught jungle fever from Six Flag's adjacent drive-through park, Wild Safari (see below). Just walking through the Kingdom, kids will be delighted to encounter pythons, monkeys, and unusual birds. Beat the heat inside the Temple of the Tiger stadium where rare Bengals strut their stuff for up to 1,000 big-cat fans at a time. Also in the Kingdom, a massive climbing structure called Balin's Jungleland stands nearly three stories tall with different levels of bridges, towers, tunnels, cargo nets, a splash section, and a play area for toddlers. SpongeBob SquarePants has his own 3-D motion-simulator ride that treats kids to a virtual underwater adventure. And the Nitro, built in 2001, a classic steel coaster with more than a mile of track, remains extremely popular each season with kids (who

---

Events: Six Flags

The Northern Star Arena hosts **concerts** throughout the season that are free with park admission; check the online calendar of events for featured artists and dates. **Saturday-night fireworks** burst in a blaze of color over the lake from the end of June through Labor Day weekend. The park's signature "thrills by day, chills by night" **Annual Fright Fest** spans the whole month of October with a "scream park" full of Halloween shows, attractions, parties, and creepy costumed characters.

Events: Zoo Dreams

For the child who wants to be a zookeeper when he or she grows up, go behind the scenes at Wild Safari in your own private Land Rover with a personal safari tour guide. Your family will feed the giraffes and African elephants, tour the Lion Compound, and take home VIP souvenir T-shirts. The 2½- to 3-hour tour costs $100 per person and must be scheduled in advance. Tour times are 10am and 1pm Monday through Saturday when the park is open. For information and reservations, call ✆ 732/928-2000, ext. 2076.

---

are 54 inches or taller), even if Kingda Ka is nearly double the height and goes more than 40 mph faster.

Hurricane Harbor, Six Flags' wet and wild water park, has its own separate entrance and separate admission ticket. (Three-park day and season passes that include Six Flags, Wild Safari, and Hurricane Harbor are available, though it's too much to tackle both the amusement rides and the water park in 1 day.) There may be no better—or wetter—way to cool off in the tri-state area once you add up the million-gallon wave pool, one of the world's largest adventure rivers, a 54-foot tower, and nearly 20 speed slides with dark tunnels, slick curves, and sudden drops. Even the tots have splash pools and sprays built just for them.

If your kids really love animals, take the time to go through **Wild Safari,** the drive-through wild-game park next to the rides. Otherwise, Six Flags has more than enough to keep the kids entertained. Admission and guided-tour shuttle service is included with your ticket if you purchase the NJ Transit–Six Flags package deal.

Note: Now that you can purchase a bus ticket separate from your admission ticket (it used to be a packaged deal only), Six Flags addicts can buy a season pass with confidence that they can get to the park to use it ($85 for theme park and safari *or* water park; $130 for theme park, safari, *and* water park). Purchase the tickets online for a discount. Also look for online specials like Print-and-Go tickets, Early-Bird Specials for the beginning of the season, and the like.

WHERE TO STAY

Sadly, no hotels are close enough to Six Flags to be able to stay the night without using a car. All the more reason that a season pass for repeat visits might be a good idea.

WHERE TO EAT

There's no shortage of food or drinks at Six Flags. Pizza, burgers, and other kid food is served throughout the park. **Granny's Country**

Kitchen is the place for fried chicken. **Best of the West** makes a nice shredded BBQ pork sandwich. **Ted's Cheesesteaks** will pile cheese fries alongside your Philly-style sandwich. A favorite stop for little ones is **The Great Character Café** in Fantasy Forest; adults might vote for grabbing nachos and a margarita at **La Cantina** instead.

WHERE TO SHOP

In amusement-park style, shops are scattered everywhere. In the Golden Kingdom, "I Survived Kingda Ka" T-shirts really get the message across to the kids back in school. The **Super Teepee** in the Frontier Adventure area takes the Western route with Native American–inspired goods. **N-B-Tween** on the Boardwalk caters to the preteen crowd with clothing and gifts, and **Totally Toddler** in the Fantasy Forest is pretty self-explanatory.

Appendix A: Resources

Here is where you can find each of the public transportation lines mentioned in this book, along with their phone numbers and websites. *Note:* These are not the addresses for the company headquarters, only the address of where to catch each of these transit options in New York City.

Academy Bus Lines
Port Authority Bus Terminal
41st Street and Eighth Avenue
✆ **800/442-7272** or 201/420-7000
www.academybus.com
Tickets available at the NJ Transit area toward the back of the South Wing.

Adirondack Trailways and Pine Hill Trailways
Port Authority Bus Terminal
41st Street and Eighth Avenue
✆ **800/776-7548**
www.trailwaysny.com
Ticket counter in the North Wing is on the subway level. Ticket counter in the South Wing is on the first floor.

Adventure Northeast Bus Lines
Departs from Second Avenue and 85th Street (northwest corner) and 79th Street between Broadway and Amsterdam at Dublin Bar
✆ **718/601-4707**
www.adventurenortheast.com
Call for reservations. Travels to Mount Snow, Stratton, Manchester, Okemo, Killington, Block Island, Martha's Vineyard, and Newport.

Amtrak
Penn Station
34th Street between Seventh and Eighth avenues
✆ **800/USA-RAIL**
www.amtrak.com
Offers online ticketing.

Block Island Ferry from New London, Connecticut
Port of Galilee
2 Ferry St.
New London, Conn.
✆ **860/444-4624**
www.goblockisland.com
Seasonal service on the high-speed ferry from New London, Connecticut, to Block Island, Rhode Island.

Bonanza Bus Lines
Port Authority Bus Terminal
41st Street and Eighth Avenue
✆ **888/751-8800**
www.bonanzabus.com
Ticket counters in both the North and South wings.

Greyhound Bus Lines
Port Authority Bus Terminal
42nd Street and Eighth Avenue
✆ **800/231-2222** or 212/971-6300
www.greyhound.com
Offers online ticketing and companion fares. Ticket counters in both the North and South wings.

Hampton Jitney Bus Lines
Four departure points on the east side of Manhattan from 40th Street to 86th Street
✆ **800/327-0732** (outside NYC) or 212/362-8400
www.hamptonjitney.com
Service to points on Long Island out to the Hamptons. Payment on board with cash or credit card. Reservations required.

IKEA Bus Shuttle to IKEA—Elizabeth, NJ
Port Authority Terminal
42nd Street and Eighth Avenue
∅ **908/289-4488**
www.ikea.com
Departs Saturday and Sunday from Gate 5 on the lower concourse near Academy Bus line. No tickets required—it's free!

Lakeland Bus Lines
Port Authority Bus Terminal
41st Street and Eighth Avenue
∅ **973/366-0600**
www.lakelandbus.com

Limoliner Bus to Boston
Hilton New York
1335 Ave. of the Americas, between 53rd and 54th streets
∅ **888/546-5469**
www.limoliner.com
Luxury 28-seat express bus from Midtown Manhattan to the Hilton Back Bay in Boston.

Long Island Rail Road (LIRR)
Penn Station
34th Street between Seventh and Eighth avenues
∅ **718/217-LIRR**
www.mta.info
One-day getaways: www.mta.info/lirr/getaways
If you live in Brooklyn, you might find it easier to use the Flatbush Avenue terminal in the Atlantic Avenue subway station at the intersection of Atlantic and Flatbush avenues and Hanson Place.

Martz Trailways Bus
Port Authority Bus Terminal
41st Street and Eighth Avenue
∅ **800/233-8604**
www.martztrailways.com
Tickets available at the NJ TRANSIT area toward the back of the South Wing.

Metro-North Railroad

Harlem, Hudson, and New Haven lines
Grand Central Terminal
42nd Street between Park and Lexington avenues
✆ **800/METRO-INFO** or 212/532-4900
www.mta.info
One-day getaways: www.mta.info/mnr/html/getaways.htm
Allows leashed pets at the conductor's discretion and bicycles during restricted hours and with a permit. Bicycle permits are $5, good for life, and available at window no. 27 in Grand Central Station.

Mitsuwa Marketplace Bus Shuttle

Port Authority Bus Terminal
41st Street and Eighth Avenue
✆ **201/941-9113**
www.mitsuwa.com
Departs from Gate 51. No tickets required—pay $2 cash (exact change) each way to the driver.

New Jersey Transit

Trains leave from Penn Station.
34th Street between Seventh and Eighth avenues
Buses leave from Port Authority Bus Terminal (toward the back of the South Wing)
41st Street and Eighth Avenue
✆ **800/772-2222**
www.njtransit.com
New Jersey Transit also has a rail terminal at Newark Penn Station in Newark, New Jersey. Be sure to confirm your trip details to avoid any confusion.

New York Waterway

Pier 78 at West 38th Street and 12th Avenue
✆ **800/53-FERRY**
www.nywaterway.com
Sightseeing cruises with stops at points of interest up and down the Hudson River.

PATH trains
Port Authority Trans-Hudson Trains
⊘ **800/234-PATH** or 212/435-7000
www.panynj.gov/path
From several points in Manhattan to Hoboken and other New Jersey destinations.

Peter Pan Bus Lines
Port Authority Bus Terminal 41st Street and Eighth Avenue
⊘ **800/343-9999** or 212/967-2900
www.peterpanbus.com
Purchase tickets at either the Greyhound or Trailways ticket counter in both the North and South wings. Buses depart from the North Wing and arrive at the South Wing.

SEPTA
Southeastern Pennsylvania Transportation Authority
Regional rail line connects in Trenton, NJ, to Philadelphia's 30th Street Station
⊘ **215/580-7800**
www.septa.org
Serving Bucks, Chester, Delaware, Montgomery, and Philadelphia counties in Pennsylvania.

Short Line/Coach USA Bus Lines
Port Authority Bus Terminal
42nd Street and Eighth Avenue
⊘ **800/631-8405** or 212/736-4700
www.coachusa.com
Ticket window is on the second floor in the North Wing.

Staten Island Ferry
Service runs continuously between the lower Manhattan terminal and Staten Island
⊘ **718/876-8441**
www.siferry.com
Trip takes 25 min.—and it's free!

Sunrise Express Coach Bus Lines
44th Street and Third Avenue (southwest corner)
⊘ **800/527-7709**
www.sunrisecoach.com
Reservations required. Travel to Long Island destinations of Riverhead (Tanger Outlets), Mattituck, Cutchogue, Southold, and Greenport.

Trans-Bridge Bus Lines
Port Authority Bus Terminal
41st Street and Eighth Avenue
℡ **610/868-6001**
www.transbridgebus.com
Tickets available at the NJ Transit area toward the back of the South Wing at ticket windows 1 through 10.

Westchester BEE-LINE bus
℡ 914/813-7777
http://beelinebus.westchestergov.com
Points throughout Westchester, including Rye Playland.

Helpful Phone Numbers & Websites

Port Authority Bus Terminal
℡ **212/564-8484**
Grand Central Terminal
www.grandcentralterminal.com

Metro-North/Grand Central Lost and Found
℡ **212/340-2555**

Amtrak/NJ Transit Lost and Found
℡ **212/630-7389**

Subway and Bus Lost and Found
℡ **212/712-4500**

Travel Information for People with Impaired Hearing
℡ **718/596-8273**

Travel Information for People with Disabilities
℡ **718/596-8585**

MTA Police
℡ **212/878-1000**

New York City Travel Transit Information Line
℡ **718/330-1234**

Port Authority of New York and New Jersey
℡ **212/435-7000**
www.panynj.gov

NYC General Information
℡ **311**
Call ℡ 311 for any city agency or related service and your call will be transferred to the appropriate department.

Other Forms of Transit

Enterprise Rent-A-Car
℘ 800/261-7331
www.enterprise.com
In Mount Kisco, New York, they will pick you up from the Metro-North train station so you can be on your way upstate: ℘ 914/241-2999.

ZipCar
℘ 866/4-ZIP-CAR
www.zipcar.com
Rental cars when and where you need them, including Cooper MINIs, Honda Elements, VW Jettas and Golfs, BMW 325s, Toyota Siennas, and the Toyota Prius.

Maps, Gear & Equipment

Eastern Mountain Sports
591 Broadway between Prince and Houston streets
℘ 212/966-8730
20 West 61st St.
℘ 212/397-4860
www.ems.com
Hiking maps, guide books, gear for hiking, camping, climbing, mountain biking, kayaking, outdoor fitness, and more. Order online and pick up at the store.

Paragon Sports
867 Broadway, at 18th Street
℘ 212/255-8036
www.paragonsports.com
Some hiking maps and outdoor guides; some camping and hiking gear; clothing; footwear; and equipment for skiing, running, swimming, biking, tennis, golf, and team sports; plus New York State fishing licenses and NYC parks' passes.

Tent & Trails
21 Park Place, at Church Street
℘ 212/227-1760
www.tenttrails.com
Lots of hiking and camping gear in a tall, crowded store near Wall Street.

Organizations

Appalachian Mountain Club—New York–North Jersey Chapter
5 Tudor City Place
℘ **212/986-1430**
www.amc-ny.org
Promotes the protection, enjoyment, and wise use of the mountains, rivers, and trails of the Appalachian region with many recreational and conservation activities open to members.

City Climbers Club
Inside the West 59 Parks Dept. Rec Center
533 W. 59th St., between 10th and 11th avenues
℘ **212/974-2250**
www.cityclimbersclub.com and www.climbnyc.com
A nonprofit rock gym and climbing community.

National Park Service
www.nps.gov
Everything you ever wanted to know about visiting any of the 328 parks in the national park system.

National Trust for Historic Preservation
℘ **800/944-6847**
www.nationaltrust.org
A private, nonprofit membership organization dedicated to saving historic places and revitalizing America's communities. Membership is $20 and gets you a tote bag, a subscription to *Preservation* magazine, free or discounted admission to 26 National Trust historic sites in the U.S., plus free or discounted admission to over 100 partner places domestically and over 500 international historic sites.

NY/NJ Trail Council
℘ **201/512-9348**
www.nynjtc.org
A federation of more than 95 hiking clubs and environmental organizations and 10,000 individuals dedicated to building and maintaining marked hiking trails and protecting related open space in the bi-state region.

Time's Up

∅ **212/802-8222**

www.times-up.org

A New York City–based not-for-profit direct-action environmental group that uses events and educational programs to promote a more sustainable, less toxic city. Known for their cycling enthusiasm, including bike-repair workshops, moonlight rides, and Critical Mass rides.

State Tourism Contacts

www.tourism.state.ct.us

∅ **888/CT-VISIT**

Tourism site for the state of Connecticut.

www.visitnj.org

∅ **800/VISIT-NJ**

The New Jersey state tourism website.

www.iloveny.com

∅ **800/CALL-NYS**

The official website for New York State tourism.

www.visitpa.com

∅ **800/VISIT-PA**

Official website for Pennsylvania tourism info.

www.visitrhodeisland.com

∅ **800/556-2484**

Rhode Island's tourism website.

www.1-800-vermont.com

∅ **800/VERMONT**

Official Vermont tourism website.

Other Travel-Related Websites

www.citysearch.com

Local guides for everything about town.

www.escapemaker.com

Online tool for getaway ideas in the Northeast.

www.gocitykids.com

The city guide for parents.

www.gorp.com
One-stop resource for outdoor recreation—hiking, biking, rafting, camping, fishing, and more. Includes info on attractions, gear, adventure travel, and national parks and wilderness areas.

www.hopstop.com
Step-by-step details on how to get from point A to point B using New York City buses and trains.

www.nymag.com
New York Magazine's site does NYC best. Find their 52 weekend getaways at www.newyorkmetro.com/travel/guides/52weekends.

www.tripadvisor.com
User reviews and forums on hotels, restaurants, attractions, and more.

Appendix B: Festivals & Special Events

Here is just a sampling of the numerous annual special events, festivals, and holiday celebrations held in the New York metropolitan area and surrounding environs.

Clearwater Festival, the Great Hudson River Revival

Croton Point Park, Croton-on-Hudson, NY 10520
⌀ **845/454-7673** · www.clearwater.org/festival.html

Getting there: Metro-North Hudson train line from Grand Central to Croton-Harmon, NY.
Subways: 4, 5, 6, 7, S to 42nd St./Grand Central.
Approximate travel time: 40–70 min., plus 5-min. free shuttle.
Schedule: Trains leave Grand Central 2–3 times an hour and return from Croton-Harmon on a similar schedule. The park and the festival are located 1 mile from the train station. Free shuttle service (5- to 7-min. trip) runs both days of the event from the Croton-Harmon Station to the festival in Croton Point Park.
Hours: Early to mid-June on a Sat and Sun 10am–dusk.
Cost: Train fare is $15 round-trip off-peak. Festival 1-day tickets, including headlining musical acts, $45; weekend tickets $60. A 2-hr. sail on the *Sloop Clearwater* is $25 for adults, $15 for children 12 and under.

One weekend each June up to 20,000 people converge on the Hudson River banks of Croton Point Park in the name of environmental education, inspiration, and activism. Music, dancing, and storytelling on six solar-powered stages plus swimming, sailing, craft and product demos, guest speakers, and interactive activities—all set to a neohippie vibe and fed with organic snack foods—has given this weekend a reputation as the "World's Fair of environmental education."

New York Renaissance Faire

Sterling Forest
600 Rte. 17A
Tuxedo, NY 18229
✆ 845/351-5174 · www.renfaire.com

Getting there: Shortline Coach USA bus line from Port Authority to the fair.
Subways: A, C, E to Port Authority or N, Q, R, S, W, 1, 2, 3, 7 to 42nd St./Times Sq.
Approximate travel time: 65 min.
Schedule: There are 2 buses a day, leaving Port Authority at 9:35 and 10am. They leave the fair at 6:45 and 7:15pm. Times change, so check schedule to be sure.
Alternate transit: NJ Transit's M&E Morristown train line to Tuxedo, NY (transferring at Secaucus Junction to get on the Main & Bergen Co. line), then a 5-min. cab ride from the station to the fair. The trip is 1 hr., 10 min., and costs $17 round-trip for off-peak tickets.
Hours: Sat-Sun from the beginning of Aug through the end of Sept (also open Labor Day), 10am to 7pm–rain or shine.
Cost: Shortline package includes round-trip bus transportation to fair, admission, and free program. (Without the bus transportation, 1-day tickets are $17 in advance, $19 at the door.)

The Renaissance Faire is set in a 65-acre "medieval village" that for nearly 30 years has been home to jugglers, jesters, magicians, storytellers, court dancers, and strolling minstrels. Aside from informal amusers scattered about, 20 stages host a carnival of acts from a full Shakespearean production to the improv comedy of *Ask the Village Idiot*. Horseback jousting and a living chess game vie for attention against the Sturdy Beggars Mud Show—a mud pit of madness and mayhem that's a perennial favorite. More than 100 craftspeople and artisans fill an elaborate Tudor-style marketplace juried by the fair. Kids' activities include maypole dances, a spot in Robin Hood's band, live shows, a petting zoo, pony rides, games, and other rides (a small fee is charged for some activities).

Belmont Stakes

Belmont Park
2150 Hempstead Tpk.
Elmont, NY 11003
℡ **516/488-6000** · www.nyra.com

Getting there: LIRR from Penn Station to Belmont Park, NY.
Subways: 1, 2, 3 to 34th St./Penn Station or A, C, E to 34th St./Eighth Ave.
Approximate travel time: 40 min.
Schedule: Trains leave Penn Station frequently throughout the day and return from Belmont on a similar schedule.
Hours: Held the 2nd Sat in June. Gates open at 8:30am and the 1st race starts at noon. The big Belmont Stakes race (the 11th out of 13 races) usually starts around 6:30pm, with the final race beginning just before 8pm.
Cost: Train fare is $12 round-trip off-peak; general admission is $10, clubhouse admission is $20.

Though it hasn't seen a Triple Crown winner here since 1978 with Affirmed (though Smarty Jones gave it his all, and Afleet Alex proudly stepped away with the Preakness), the horse races of the Belmont Stakes are always worth a trip to this legendary track. Belmont Stakes starts with a full day of 13 races, the first beginning at noon. The all-day races, betting, speculating, and snacking lead up to the evening's big race, the Belmont Stakes. The 1½-mile Stakes is the third leg of the Triple Crown, following the Kentucky Derby and the Preakness Stakes. Three-year-old thoroughbreds compete to, ideally, take first prize in all three races. *Note:* Belmont's other big race, the Breeders' Cup World Thoroughbred Championships, takes place around the end of October.

Arts & Ideas Festival

Downtown New Haven, CT 06510
℡ **888/ART-IDEA** · www.artidea.org

Getting there: Metro-North New Haven Line from Grand Central to New Haven, Conn.
Subways: 4, 5, 6, 7, S to 42nd St./Grand Central.
Approximate travel time: 1 hr., 50 min.
Schedule: Trains leave hourly from Grand Central and return from New Haven on a similar schedule. New Haven is the last stop on the Metro-North train line with the same name. From the train station, downtown is a 10- to 15-min. walk. Follow Union St. under I-95 and it turns into State St.

When you hit Chapel St., turn left and you'll bump into The Green after several blocks. Should you need a lift, you can try **Metro Taxi** at ✆ **203/777-7777, New Haven Taxi Co.** at ✆ **203/877-0000,** or **Yellow Cab Co.** at ✆ **203/777-5555.**
Hours: Daily for 2 weeks in mid-June; check schedule for dates and times.
Cost: Train fare is $33 round-trip off-peak. Most festival events are free.

The "culture capital of Connecticut" plays host to this annual festival spanning 2 weeks and packing in hundreds of events. Music, dance, theater, exhibits, and special events are spread out around the city. Named one of the country's 10 most beautiful public spaces, the New Haven Green is at the festival's heart. At opposite ends of the green, the World Stage and the Family Stage present a lineup of concerts, art activities, and street performances. Festival events are also held in the Long Wharf Theatre and the Shubert Theater, and in the courtyards, auditoriums, and theaters of Yale. Your day in town could encapsulate jazz, folk, funk, or opera performances, a rock concert, a Shakespearean drama, a poetry slam, a reading, and a puppet show. *Note:* More than 85% of Arts & Ideas events are free.

Hudson Valley Garlic Festival

Cantine Field
Saugerties, NY 12477
✆ **845/246-3090** • www.hvgf.org

Getting there: Adirondack Trailways bus line from Port Authority to Saugerties, NY.
Subways: A, C, E to 42nd St./Port Authority or N, Q, R, S, W, 1, 2, 3, 7 to 42nd St./Times Sq.
Approximate travel time: 2 hr., 25 min., plus free shuttle.
Schedule: Buses leave Port Authority once in the morning and once in the evening. They leave Saugerties for NYC on a similar schedule. If you're just there for the day, take a cab from the bus stop out to the festival. The only Saugerties-based taxi company is **S&K Car Service** (✆ **845/247-4444**).
Hours: The last full weekend in Sept, Sat 10am–6pm, Sun 10am–5pm–rain or shine.
Cost: Bus fare is $48 round-trip. Admission is $7 at the door, $5 in advance.

The Hudson Valley Garlic Festival attracts gardeners, chefs, educators, and photographers. Visitors can buy garlic seed direct from garlic growers, browse garlic crafts, attend cooking demos, and taste more than 40 varieties of garlic—with names like Danube Rose, Killarney Red, Russian White, Sicilian Gold, and Spanish Roja. Food vendors sell garlic soup, garlic mozzarella, garlic mashed potatoes, garlic pretzels, garlic sauerkraut, garlic ice cream, garlic steak, garlic chili, garlic pasta, and garlic pickles. Garlic aside, the festival features four stages of live entertainment, a children's area with a climbing wall and bouncy tent, and a garlic-braiding how-to. Last year's musical entertainment included bluegrass, Dixieland, zydeco, folk, Celtic, and a German-Austrian band beloved for its polkas and fox trots. *Note:* Money raised from the Garlic Festival goes toward scholarships for local service-minded students, Hudson Valley nonprofit organizations, and community improvements.

Festival of Light

Constitution Plaza
Downtown Hartford, CT 06103
⌀ **860/525-8629** • www.connectthedots.org

Getting there: Amtrak from Penn Station to Hartford, CT.
Subways: 1, 2, 3 to 34th St./Penn Station or A, C, E to 34th St./Eighth Ave.
Approximate travel time: 2 hr., 40 min.
Schedule: Trains leave NY several times throughout the day and evening and return from Hartford on a similar schedule.
Alternate transit: Peter Pan bus lines leave about once an hour from Penn Station en route to 1 Union Place in Hartford. Travel time is roughly 2 hr., 35 min., and costs $49 round-trip (*⌀* **800/343-9999;** www.peter panbus.com).
Hours: Weekend events kick off at 5:30pm on the Fri after Thanksgiving and lights turn on each night until Three Kings Day in early Jan.
Cost: Train fare is $82 round-trip; event is free.

For 43 years, Hartford's Constitution Plaza has hosted the brilliant Festival of Light. Santa arrives in his sleigh to turn on 250,000 twinkling white lights, carols play, and hot chocolate is for sale.

The Three Feasts of Hoboken

Hoboken, NJ 07030
www.hobokennj.org or www.hobokeni.com

Getting there: PATH train from Manhattan to Hoboken, NJ.
Subways: F train to a PATH stop (located on Sixth Ave. at 33rd St., 23rd

St., 14th St., or 9th St; or Hudson St. and Christopher St.).
Approximate travel time: 30 min.
Schedule: PATH trains run about every 15 min. on weekends. Make sure you're boarding the blue-line train to Hoboken. Festivals are within walking distance of the PATH station in Hoboken.
Hours: June–Sept–see details below for each one.
Cost: PATH train costs $3 round-trip, festivals are free.

The city where Sinatra was born and its large Italian population celebrate three annual feasts. The **Feast of St. Anthony** (mid-June), the smallest of the three feasts, is sponsored by St. Francis Church (3rd and Jefferson sts.; ✆ **201/659-1772**). Like the larger fests, music, food, and children's activities lead up to a procession through the streets. The feast's claim to fame: the best zeppole of the all local festivals.

The **Feast of St. Ann** (mid- to late July), sponsored by St. Ann's Church (701 Jefferson St., at 7th St.; ✆ **201/659-1114**), spans 7 days, starting with evening-only activities and culminating in up to 12 hours a day of feasting. Live music from Latin to swing, food, games, rides, and a procession through the streets. Last year comedian Joe Piscopo performed a tribute to Frank Sinatra and Hoboken with his big band.

The **Feast of Madonna dei Martiri, aka the Hoboken Italian Festival** (the weekend after Labor Day; www.hobokenitalianfestival.com), more than 75 years old, is the star Italian-American festival in the New Jersey tri-state area. This 4-day feast held in Sinatra Park (on the Hoboken waterfront) kicks off on Thursday and Friday nights, then offers nonstop entertainment from noon to late on Saturday and Sunday, including music (from standards to rock to Rod Stewart tributes), singing, dancing, comedy, international foods, and more than 50,000 boisterous partakers. Saturday is the day of Catholic pageantry, when a Mass, a procession through the streets, and a harbor fleet blessing are highlights. The 800-pound Madonna is paraded through the streets, placed on a boat, and floated in the Hudson to bless the boats and ships nearby. More music and a glittering fireworks display end the evening's festivities.

Annual Blessing of the Fleet

Water St.
Stonington, CT 06378
✆ **860/535-3150** • www.mysticmore.com

Getting there: Amtrak train from Penn Station to Mystic, CT, then a taxi 4 miles to Stonington.

Subways: 1, 2, 3 to 34th St./Penn Station or A, C, E to 34th St./Eighth Ave.
Approximate travel time: 2 hr., 40 min., to 3 hr.
Schedule: Trains leave NY every few hours and return from Mystic on a similar schedule. Taxis will be waiting at the Mystic Amtrak station to take you to Stonington.
Hours: Last weekend in July.
Cost: Train fare is $98 round-trip; festival is free.

This 2-day festival celebrating the blessing of the local dock's fleet of ships has been a tradition here since 1956. Stonington is Connecticut's oldest borough—a charming seaside village with colonial flavor and grand Federal and Greek Revival houses set along the main streets. From the docks—a popular hangout for both locals and visitors—the town's collection of busy sea vessels can be seen sailing by at all hours of the day. Each June the Blessing of the Fleet weekend features parades, bands, food tents selling local specialties like seafood salad rolls and bowls of clam chowder, music, dancing on the docks, and a Sunday Mass. The epicenter of the festival is the Stonington harbor docks.

United States Open Tennis Championship

National Tennis Center, Flushing Meadows Corona Park,
Flushing, NY 11368
∅ **718/592-0711** • www.usopen.org

Getting there: From Times Square or Grand Central, 7 train to Shea Stadium/Willets Point Station; from Penn Station, LIRR to USTA National Tennis Center (Shea Stadium/Willets Point Station).
Subways: 7 train.
Approximate travel time: 45 min. on 7 train, 15 min. on the LIRR.
Schedule: Subway trains depart regularly. Extra trains are made available for tennisgoers.
Cost: Grounds passes are $43 and $47, depending on date. Stadium seats go for up to $457, depending on date and seats.
Hours: Day and night late Aug through mid-Sept.

As the summer nears its end in New York, an excitement begins to grip the city. You feel it on trains and in taverns, in parks and penthouses alike. No, it isn't back-to-school jitters; tennis fever has struck, and its epicenter is Flushing Meadows in Queens, at the National Tennis Center. There, in late August and early September, the best tennis players from around the world gather to compete for one of tennis's most prized possessions, a Grand Slam trophy—not to mention the more-than-$1-million first prize. It's no wonder New Yorkers get pumped up: One of the four most important tournaments of the year—the most important on American soil—is right in their backyard. And with such a spectacle only a $2 subway ride away, not catching at least 1 day of tennis is almost criminal.

There are two ways to get in on the action in Flushing—in Arthur Ashe Stadium and on the outer courts. With its 23,326 seats, Arthur Ashe Stadium is the centerpiece of the Tennis Center's remarkable facility, but it is hardly the only place to catch great tennis. In fact, early on in the tournament, the better matches often take place on the outer courts. Big-name players like Federer, Hewitt, and Roddick will likely receive center-court billing, but in the early rounds they will be playing the weakest players in the draw. (No sense paying for stadium seating just for that!) These matches will be quick—and ugly.

If hotly contested matches are what you are after, you are better off buying a grounds pass (which excludes admission to Arthur Ashe Stadium). Not only is this cheaper than the stadium option, but it often lets you get much closer to all that sweating and grunting, sometimes only a few feet away from the court. Seeing world-class players slug it out from that close is incredibly thrilling. As the tournament progresses, the best players will creep toward each other in the narrowing draw, and a stadium seat becomes a better idea. (The night sessions being particularly exciting.) Be warned, however: Arthur Ashe stadium is *huge*—if you have seats in the upper tiers, you'll need to squint a bit to see the players.

Tennis is, of course, the primary attraction at the Open, but if you need a break from the matches, there are plenty of places to eat, shop, sit, or stroll. A food village offers 14 different dining options, and there are an additional 6 upscale restaurants around the facility. For shoppers, sponsor stores offer racquets, clothing, and other memorabilia. Last year, even the George Foreman Grill made a special appearance, using grilled meat on toothpicks to reel in passersby.

If you play or watch tennis frequently, then you will be in heaven at the Open, yet you needn't be a tennis maven to enjoy the tournament. Simply spending a day out in the sun, enjoying the beautiful grounds, and witnessing the mastery and fitness of these amazing athletes is enough to provide plenty of outdoor entertainment—or, quite possibly, enough motivation to convince you to pick up a racquet and try the sport for yourself.

—Alex Altman

Haunted Happenings in Salem, MA

Salem, MA, 01970

✆ 877/SALEM-MA • www.hauntedhappenings.org

Getting there: Peter Pan, Greyhound (or a number of other bus lines) from Port Authority to Boston's South Station. Take the T from South Station to North Station and switch to the Newburyport/Rockport commuter rail line, which you'll take from Boston's North Station 4 stops to Salem.

Subways: A, C, E to 42nd St./Port Authority or N, Q, R, S, W, 1, 2, 3, 7 to 42nd St./Times Sq.

Approximate travel time: Minimum of 4 hr. to Boston (could be as much as 5½ or more depending on the route), then a 35-min. subway ride to Salem.

Schedule: Buses leave Port Authority roughly every half-hour. They leave Boston on a similar schedule. The commuter rail between Salem and Boston runs hourly, and sometimes more often during busy times of day.

Cost: $49–$65 R/T plus $7.50 R/T for the train to Salem. (These are Greyhound's regular R/T fares, but they often run specials for $36 R/T and periodically offer 50% off companion fares.)

Hours: Varied (though you can usually find something going on at any time of the day during the month of Oct).

In what's been called an autumnal-themed "Mardi Gras of the North," from early October to Halloween itself, streets are filled with parades, merchants, dramatic productions, psychic fairs, and games. Visit haunted houses and graveyards, take a ghost or haunted trolley tour, witness a pie-eating contest, attend a costume party, see local art students do pumpkin-carving demos, and more, in this notorious little town with the witchy reputation that—somewhat ironically—takes its name from the word "shalom," meaning "peace." Drive through a haunted car wash (yes, really!), go to a witch museum or dungeon, and take in a performance by the Salem Theatre Company.

Halloween in Salem is like Times Square on New Year's Eve. Make reservations 6 months to a year in advance if you plan to party with the hometown ghosts, goblins, and ghouls. Okay, and witches. The ominous music, eerie lighting, and Vincent Price-ish voiceovers do border on melodramatic, but these *were* dramatic times for a hard-working New England town that believed its dwellers had become possessed. Besides, the witch-related attractions strive to captivate children as well as adults—so those moments of hokeyness might not seem so to younger minds.

The **Salem Witch Museum** (Washington Sq. N.; ✆ 978/744-1692; www.salemwitchmuseum.com) provides a 30-minute presentation in the round. Visitors take a seat in the middle of the theater while recorded narration accompanies the ring of still-life scenes around the perimeter.

In 1956, the local telephone company discovered the original cells used for the accused—150 of them, with shackles and chains intact. The cells were then recreated below an old church as the **Witch Dungeon Museum** (16 Lynde St.; ✆ 978/741-3570; www.witchdungeon. com).

The nation's oldest continually operating museum, the **Peabody Essex Museum** (E. India Sq.; ✆ 978/745-9500; www.pem.org), is also one of its most incredible. A modern building with a skylit inner courtyard topped by a stunning glass atrium houses Asian, African, Oceanic, Native American, and regional art through the ages.

Built in 1668 for Captain John Turner, three generations of Turners lived in the **House of Seven Gables** (54 Turner St.; ✆ 978/744-0991; www.7gables.org), followed by Nathaniel Hawthorne's relatives, the Ingersolls. Hawthorne's visits to the Turner-Ingersoll house, now New England's oldest standing wooden mansion, inspired him to pen *The House of the Seven Gables* as well as *The Scarlet Letter*. The very home where he was born was later moved to the same location and now lies just feet away from the home made famous in fiction.

The **Salem Visitor's Center** (2 New Liberty St.; ✆ 978/740-1650) is a good place to pick up maps, brochures, and information. You can also download the Salem Visitors Guide before you go at www.salem. org. See www.hauntedhappenings.org for more details.

Index

See also Accommodations and Restaurant indexes, below.

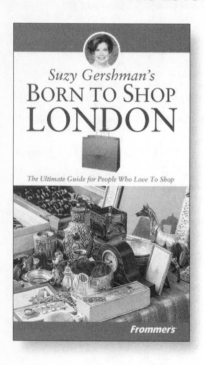
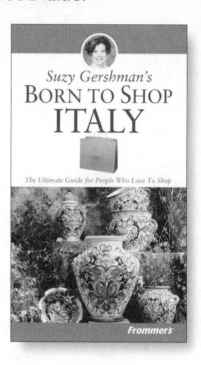

Destinations in a Nutshell

Frommer's®

 WILEY

FROMMER'S® DAY BY DAY GUIDES

Amsterdam
Chicago
Florence & Tuscany

London
New York City
Paris

Rome
San Francisco
Venice

FROMMER'S® NATIONAL PARK GUIDES

Algonquin Provincial Park
Banff & Jasper
Grand Canyon

National Parks of the American West
Rocky Mountain
Yellowstone & Grand Teton

Yosemite and Sequoia & Kings
  Canyon
Zion & Bryce Canyon

FROMMER'S® MEMORABLE WALKS

Chicago
London

New York
Paris

Rome
San Francisco

FROMMER'S® WITH KIDS GUIDES

Chicago
Hawaii
Las Vegas
London

National Parks
New York City
San Francisco

Toronto
Walt Disney World® & Orlando
Washington, D.C.

SUZY GERSHMAN'S BORN TO SHOP GUIDES

Born to Shop: France
Born to Shop: Hong Kong, Shanghai
  & Beijing

Born to Shop: Italy
Born to Shop: London

Born to Shop: New York
Born to Shop: Paris

FROMMER'S® IRREVERENT GUIDES

Amsterdam
Boston
Chicago
Las Vegas
London

Los Angeles
Manhattan
New Orleans
Paris

Rome
San Francisco
Walt Disney World®
Washington, D.C.

FROMMER'S® BEST-LOVED DRIVING TOURS

Austria
Britain
California
France

Germany
Ireland
Italy
New England

Northern Italy
Scotland
Spain
Tuscany & Umbria

THE UNOFFICIAL GUIDES®

Adventure Travel in Alaska
Beyond Disney
California with Kids
Central Italy
Chicago
Cruises
Disneyland®
England
Florida
Florida with Kids

Hawaii
Ireland
Las Vegas
London
Maui
Mexico's Best Beach Resorts
Mini Las Vegas
Mini Mickey
New Orleans
New York City

Paris
San Francisco
South Florida including Miami &
  the Keys
Walt Disney World®
Walt Disney World® for
  Grown-ups
Walt Disney World® with Kids
Washington, D.C.

SPECIAL-INTEREST TITLES

Athens Past & Present
Cities Ranked & Rated
Frommer's Best Day Trips from London
Frommer's Best RV & Tent Campgrounds
  in the U.S.A.

Frommer's Exploring America by RV
Frommer's NYC Free & Dirt Cheap
Frommer's Road Atlas Europe
Frommer's Road Atlas Ireland
Retirement Places Rated

FROMMER'S® PHRASEFINDER DICTIONARY GUIDES

French

Italian

Spanish